CAMI … :S

General Editors

W. K. C. GUTHRIE A. H. M. JONES D. L. PAGE

AN HISTORICAL COMMENTARY ON THE 'HELLENICA OXYRHYNCHIA'

AN HISTORICAL COMMENTARY ON THE 'HELLENICA OXYRHYNCHIA'

BY

I. A. F. BRUCE

Assistant Professor of Classics in the Memorial University of Newfoundland

CAMBRIDGE
AT THE UNIVERSITY PRESS
1967

CAMBRIDGE UNIVERSITY PRESS
Cambridge, New York, Melbourne, Madrid, Cape Town, Singapore, São Paulo

Cambridge University Press
The Edinburgh Building, Cambridge CB2 2RU, UK

Published in the United States of America by Cambridge University Press, New York

www.cambridge.org
Information on this title: www.cambridge.org/9780521043526

First published 1967
This digitally printed first paperback version 2006

A catalogue record for this publication is available from the British Library

Library of Congress Catalogue Card Number: 66-19605

ISBN-13 978-0-521-04352-6 hardback
ISBN-10 0-521-04352-2 hardback

ISBN-13 978-0-521-03412-8 paperback
ISBN-10 0-521-03412-4 paperback

TO MY FATHER AND MOTHER

CONTENTS

PREFACE

This historical commentary is the major part of a doctoral dissertation submitted to the University of Sheffield in 1963. It is based upon the most recent and most reliable edition of the *Hellenica Oxyrhynchia*, that of V. Bartoletti, published in 1959 in the Teubner series of classical texts. The following signs are used as in Bartoletti's edition:

α̣α̣α̣α̣	uncertain letters
. . . .	letters of which only the slightest trace remains
[. . .]	lost letters
[– – –]	lacuna of indeterminate number of letters
[ααα]	letters supplied by conjecture
⟨ααα⟩	letters to be inserted
{ααα}	letters to be deleted

I have not, however, adopted in its entirety the new system of chapter numbering devised by Bartoletti, by which the Florence papyrus contains I–V and the London papyrus VI–XXII. Instead, while using Bartoletti's chapter divisions in the Florence papyrus, I have considered it more convenient to retain the numbering of the chapters in the London papyrus from I to XVII, as established by Grenfell and Hunt in the first edition. Since this numbering appears in Bartoletti's edition along with his own it provides a uniform standard of reference to all the editions of the text. Notes on variant textual restorations are few and mainly confined to points which might alter the sense of the narrative. These observations on the text are based on a study of photostat copies of the papyri. I refer to the author, for the sake of brevity, by the letter P. A lower-case p in notes on the text indicates the papyrus reading.

Five essays which were incorporated in my dissertation have been omitted because they are published elsewhere; they are listed under my name in the Bibliography.

How much I owe to the published work of various scholars, in particular the first editors, will be obvious. I should also like to express my thanks to Professor R. J. Hopper, who supervised the preparation of the original thesis, for his guidance and advice;

to Professor R. E. Smith for the constructive criticisms he offered as examiner; and to Mr G. T. Griffith, not only for reading my typescript and making many valuable comments on it, but also for his kindly interest in my work, which has been a source of much encouragement. Wherever my commentary appears inadequate it will be safe to assume that I have stubbornly ignored the suggestions or criticisms of these scholars.

Editions of the *Hellenica Oxyrhynchia* are cited as follows:

ed.pr.	editio princeps, i.e., in notes on the London papyrus, Grenfell and Hunt, *Oxyrhynchus Papyri* v, 110–242; in notes on the Florence papyrus, Bartoletti, *Papiri greci e latini* XIII, 1, pp. 61–81
OCT	Grenfell and Hunt, *Hellenica Oxyrhynchia cum Theopompi et Cratippi Fragmentis*, Oxford Classical Texts
Meyer	Meyer, *Theopomps Hellenika*
Lipsius	Lipsius, *Cratippi Hellenicorum Fragmenta Oxyrhynchia*
F.Gr.Hist.	Jacoby, *Die Fragmente der griechischen Historiker* II A, pp. 17–35; II C, pp. 6–20
Kalinka	Kalinka, *Hellenica Oxyrhynchia*, Teubner
Gigante	Gigante, *Le Elleniche di Ossirinco*
Maas	Maas, 'Nova Hellenicorum Oxyrhynchiorum Fragmenta', in *Classical Quarterly* XLIV (1950)
Bartoletti	Bartoletti, *Hellenica Oxyrhynchia*, Teubner

Standard abbreviations for modern works of reference and periodicals are used, notably the following:

AJA	*American Journal of Archaeology*
BCH	*Bulletin de Correspondance Hellénique*
Beloch, *Gr.Gesch.*	K. J. Beloch, *Griechische Geschichte*
Berl.Phil.Woch.	*Berliner Philologische Wochenschrift*
Boll.Fil.Class.	*Bollettino di Filologia Classica*
CAH	*Cambridge Ancient History*
CIA	*Corpus Inscriptionum Atticarum*
CJ	*Classical Journal*
CP	*Classical Philology*
CQ	*Classical Quarterly*
CR	*Classical Review*
CRAI	*Comptes Rendus de l'Académie des Inscriptions et Belles-Lettres*
F.Gr.Hist.	F. Jacoby, *Die Fragmente der griechischen Historiker*
GHI	M. N. Tod, *Greek Historical Inscriptions*

HSCP	*Harvard Studies in Classical Philology*
IG	*Inscriptiones Graecae*
Inscr.Gr.Septent.	*Corpus Inscriptionum Graecarum Graeciae Septentrionalis*
JHS	*Journal of Hellenic Studies*
L'Ant.Cl.	*L'Antiquité Classique*
PA	J. Kirchner, *Prosopographia Attica*
Philol.	*Philologus*
Phil.Woch.	*Philologische Wochenschrift*
P.Lak.	P. Poralla, *Prosopographie der Lakedaimonier*
RE	Pauly–Wissowa–Kroll, *Realencyclopädie der klassischen Altertumswissenschaft*
REA	*Revue des Études Anciennes*
REG	*Revue des Études Grecques*
Rhein.Mus.	*Rheinisches Museum*
Riv.Fil.	*Rivista di Filologia e d'Istruzione Classica*
St.It.Fil.Class.	*Studi Italiani di Filologia Classica*
TAPA	*Transactions of the American Philological Association*

INTRODUCTION

I. THE PAPYRI

Two separate papyrus discoveries made at Oxyrhynchus form the portions which we possess of the work of a Greek historian whose identity has not been established and whose history is consequently known as the *Hellenica Oxyrhynchia*.

The larger of the two papyri was discovered in 1906 and was first published in 1908 by B. P. Grenfell and A. S. Hunt as P.Oxy. 842 in volume v of *Oxyrhynchus Papyri*. It is now housed in the British Museum as papyrus 1843 in the Department of Manuscripts. It originally consisted of about 230 fragments of varying size which were pieced together by the first editors so as to leave only some 57 small fragments unplaced. The papyrus contains some sections of the history dealing in considerable detail with events of the Greek world in 396–395 B.C. The historical work is written on the verso of an official document, a land-survey register of the Arsinoite nome (P.Oxy. 918), which, apart from its own interest, was of great help to the editors in determining the position of the detached fragments of the history. Twenty-one columns of the *Hellenica* can be distinguished. These are not continuous, but are divided into four distinct sections, called by the editors A, B, C, and D. Section A contains columns i–iv and fragments 1 and 2; B contains columns v–viii with fragments 3–7; C, which is very badly mutilated, consists of columns ix and x, and fragments 8–15 were also attributed to this section. D contains the best preserved columns, xi–xxi, which are continuous. Within A, columns i–ii and iii–iv are continuous, and both internal evidence and the text of the land-survey show that column iii follows column ii. Within B, columns v–vi and the beginnings of lines in column vii are on the same piece of papyrus; column viii (all of which is contained in fragment 7) is known to follow column vii both from consideration of its content and since certain white stains on the recto of column vii are also present on the recto of column viii. Between each of the sections A, B, C, and D a number of columns may be lost. The manuscript is the work of two scribes, the first being responsible for columns i–iv, vi, line 27–

xxi, and all but one or two of the unplaced fragments. The columns measure about 16·7×9 cm., but the number of lines in a column varies from 37 (col. i) to 45 (col. vii) in the first hand, while column v, the only one written entirely in the second hand, which is smaller than the first, contains 60 lines. As regards the date of the manuscript, the land-survey is placed by the handwriting in the second century A.D., but, from internal evidence, before the principate of Commodus. The text of the *Hellenica* is dated to the end of the second century or the early part of the third, the scribe responsible for by far the greater part of it employing a small, sloping uncial which the first editors considered to represent 'a transitional stage between the earlier specimens of this style of the late first or early second century, and the ordinary third century type' (ed.pr. p. 111).

The other papyrus, found at Oxyrhynchus in 1934, was first published by V. Bartoletti as P.S.I. 1304 in *Papiri greci e latini*, vol. XIII (1949),[1] and is kept in Florence in the library of the Istituto Papirologico 'G. Vitelli' della Università di Firenze. The script is on the recto of the papyrus, the verso being unused. There are three quite large fragments, labelled by Bartoletti A (13·7×15·5 cm.), B (10·7×21 cm.), and C (14·5×10·5 cm.), which contain parts of six columns. A smaller fragment, D (2·4×3·2 cm.), is badly mutilated, and a further fragment (2×4·8 cm.), labelled E in the editio princeps, has been seen to belong to the first eleven lines of the second column of A. The columns are 9 cm. in width, and have about 30 letters to a line; the height is not certain as the initial lines of all the columns are missing, but in column ii of B there are as many as 40 lines. The handwriting, a clear uncial, is thought by Bartoletti to belong to the end of the second century A.D. That the text of this papyrus is the work of the author of the London papyrus appears certain. Not only does the Florence papyrus reveal many characteristics already observed in the London papyrus—a lucid, but colourless and unrhetorical style (apart from a general avoidance of hiatus), restricted vocabulary and repetition of favourite words or expressions, wealth of detail in the narrative and absence of subjective comment—but, as is true of the London papyrus for the years 396/5 B.C., the new fragments appear without doubt to have been the main source, entirely independent of Xenophon, used by

[1] On the circumstances of this considerable delay between the discovery and the publication of the papyrus see Bartoletti, ed.pr. p. 61 n. 2, and p. 71.

Ephorus and, through him, by Diodorus, for the years to which the fragments refer, 410–407 B.C. The content of the Florence papyrus thus helps to substantiate the view of Grenfell and Hunt (ed.pr. p. 122) that the Oxyrhynchus historian intended his work to be a continuation of Thucydides' history, and that his narrative therefore began with the events of 411 B.C.

II. THE 'HELLENICA'

1. *The scope of the history and its date of composition*

If one cannot state with absolute certainty the points at which the narrative of the *Hellenica* began and terminated, one can, at least, make a very reasonable conjecture about the scope of the work from the available evidence. In the London papyrus, at II, 4, the author refers back to his earlier mention of a sea-battle near Amphipolis in which Timolaus, the Corinthian, defeated an Athenian general whose name appears to have been Simichus. The most likely date for this episode is the latter part of 411 B.C., in other words, shortly after the point at which Thucydides' history comes to an end.[1] It seems to have been P's practice, when making a passing reference to a subject he had previously dealt with, to indicate that he had done so by the use of such a phrase as ὥσπερ εἴρηκά που καὶ πρότερον (cf. Lond.pap. II, 2, 4, 5; XII, 1), yet at XII, 4–5, while recalling certain consequences of the Spartan occupation of Decelea, he gives no such notice of a former treatment of these matters, and it has been sensibly suggested[2] that the narrative to which P's note here is supplementary is not his own, but that of Thucydides. This is not, of course, conclusive proof that P had not given an account of the beginning of the Decelean War himself, for at XIV, 2, in a note on the inadequacy of Persian financial support to the Spartan fleet at that period, P omits to cite a passage which must surely have been contained in his earlier narrative. A more convincing hint, however, appears in the Florence papyrus, in chapter II of which P actually cites Thucydides, in the course of a digression on the activity of the Spartan, Pedaritus, at Chios in 412 B.C. (cf. Thuc. VIII, 28 ff.). One may thus infer, it seems, that P's own narrative began after 412, and

[1] Cf. ed.pr. p. 206 n. ii, 21–32.

[2] Cf. Hardy, *CP* XXI (1926), 355 and Bloch, *HSCP*, supp. vol. I (1940), p. 326.

since it included the exploits of Timolaus at Amphipolis (noted above) and the extant account of the battle of 'The Horns' near Megara in 410 or 409 (Flor.pap. I) there are good grounds for the assumption that the work was undertaken as a continuation to the history of Thucydides.

The surviving portions of the work seem to indicate that it was written more on the scale of Thucydides' history than of, say, Xenophon's *Hellenica*, and the inference may perhaps be made that it did not cover many more years than Thucydides' work. Of course, it *could* have done, but the detail in which all the extant parts of the narrative and digressions are rich makes this rather improbable; otherwise the work would have been very much longer than either Thucydides' or Xenophon's histories. Two dates which might be suitable closing points for P's work suggest themselves: 394, the year of the battle of Cnidus (with which Theopompus concluded his *Hellenica*), and 386, the Peace of Antalcidas. Of these the latter appears the more probable, for the history of Diodorus, whose main source for the events covered by both the Florence and London papyri was without question the Oxyrhynchus historian, albeit with Ephorus as intermediary, has been demonstrated[1] to rest on such a source for the whole period 411–386, and the assumption may fairly be made that that source for the whole period, entirely independent of the tradition preserved by Xenophon, was the work of P.

The date of composition can be fixed within certain limits from internal evidence. In introducing an excursus on the constitution of Boeotia by the words εἶχεν δὲ τὰ πράγματα τότε κατὰ τὴν Βοιωτίαν οὕτως (Lond.pap. XI, 2), the historian seems to indicate that he was writing later than the dissolution of that constitution in 386. As for the *terminus ad quem*, the passage relating to the disputed territory between Phocis and Locris (Lond.pap. XIII, 3), ἔ σ τ ι τοῖς ἔθνεσιν τούτοις ἀμφισβητήσιμος χώρα περὶ τὸν Παρνασσόν, suggests that the author was ignorant of the Sacred War, and was therefore writing before its outbreak in 356.[2] At any

[1] Cf. Accame, *Ricerche intorno alla guerra corinzia*, ch. I (also in *Rend. Accad. Lincei* XIV (1938), 433 f. and *Riv.Fil.* XXVIII (1950), 30ff.). Grenfell and Hunt (ed.pr. p. 122), however, considered there was no evidence that the work went further than the battle of Cnidus. This would, of course, be an attractive possibility for those who wished to attribute the work to Theopompus.

[2] Cf. Walker, *Klio* VIII (1908), 361.

rate it is safe to conclude with the first editors (ed.pr. p. 122) that the composition preceded the conclusion of the Sacred War in 346. A further passage (Lond.pap. XIV, 2), although not of great importance in view of the satisfactory nature of the above argument, reveals that the work was composed before the collapse of the Persian Empire. The remarkable detail of P's narrative makes it highly unlikely that any great lapse of time occurred between the events he describes and his time of writing, and many of his informants would seem to have been eyewitnesses. With this in mind I have suggested[1] a date as early as 374 for the composition of the work, or part of it, but this cannot be claimed as more than speculative, for my argument was based on a conjecture about the constitution of the renewed Boeotian League which cannot be proved correct.

2. *P's sources*

In the extant fragments, P makes mention of only one literary source, Thucydides, and that in connection with the Spartan, Pedaritus, whose death occurred earlier than the date at which I have assumed that P's narrative began. It is quite possible, further, that XII, 5 of the London papyrus reveals knowledge of the parts of Thucydides' work relating to the Archidamian invasions of Attica and those of the Decelean War period.

Supposing P's starting point to have been that at which Thucydides' history ended, did P make use of any literary sources for the period covered by his main narrative? He notes at II, 2 of the London papyrus that certain men (τινές) believed the receipt of Persian gold brought by Timocrates to have been the cause of hostility to Sparta on the part of Epicrates and Cephalus at Athens and the party of Ismenias at Thebes. It is perhaps likely, although not certain, that the persons to whom P refers were writers, but his critical view of their judgement implies only acquaintance with, and not dependence upon, their works.

Indeed, the only literary authorities known to us whom P could have used are those with whom he has been identified from time to time, Cratippus and Daimachus (for P is clearly independent of Xenophon and possibly completed his work before the publication of Xenophon's *Hellenica*,[2] and certainly did so earlier than the

[1] In *Emerita* XXVIII (1960), 86.

[2] Cf. Grenfell and Hunt, ed.pr. pp. 124–5.

appearance of Theopompus' *Hellenica*), and of these Daimachus cannot be said with certainty to have covered the same period as P.

The nature of P's history, as it appears to me, does not, in fact, suggest much use of literary sources, but rather gives the impression that his choice of source material has much in common with that professed by Thucydides.[1] Nor would it be surprising to find that P had modelled his work on that of Thucydides in this respect, for it is clear that he did so in the matter of chronological organization of the history.

Of the narrative passages, the account of the mutiny of Conon's troops at Caunus (Lond.pap. xv) above all has every indication of having been communicated to P by an eyewitness. The details that Conon, while on his way with the leader of the mutineers to address the Cypriot soldiers, happened to pass through the city gate first, and that the Carpasian happened to be just in the gateway when he was seized by some of the Messenians, are of no special relevance, but are exactly the sort of minutiae which an eyewitness might remember and relate.

P's intimate knowledge of the preparations for the *coup d'état* at Rhodes and its execution by the adherents of Dorimachus suggests that his informant had been in Rhodes at the time and had perhaps actually been in the agora when Dorimachus stood on the pedestal from which the herald was accustomed to make his pronouncements and exhorted his band of assassins with the words ἴωμεν, ὦ ἄνδρες πολῖται, ἐπὶ τοὺς τυράννους τὴν ταχίστην (x, 2). We have not, of course, sufficient evidence to say whether P made use of speeches or not, but this, the only direct speech in the extant fragments, is not at all a speech of the Thucydidean type and must have been inserted either for dramatic effect (which would seem not to accord well with P's general avoidance of sensational writing) or as words reported by someone who had actually heard them.

In general, the passages relating to the naval operations of Conon have appeared to commentators to be based on the

[1] Thuc. I, 22. 2–3: τὰ δ' ἔργα τῶν πραχθέντων ἐν τῷ πολέμῳ οὐκ ἐκ τοῦ παρατυχόντος πυνθανόμενος ἠξίωσα γράφειν, οὐδ' ὡς ἐμοὶ ἐδόκει, ἀλλ' οἷς τε αὐτὸς παρῆν καὶ παρὰ τῶν ἄλλων ὅσον δυνατὸν ἀκριβείᾳ περὶ ἑκάστου ἐπεξελθών. ἐπιπόνως δὲ ηὑρίσκετο, διότι οἱ παρόντες τοῖς ἔργοις ἑκάστοις οὐ ταὐτὰ περὶ τῶν αὐτῶν ἔλεγον, ἀλλ' ὡς ἑκατέρων τις εὐνοίας ἢ μνήμης ἔχοι.

accounts of eyewitnesses or on the personal, or official, diaries of participants.[1]

On the subject of Agesilaus' campaigns in Asia Minor, P must be credited with having troubled to obtain and record much more detailed information on the movements of the Spartan army than did Xenophon, despite the latter's presence in Asia at the time, a good part of it being spent in the Spartan camp. Some pertinent comments on P's probable sources here have been made by Ch. Dugas (*BCH* XXXIV (1910), 92), and these I quote:

'Quant au récit de P, il est difficile, vu sa précision, de ne pas chercher la source dans les notes d'un témoin oculaire. Or, ce qui étonne un peu chez P, c'est, à côté de sa diligence lorsqu'il décrit des mouvements de troupes, sa brièveté lorsqu'il s'agit de négociations; il semble que l'auteur utilisé par lui ait suivi la campagne de très près, mais n'ait pris ni part ni intérêt aux délibérations des chefs et aux pourparlers avec les alliés. L'hypothèse que P se serait servi d'un journal de route tenu par un officier rendrait compte à la fois de cette exactitude et de ces lacunes.'

It appears from the short surviving fragments of the Florence papyrus which also deal with military affairs (chs. I and V) that P was no less careful there to obtain the most accurate information available, no doubt from a similar source.

It is not so easy, however, to attribute the story of the execution of Tissaphernes (Lond.pap. VIII) to such a source; here it is possible that P made use of some other literary work; but it is also probably true that the news of this event and the way in which it was planned would have spread widely in Asia Minor by word of mouth, for it is that sort of news about a notable figure which often arouses public interest. Wherever P got his information, he obviously made sure that he obtained as much detail as was possible, to judge by the length and the intelligible fragments of his account.

P's description of the battle of Notium (Flor.pap. IV) strongly suggests the use of an Athenian source. This, in itself, might go far to explain his differences here from Xenophon on points of detail, for Xenophon's source was most probably Spartan. De Sanctis (*Riv.Fil.* IX (1931), 229) even suggested that P's account (not then

[1] Cf. Judeich, *Rhein.Mus.* LXVI (1911), 98 n. 1; Walker, in Powell–Barber, *New Chapters in the History of Greek Literature* (1921), p. 126; Jacoby, *F.Gr.Hist.* II C, 18; Gigante, p. xxxiv.

discovered, but preserved in part through Diodorus) derived from official reports sent to the Athenian boule by the generals. If not, it assuredly bears every sign of having been based on some report, more probably written at the time than given orally later, from a participant in the battle.

In writing on political history P appears to have been no less diligent in his choice of well informed sources. Although his summary of the Boeotian Constitution could perhaps have been obtained from some documentary source, the passages which discuss the rivalries and policies of the leading factions in both Athens and Thebes can only have derived from information provided by someone who had been in these cities at the time and had taken a keen interest in politics. The bias which appears against the anti-Spartan group in Thebes and the extremist anti-Spartan democrats at Athens could thus be attributed either to P himself or to the political sentiments of his informant, or to both. It is quite possible, of course, that in the case of one of these cities P might himself have been the eyewitness observer of the political scene, at Athens, for instance, if he were in fact Cratippus.

To sum up, this brief discussion of likely sources for particular sections of the history may indicate the probability that P learned much from Thucydides in his choice of source material.

3. *Chronology*

There does not seem to be any doubt (from Lond.pap. IV, I) that P modelled his chronological system on that of Thucydides, by which events γέγραπται...ἑξῆς ὡς ἕκαστα ἐγίγνετο κατὰ θέρος καὶ χειμῶνα.[1] However, just how closely P followed Thucydides in choosing the point in the year at which his 'summers' and 'winters' began is open to dispute. A number of notable scholars, among them Meyer, Jacoby, Bloch and Bartoletti, have argued forcibly that P, like Thucydides, reckoned his 'summers' as beginning in the spring. Despite the attractiveness of this view and the weight which must be attached to the arguments in its favour, I personally incline to the view of Grenfell and Hunt that the summer from which P reckoned the beginning of the eighth year (after some such event as the restoration of the Athenian democracy)

[1] Thuc. II, I.

refers to midsummer; in this the first editors have been supported by De Sanctis, Gigante and Barbieri. The whole question is discussed in some detail in my commentary on chapter IV of the London papyrus.

In order to synchronize the events of different areas of the Greek world P made use of the customary Thucydidean formulae, of which I list a few examples:

(i) ὑπὸ δὲ τοὺ[ς αὐτοὺς χρόνο]υς (Lond.pap. I, 1); cf. Thuc. II, 95. 1 *et passim*.

(ii) κατὰ δὲ τὸν αὐ]τὸν χρόνον (Lond.pap. IV, 2); cf. Thuc. IV, 7; 46. 1 *et passim*.

(iii) τούτου τοῦ θέρους (Lond.pap. XI, 1); cf. the similar use of τοῦ δ' αὐτοῦ θέρους in Thuc. II, 80; IV, 42. 1 *et passim*.

We may further note that P employs the simple form of transition from one scene to another which is well known from Thucydides; cf. Βοιωτοὶ μὲν ο[ὖ]ν τοσαῦτα κακὰ ποιήσαντες [τ]οὺς Φωκέ[α]ς ἀπῆλθον εἰς τὴν ἑαυτῶν. Κόνων δέ,... (Lond.pap. XIII, 5–XIV, 1) and, e.g., Thuc. I, 93. 8–94. 1: 'Αθηναῖοι μὲν οὖν οὕτως ἐτειχίσθησαν...Παυσανίας δὲ ὁ Κλεομβρότου...

P's chronological method is therefore open to all the criticisms which have been directed against Thucydides' method, but whatever the failings of this system the serious historian is likely to feel that they are outweighed by the general reliability of the method in providing secure dates which are seldom matched by ancient writers.

4. *P's bias and judgement*

P is not much given to offering personal comment, and such bias as appears is found only in the point of view from which he narrates various episodes of political history. Here it is not by any means clear whether the bias which emerges is that of the historian himself or of his informants, but as a fairly consistent pattern seems perceptible there is good reason to suppose that some part of the bias represents P's own standpoint.

The terminology which he uses of the Athenian party opposed to the provocative acts of the extreme democrats in sending assistance to the enemies of Sparta (γνώριμοι καὶ χαρίεντες, οἱ ἐπιεικεῖς καὶ τὰς οὐσίας ἔχοντες, Lond.pap. I, 2–3), and the motives of personal greed and ambition which he attributes to Epicrates and Cephalus who led the group anxious, or at least willing, to engage the city in a war against Sparta (Lond.pap. II, 2), indicate a bias against the popular faction. Further, the impression he gives that the anti-Spartan leaders in Thebes were the sole instigators of the Corinthian War (Lond.pap. XI, 1; XIII), and that the outbreak of the war was engineered by means of a clever stratagem, suggests a fair degree of sympathy with Sparta. Although it is quite possible that P's informants represented the oligarchic viewpoint in the case of Athens and the pro-Spartan attitude in the case of Thebes, one may well ask why P chose to obtain his information from such sources, or to reproduce their views in preference to those of their political opponents if he troubled to learn the opinions of both sides, unless his own sympathies coincided with those he has reproduced. It is, of course, well-nigh impossible to write a history without some bias, be it conscious or unconscious, and to make such observations as I have is far from alleging that P's history is written with a strong bias. On the contrary, the reader cannot fail to be impressed by the general fairness of P. Those who suffer most at his hand are Ismenias and his Theban colleagues, yet the historian takes the trouble to absolve them from the charge which their contemporaries made against them, that of atticizing. Again, P appears to have admired at the same time Agesilaus and Conon, despite the latter's leadership of the Great King's navy against the Spartans. Indeed he seems to admire Conon more than Agesilaus, and thus reveals independence from the bias in favour of Sparta which other parts of his work indicate.

The historian's judgement can be assessed in two respects. The first concerns the relative importance which he attaches to the various branches of the history of his period, and on this point he is at great divergence from Xenophon. For P, political history (most notably in the extant fragments concerning Boeotia), military history (the campaigns of Agesilaus, the battle of 'The Horns', the episode in Flor.pap. V) and naval warfare (the battle of Notium, Conon's operations at Rhodes and Caunus) all appear to have been of equal significance, and have consequently been described in equal detail. In particular, in the London papyrus, P seems to have realized that the naval war was as important as, if not more important, for the ultimate conclusion of the struggle against the Spartan supremacy, than the land warfare in Asia. In this his judgement was surely right; on the other hand Xenophon ignored completely the naval operations of the years recorded in our papyrus, and gave relatively little attention to the domestic politics of European Greek cities. His judgement of the relevance of these various fields in a truly comprehensive and balanced history of the Greek world falls short indeed of the judgement of P.

The second respect in which we may consider the powers of judgement of the historian arises from his interest in causation, in that we may criticize his assessment of causes. His habit of presenting to the reader a motive for most of the actions of leading characters, or a reason for the policies of cities in their relations with one another, is discussed in the next section of the Introduction. Here, however, we may note that some of the reasons given are self-evident from the situation and the consequences of the action, some may have been explained by the persons in question and others suggested by P's informants, while some are obviously P's own judgements. Of these one or two are worthy of attention now. His assessment of the responsibility for the habitual shortage of pay for those in the service of the Great King (Lond.pap. XIV, 2) appears to us to be sound in the light of our knowledge from other sources of the experiences of those in that situation. His argument (Lond.pap. II, 2), designed to correct a mistaken and apparently widespread view, that Timocrates' bribes were not the major cause of antipathy to Sparta in 396 is well presented and convincing. In presenting alternative reasons for the hostility to Sparta in the Greek cities, however, P's judgement does not convince me, and my doubts on this point are expressed in *Emerita* XXVIII (1960), 75 ff. If I, personally, do not find P's view satisfactory in this particular instance, it is, nevertheless, the result of some penetrating investigation and study, and on the whole his judgement must appear to be remarkably sound.

5. *Digression and causation*

The relative frequency with which digressions from the main narrative appear in the short portions of the *Hellenica* which survive has led most commentators to remark upon this feature of the author's style. His use of digression, however, is more than a stylistic peculiarity; it is a part of his historical method, employed either to elucidate the background, often the political background, against which the events of the narrative took place, or to provide an explanation of the long-standing causes of the more important events or trends in the history. It thus appears that to a certain extent these digressions fulfil the same function as do some of the speeches in Thucydides' history.

There are some eight main digressions from the narrative in the extant portions of the work, and one of these is in fact made up of two consecutive digressions, while another consists of three. The digressions on Pedaritus (Flor.pap. II), the Boeotian Constitution (Lond.pap. XI) and the increasing affluence of Boeotia consequent on the Spartan occupation of Decelea (Lond.pap. XII, 4–5), I have discussed in *Phoenix* XVIII (1964), 272 ff., and therefore dismiss here with the brief statement that I believe they are all examples of a type of excursus designed to illuminate and clarify a political situation of some complexity. The remaining five digressions are worthy of some further comment here.

(i) After relating the reaction of the various Athenian political groups to the expedition of Demaenetus (Lond.pap. I), P embarks on three digressions which immediately follow one another:

(*a*) It was first noticed by De Sanctis[1] that the passage (I, 3–II, 1) recording the positive acts of hostility to Sparta before the adventure of Demaenetus is in fact a digression from the main narrative, which is not resumed until chapter III. This brief excursus recalls the sending of arms and sailors to assist Conon, and the mission to the Great King of certain ambassadors who had the misfortune to be arrested by Pharax, the Spartan nauarch, and were subsequently executed. These activities had been instigated by the adherents of Epicrates and Cephalus, and are recorded at this point by P to emphasize the contrast between the former policy of the group and its willingness on the present occasion to agree that the behaviour of Demaenetus should be publicly disowned, and that the Spartan harmost of Aegina be informed that he could punish Demaenetus with the consent of the Athenian people. The agree-

[1] 'Nuovi studi sulle "Elleniche" di Oxyrhynchos', in *Atti Accad. Torino* LXVI (1931), 157 ff. Whether or not this section is to be regarded as part of the digression has an important bearing on the date of the visit to Greece of Timocrates, the Rhodian, and it was in this connection that De Sanctis made his point. For a more recent study of the question of the date of Timocrates' visit, based on De Sanctis' argument, see Barbieri, *Conone*, pp. 90–100, especially p. 91.

ment of the group to this course, we are told, was due to fear, on being made aware of the dangerous consequences of the venture should the Spartans regard it as an act of aggression.

(*b*) P goes on to indicate (II, 2) that Epicrates and Cephalus had favoured a policy of open hostility to Sparta even before the visit of Timocrates with his offer of Persian gold, and that, therefore, contrary to the opinions of some, this was not the cause of their anti-Laconism. The same is true of Boeotia and the other places in Greece visited by Timocrates. P then suggests as a deeper cause that the Spartans had 'treated as friends' the political opponents of the Boeotians and Argives, by whom, one must assume, he means the majority or ascendant parties in these areas. In the case of the Athenians, P makes the rather unconvincing claim that the opponents of Sparta saw in war an opportunity to increase their personal fortunes out of state funds. Those of the Corinthians who favoured a change of policy or government hated the Spartans for reasons similar to those applicable in Boeotia and Argos.

This digression obviously illustrates P's interest in penetrating the longer-standing causes of events and his unwillingness to accept what are at best only immediate causes. He is not, however, giving the cause of some event described at this point in his narrative, for the excursus is occasioned by the mention of the policy of Epicrates and Cephalus before their meeting with Timocrates. Further, the causes of anti-Laconism in cities other than Athens are not really relevant even to the earlier comments on Epicrates and Cephalus. Yet, if it is an historian's duty to attempt to discover causes, one cannot dismiss the attempt made here as no more than an irrelevant digression, for the Corinthian War, the immediate antecedents of which are described in chapter XIII, and the course of which must have been narrated later, was an event of some magnitude, and the causes of opposition to Sparta in Greece are in fact the long-standing causes of the alliance against Sparta in 395, and of the war itself. It may still appear, at first sight, that P has chosen rather an inappropriate juncture at which to discuss these causes, but the result of his chronological arrangement, which of necessity prevents continuity in the narrative of any event of considerable duration, is that he would otherwise be obliged to insert these causes either immediately before relating the direct antecedent of the war, the outbreak of hostilities between Boeotia and Phocis (at which point reference to Argos, Corinth and Athens would scarcely be relevant), or before the alliance of these cities with Boeotia (by which time, with the possible exception of the Boeotian alliance with Athens, the war had already begun). Neither of these points, then, would seem to be any more appropriate for a review of long-standing causes of antipathy to Sparta.

(*c*) Having explained the hostility of a party of the Corinthians to Sparta, P singles out Timolaus as opposing the Spartans for personal reasons (II, 3–4). It is not at all surprising that particular mention should be made of Timolaus, for P is here correcting the mistaken view that the receipt of money from Timocrates was the reason for anti-Spartan activity, and Timolaus is alleged to have been among those who accepted bribes from Timocrates.[1] P remarks that Timolaus had formerly been a notable supporter of Sparta, and then digresses on his activities in the Decelean War by way of proof of his former sympathy. This short digression would have been more interesting, and perhaps more relevant, if P had told us what the personal reasons were for Timolaus' change of attitude. But perhaps he did not know, and the statement that Timolaus now opposed the Spartans ἰδίων ἐγκλημάτων ἕνεκα may simply be an assumption based upon the details provided about his former exploits.

(ii) London papyrus IX, although severely mutilated, clearly contained a character-sketch of some notable person whose identity cannot be determined with certainty. If Bartoletti's view[2] that the subject is Cyrus the Younger is to be accepted, the passage constitutes a major digression from the narrative. Assuming that the accounts of the death of Tissaphernes in Polyaenus VII, 16. 1 and Diodorus XIV, 80. 6–8 are derived from that in P (Lond.pap. VIII), P would, like these two authors, have mentioned the death of Cyrus as the reason for Parysatis' hatred of Tissaphernes. The character-sketch of Cyrus would thus have been occasioned solely by this incidental reference to him, and would thus appear to be an almost entirely irrelevant digression indicative only of a certain tendency to be led away from the main subject on the part of the author.

[1] Xen. *Hell.* III, 5. 1 and Paus. III, 9. 8.

[2] Bartoletti, pp. xvi–xvii. While I personally find this view more satisfactory than previous suggestions about the subject of the passage, it has not met with universal acceptance; cf., e.g., Westlake, *CR* n.s. X (1960), 209.

(iii) There is a somewhat similar excursus at XVI, 4 of the London papyrus, on Spithridates, but here the object is clearly to provide some information about a newly introduced character who would not, in all probability, be known to Greek readers. Spithridates' background is of further relevance in explaining why Agesilaus thought he would be a useful ally.

(iv) There is something of a digression at XIII, 3 on the disputed territory between Phocis and Locris, and the customary course of the border incidents which resulted from time to time. Knowledge of this cause of frequent disputes is essential for an understanding of the stratagem whereby the Thebans were said to have engineered the outbreak of war between themselves and the Phocians, and subsequently the Spartans also.

(v) Conon's visit to Tithraustes and Pharnabazus to obtain arrears of pay for his troops gives rise to an excursus on the Great King's reluctance to provide the remuneration due to those in his service (XIV, 2). This excursus could possibly be interpreted as giving the reason for the pay having been withheld, i.e. that this was the normal practice of the King, but the situation caused by the King's practice, although the historian does not say so in as many words, is of particular significance as being the chief cause of the serious mutiny of the Cypriot land forces under Conon's command which is described in detail in chapter XV.

It may, therefore, be claimed that three or even four of these five digressions illustrate P's interest in causation, especially in causes which are not readily apparent. That immediate causes also interested P is most evident to the reader from the constant explanation of the motives of individuals or parties for their actions. P consistently introduces these motives by the use of a participle, usually βουλόμενος or βουλόμενοι.[1] There can be no doubt that these observations on causation enhance the value of P's history, and his attempts to probe the deeper causes of important events represent another feature of his work which, by modern standards of criticism, entitles him to a place among the best of the ancient historians.

[1] The following are examples of this use of βουλόμενος in the London papyrus: IV, 1; VIII, 1; X, 1 *bis*; XIII, 1 (βουλόμενοι); XIV, 1; XVI, 1. Cf. also the uses of λεγόντων ὅτι (I, 2), φοβηθέντες (I, 3), προφασιζόμενος (X, 1), ὁρῶν... καὶ βουλόμενος (XVI, 2).

6. *P's treatment of leading characters*

If P's comments on some of the less notable characters[1] in his history appear to be influenced at times by his general sympathy with the supporters of Sparta or of oligarchy, his presentation of the outstanding personalities suggests an honest attempt to be a fair and trustworthy reporter. Thus, in contrast to Xenophon, P writes of Agesilaus' failures as well as his successes. Yet P too is unable to conceal the admiration which he feels for a great personality, even when that personality, namely Conon, was engaged in a struggle in which P's own sympathies may well have been with the opposing side. Since Agesilaus and Conon, from the Greek point of view at any rate, are the leading figures in the surviving fragments of P's work, it is to these that I confine most of my remarks.

P's method of presenting Agesilaus is altogether different from that employed by Xenophon in the *Hellenica*; while Xenophon's admiration and enthusiasm for the Spartan king seem to have blinded him to Agesilaus' failings, P portrays him as a more convincing and human figure, yet still as an adaptable and experienced tactician and general. A few incidents from the Phrygian campaign of autumn 395, as narrated by P (Lond.pap. XVI–XVII), may illustrate the point.

After scrupulously adhering to the terms of his agreement with Tithraustes in restraining his soldiers from pillage while marching through Lydia, Agesilaus adopted a high-handed policy towards the people of Mysia, who were independent of the King, demanding enlistment under himself, the penalty for refusal being to suffer the ravages of his army. Very soon, however, Agesilaus found himself in difficulties in the mountainous country and naïvely assumed, or hoped, that the Mysians would abide by a hastily arranged truce. When they, naturally, seized the opportunity thus afforded for revenge upon the Greeks, Agesilaus was able to extricate his army from danger by a well conceived and well executed ambush. By recording this episode in a degree of detail which is never matched by Xenophon in his accounts of military operations in this campaign, P presents to his reader several sides of Agesilaus' character; he is a

[1] Particularly his treatment of the Athenians Epicrates and Cephalus (Lond. pap. II), and the Thebans Ismenias and Androcleidas (Lond.pap. XI, I and XIII).

man of his word; he is a capable and confident general, but he is not more than human, and at times he falls into error. During the same campaign he made assaults on three fortified towns and was unable to capture any of them. It may have been a consequence of these failures that, on reaching the lake close by Dascylium, he made no attempt on that city. Perhaps he had come to realize that the great strength of his army was to be found rather in a systematic pillage of the countryside of Asia Minor. P enables his reader to see Agesilaus as an outstanding soldier, but as one who is subject to the limitations imposed by circumstances. Xenophon presents only the picture of success: 'he burned and ravaged the land, and he captured the cities, some by force and others of their own will' (*Hell.* IV, I. I).

By comparison with the rather lesser characters in Athens who supported him, Conon, despite his anti-Spartan activity, has been most fairly treated by P. Indeed the favourable picture which he presents of Conon might suggest that much of the apparent hostility of P towards those in Athens and Thebes who were actively opposed to the Spartans may reflect more the sympathies of P's informants than his own; if not, one must credit P with the willingness to rise above the prejudices of his personal views and appreciate the outstanding qualities of one whose energies were directed towards ends of which he probably disapproved. The simple fact emerges, even from the dispassionate writing of P, that he admired Conon greatly. Such small detail as that the arrest of the Carpasian during the mutiny at Caunus (Lond.pap. XV) was made without Conon's consent or command (lest he should seem to have broken faith with the Carpasian) suggests the author's concern to give a good impression of Conon, although it could, possibly, have been due to P's informant. However that may be, the comment with which the narrative of this event is concluded, τὸ μὲν οὖν βασιλικὸν στρατό[πεδον οὕτ]ως εἰς μέγαν κίνδυνον προελθὸν διὰ Κόνων[α καὶ] τὴν ἐκείνου προθυμίαν ἐπαύσατο τῆς ταραχῆ[ς (XV, 6), is surely P's own, and one which suggests unconcealed admiration, for the remark is not at all essential to a straightforward narration of the facts. It is the more striking in that it comes from an historian so little inclined to offer subjective comment.

On this last point the fragmentary chapter IX of the London papyrus comes tantalizingly close to shedding more light. Here it appears that P digressed at some length on the character of some notable personality. The indications, insubstantial as they are, are that this passage contained a good deal of personal comment, favourable so far as we can tell, and it is remarkable that we should find a digression of this sort from P when the most part of his work strikes the reader as so objective. It is perhaps a fair supposition that other such chapters on the character of leading figures appeared elsewhere in the *Hellenica*, and, if so, would represent an important aspect of P's conception of his duties as an historian in respect of the outstanding personalities of the period about which he wrote. It is possible that there is some favourable observation on the character of Pedaritus in Florence papyrus II (οὐδ[– – –φι]λοτιμίας ἀπε.[– – –]), and the very poor state of preservation of this passage and of that in London papyrus IX is much to be deplored since it deprives us of insight into an important feature of P's treatment of his leading characters. Our general conclusion from the extant fragments, however, must be that P prefers not to comment, but to let his characters' actions speak for themselves.

7. *P's style and vocabulary*

P writes a pure Attic Greek[1] in which simplicity of diction and clarity of expression are striking features. These characteristics, when combined with P's relative impartiality,[2] serious approach[3] and wealth of detailed information, render him, on historical grounds, an excellent narrator of events. From the point of view of the literary critic, however, they expose him to censure, for his simplicity does not avoid monotony. Dramatic colour is conspicuously lacking, except in the one short direct speech, consisting of nine words, in the account of the revolution at Rhodes (Lond.pap. X). Grenfell and Hunt (ed.pr. p. 124) pronounced P's style 'frigid, colourless and verbose'. The general absence of direct speeches, however, may not represent a literary desire to avoid a particular rhetorical influence so much as the abandonment of the device by which Thucydides presented an explanation of motives or an

[1] A fact which, incidentally, may suggest that he was an Athenian, although, of course, we know of non-Athenians who wrote in pure Attic.

[2] Relative to, for instance, Xenophon.

[3] Illustrated well by the choice of material regarding Spithridates which is selected for presentation by P (Lond.pap. XVI–XVII) and Xenophon (*Hell.* IV, I. 2ff.) respectively.

elucidation of the circumstances against the background of which particular episodes occurred. (It should be noted that the extant fragments do not contain many suitable places for the composition of speeches on the Thucydidean pattern, and so it does not necessarily follow that P made no use of them elsewhere; it is probable, however, that he did not, partly because he may well have taken Book VIII of Thucydides as his model, but more importantly, I feel, because he invented an alternative device to perform the function of Thucydides' speeches.) P makes frequent use of digressions to explain causes or to acquaint his reader with essential background information, and I prefer to regard these as a feature of his historical method rather than of his literary style.

Generally speaking, P, unlike many of his contemporaries, was very little influenced by rhetoric, and this may well have been one reason for his apparent neglect at the hands of ancient scholars. One or two characteristics of rhetorical style can, however, be observed in P's work. For the most part hiatus is avoided (although some ten or eleven do occur in the two papyri), occasionally at the cost of an unnatural word order, as in ἐπηρμένοι μισεῖν ἦ̣[σ]α̣ν̣ τοὺς Λακεδαιμονίους (Lond.pap. II, 5) or [ἴ]ω̣μεν, ὦ ἄνδρες, ἔφη, πολῖται (Lond.pap. X, 2). Antithesis is frequently striking, especially, for example, in London papyrus XII, where P describes the Theban political situation and contrasts the two rival parties. Μέν and δέ, as Grenfell and Hunt observed (ed.pr. p. 124), recur 'with dull regularity'. There are a number of instances of litotes, for example in the London papyrus at I, 1 [οὐ μετὰ τῆς τοῦ] δήμου γνώμης, I, 3 ο[ὐ με]τὰ τῆς πόλεως, XIV, 3 οὐκ εὐλόγως and XV, 3 [οὐ] μετὰ τῆς ἐκείνου γν[ώ]μης.

P does not construct complex sentences and *varietas* is largely lacking both in his forms of expression and in his choice of vocabulary. Participles are used a great deal, at times to an excess, and this produces a heavy effect, especially in combination with the parentheses which P inserts with some frequency. Of the verbs for which P appears to have a particular preference we may note τυγχάνειν with the participle (which occurs 11 times), βαδίζειν (11 times), ἐπακολουθεῖν and ἐπιχειρεῖν (5 times each), καταβάλλειν (4 times) and παροξύνειν (3 times).

To sum up, those aspects of P's style which have a direct bearing on his qualities as an historical source, some, at least, of which he may have acquired from an acquaintance with the work of Thucydides, are to be admired by those whose chief concern is the history of the period P describes. From a purely literary standpoint, however, there is little to arouse enthusiasm in the reader, and not a little which is open to criticism.

8. *The importance of the work*

The work of P does not appear to have been widely read in antiquity. This we may infer from the fact that ancient critics of Thucydides' διαίρεσις, which P is the only Greek historian to adopt, so far as we know, reveal no knowledge of any writer other than Thucydides to employ it. Indeed Dionysius of Halicarnassus[1] expressly states that there were none to do so: οὐδεὶς γὰρ τῶν μεταγενεστέρων συγγραφέων θερείαις καὶ χειμῶσι διεῖλε τὴν ἱστορίαν. ἀλλὰ πάντες τὰς τετριμμένας ⟨ὁδοὺς καὶ δυναμένας⟩ ἄγειν ἐπὶ τὴν σαφήνειαν μετῆλθον. Dionysius thus seems to indicate that he did not know the work of P. (This passage is discussed further in my remarks on the question of the authorship of the work.)

Possible reasons for the obscurity of P in ancient times are not hard to suggest. His unrhetorical, and in some ways unattractive, style may not have encouraged reading; his presentation of historical fact, without much personal comment, without set speeches, and arranged chronologically by summers and winters (if the extant fragments are truly representative of the whole work in these respects), obviously had many critics; perhaps most significantly, the substance of his history was largely absorbed in the later work of Ephorus. The analogy of Livy's work superseding all earlier annalistic literature has been cited,[2] and appears a good one.

The chance that Ephorus made use of P as his main source for the period from 411 to 386[3] may, however, have been the means of preserving the researches of our historian from total oblivion, excepting the copies which were kept by some scholars, no doubt very few, to one of whom we are indebted for the London papyrus which we now possess, and to another, perhaps, for the Florence fragments. Diodorus, most notably, reproduces much of the substance of P's history by reason of his recourse to Ephorus as a source; in all the passages of Diodorus which are parallel to the

[1] *De Thuc.* 9. [2] Cf. Bloch, *HSCP*, supp. vol. 1 (1940), p. 339 n. 4.

[3] See p. 4 n. 1.

extant fragments of P there can be no doubt that the narrative of the former derives ultimately from that of the latter. Polyaenus, too, shows some noteworthy agreement with P, particularly in his account of the execution of Tissaphernes (VII, 16. 1; cf. Lond.pap. VIII). He is, further, the only ancient authority to concur with P in associating the mission of Timocrates with Pharnabazus and not Tithraustes (I, 48. 3; cf. Lond.pap. II, 5). Pausanias, on some points, appears to have used as a source some account deriving from P, as for instance in the assertion that Epicrates and Cephalus at Athens did indeed accept the bribes which Timocrates offered (III, 9. 8; cf. Lond.pap. II, 2), but on a number of other matters he shows marked agreement with Xenophon as against P. The mutiny of Conon's troops in the summer of 395, which P describes in great detail, is recorded by only one other ancient writer, very briefly it is true, and that is Justin. It may be a fair inference that Justin's statement (VI, 2. 11) derived from P. Grenfell and Hunt (ed.pr. p. 125) professed themselves unable to find any trace of P's influence in either Plutarch or Nepos, and we may now add that Plutarch's version of the battle of Notium in the *Lysander* and *Alcibiades* reveals no knowledge of P's account, or at least no use of it.

What, then, of P's significance for modern students of Greek history? Obviously for the year 396/5, and for the battle of Notium in the Florence papyrus, P is a source of the highest importance. The scale of his work renders him our most informative authority when his full narrative has survived, and the care with which, so far as we can judge, he gathered his information, organized it for presentation and attempted some analysis of cause and effect leads me to the opinion that he is a more reliable source than Xenophon. Indeed, had his entire work survived, he might well have earned the reputation now of being, if inferior to Thucydides, second to none of the post-Thucydidean Greek historians. However, the wider significance of the discovery of these two papyri lies in the established fact that P was indirectly a source of Diodorus, and, if the conclusion of Accame[1] be accepted, as I believe it must be, the main source of Diodorus, through Ephorus, for the entire period 411–386. It has been the general practice of modern historians to prefer Xenophon to Diodorus on points on which the two differ. Now

[1] *Ricerche intorno alla guerra corinzia*, ch. 1; *Rend. Accad. Lincei* XIV (1938), 433f.

that we can see the quality of Diodorus' source, his history of this period must be approached with greater respect when it is found to be at variance with Xenophon. The need has arisen for what Accame has called 'una profonda revisione'[1] of the traditional versions of the history of the years 411–386, and this need has, in fact, been recognized by some of the scholars who in more recent years have studied afresh the events of this period of Greek history.

9. *Authorship*

So much has been written on the question of the identity of P, and so little progress made towards the discovery of a really convincing answer after exhausting the evidence at our disposal, that I feel another lengthy inquiry would not be fruitful.[2] It is therefore my intention to give a brief survey of the main arguments which have already been advanced, and to state the conclusions which I, personally, have reached.

It is rather difficult now to understand why so many scholars of the highest reputation[3] attributed the work to Theopompus, for the

[1] *Riv.Fil.* XXVIII (1950), 49.

[2] Cf. Westlake, *CR* n.s. X (1960), 210: 'This fascinating but almost hopeless pursuit of the author...has tended to bedevil the study of the *Hellenica Oxyrhynchia*, which might profitably turn in other directions'; cf. also Gomme, *A Historical Commentary on Thucydides*, I, 49 n. 3: 'That eminent scholars have disputed the authorship of the *Hellenika Oxyrhynchia* between Ephoros and Theopompos, confidently attributing it to one or to the other, is only a measure of our lack of judgement or our ignorance... To argue for Kratippos or Daimachos of Plataia is...to say that it is by X; for they certainly are only names to us.' For a full, and scholarly, discussion of the problem, see Bloch, 'Studies in Historical Literature of the Fourth Century B.C.: I. The "Hellenica of Oxyrhynchus" and its Authorship', in *HSCP*, supp. vol. I (1940), pp. 303–41. Bloch argues against Theopompus, Cratippus, Ephorus, Androtion and Daimachus, and in favour of anonymity. For an excellent objective summary of the problem, see Griffith, 'The Greek Historians', in *Fifty Years of Classical Scholarship* (Oxford, 1954), pp. 160–2. Bloch (*loc. cit.*) lists all the scholars who, previous to 1940, argued for or against any of the names proposed; all relevant publications are to be found in the *studiorum conspectus* of Bartoletti's Teubner edition.

[3] Notably, in addition to Grenfell and Hunt whose first edition was published as 'Theopompus (or Cratippus), *Hellenica*', Meyer (*Theopomps Hellenika*), Busolt (*Hermes* XLIII (1908), 255 ff.), Wilcken (*Hermes* XLIII (1908), 475 ff.), Swoboda (*Klio* X (1910), 315 ff.), and Wilamowitz-Moellendorff ('Die griechische Literatur des Altertums' (*Die Kultur der Gegenwart*, I, 8[3]), p. 116).

objections to this hypothesis, which I recall briefly here, seem insuperable.

(i) Born in 377/6, Theopompus could hardly have written the tenth book of his *Hellenica*, concerning the years 396–395, before 356, which seems to be the *terminus ad quem* for the composition of P's work, especially as he was converted late from the study of rhetoric to the writing of history.

(ii) In the matter of style, P and Theopompus have nothing in common. The rhetoric perceptible in the extant fragments of Theopompus is in marked contrast to the colourless style of P. Nowhere in P's work is to be found the *elatio atque altitudo orationis* which Cicero (*Brutus* 66) attributes to Theopompus. Nor are there to be found in our papyri examples of the ψυχρότης[1] with which both Speusippus (*F.Gr.Hist.* 115 T 7)[2] and Demetrius (*F.Gr.Hist.* 115 T 44)[3] reproach Theopompus. P clearly did not indulge in passionate diatribes such as that of Theopompus against the friends of Philip (*F.Gr.Hist.* 115 F 225 *c*). Again, the apparent absence of speeches in P's history may be contrasted with the use made of them by Theopompus (cf. Plut. *Mor.* 803 B and *F.Gr.Hist.* 115 F 164 and F 166).

(iii) Then there is the statement of Porphyry (*ap.* Euseb. *Praep. Evang.* p. 465 B–C) that Theopompus plagiarized from Xenophon (cf. *F.Gr.Hist.* 115 F 21).

These few points may be sufficient to illustrate the case against Theopompus, which has for some time now been considered overwhelming.[4]

Many scholars have argued in favour of Ephorus,[5] although this

1 Cf. the definition (Demetrius, Περὶ Ἑρμηνείας 114): ὁρίζεται δὲ τὸ ψυχρὸν Θεόφραστος οὕτως. ψυχρόν ἐστι τὸ ὑπερβάλλον τὴν οἰκείαν ἀπαγγελίαν.

2 πυνθάνομαι δὲ καὶ Θεόπομπον παρ' ὑμῖν μὲν εἶναι πάνυ ψυχρόν...

3 ὄγκον γὰρ ποιοῦσιν, οὐ δεινότητα, πολλαχοῦ δὲ καὶ ψυχρότητα ἀντὶ δεινότητος, οἷον ὡς ὁ Θεόπομπος κατὰ τῶν ἑταίρων τῶν Φιλίππου λέγων ἔλυσεν τῇ ἀντιθέσει τὴν δεινότητα, 'ἀνδροφόνοι δὲ τὴν φύσιν ὄντες', λέγων, 'ἀνδρόπορνοι τὸν τρόπον ἦσαν'.

4 Cf. Jacoby, *Nachr. Ges. Wiss. zu Göttingen*, 1924, p. 13.

5 The earliest being Reuss, *Jahresbericht über die Fortschritte der klass. Altertumswiss.* CXLII (1909), 36–41; Bauer, *Wiener Studien* XXXII (1910), 296–314; Judeich, *Rhein.Mus.* LXVI (1911), 94–139; Walker, *The Hellenica Oxyrhynchia, its Authorship and Authority* (1913).

view is no longer held to be worthy of serious consideration.[1] Barber (*The Historian Ephorus*, pp. 49–67) brought out well the fact that P was not used directly by Diodorus, but by Ephorus, whose work was the medium between P and Diodorus. Bloch (art. cit.) further demonstrated from the Ephorus papyrus (P.Oxy. 1610)[2] published in 1919 that the very close verbal agreements between *F.Gr.Hist.* 70 F 191.3 and Diodorus XI, 59. 3, and between *F.Gr.Hist.* 70 F 191.8 and Diodorus XI, 60. 4, are not at all representative of the relationship evident between P and Diodorus, but are in fact much closer.[3]

On chronological grounds,[4] Ephorus could not possibly have been P, since he wrote his fourth Book after 356, and Books XX ff. after the publication of Callisthenes' *Hellenica* (343–335), which he used as a source (cf. *F.Gr.Hist.* 70 T 17). The year 396/5 would have appeared in Book XVIII or XIX.

Other points which can scarcely be reconciled with the view that P is Ephorus, are the contrast between P's lucid chronological system and Diodorus' confused chronology,[5] the fact that Diodorus XIV, 80. 2 records the destruction of Tissaphernes' gardens by Agesilaus' troops, whereas P does not (hence P is not the direct source of Diodorus on this subject), the absence in Diodorus of any trace of P's account of the Boeotian Constitution, the contrast

[1] Cf. e.g. Gomme, *loc. cit.*, 'These two men [viz. Theopompus and Ephorus] were of such contrary temper that we may be sure that a *History* which can be attributed to both was the work of neither'.

[2] = *F.Gr.Hist.* 70 F 191.

[3] Ephorus F 191.3: ἐκ[εῖνον] μὲν ὑπὸ τῆς πόλε[ως] ἠτιμασμένον, τ[ὴ]ν δὲ πόλιν διὰ τ[ὰ]ς ἐκείνου πράξε[ι]ς τῆς μεγίστης τιμῆς ὑπὸ τῶν Ἑλλήνων ἀξιωθεῖσαν Diod. XI, 59. 3: διόπερ, ὅταν...σκοποῦντες τὰ κατὰ μέρος εὕρωμεν ἐκεῖνον μὲν ὑπὸ τῆς πόλεως ἠτιμασμένον, τὴν δὲ πόλιν διὰ τὰς ἐκείνου πράξεις ἐπαιρομένην...

Ephorus F 191.8: παραθ]αλα[ττίων καλο]υμένω[ν πόλεων ὅσ]αι μὲν ἐκ τ[ῆς Ἑλλά]δος ἦσα[ν ἀπῳ]κισμέναι π[αρα]χρῆμα συν[έπεισε Diod. XI, 60. 4: πλεύσας οὖν μετὰ παντὸς τοῦ στόλου πρὸς τὴν Καρίαν, τῶν παραθαλαττίων πόλεων ὅσαι μὲν ἦσαν ἐκ τῆς Ἑλλάδος ἀπῳκισμέναι, ταύτας παραχρῆμα συνέπεισεν ἀποστῆναι τῶν Περσῶν.

[4] For full discussion, see Jacoby, *Nachr. Ges. Wiss. zu Göttingen*, 1924, pp. 13–18, Bloch, *HSCP*, supp. vol. I (1940), p. 323, and Barber, *The Historian Ephorus*, pp. 49–67.

[5] Suggesting that Diodorus could not have used P directly as a source, as would be the case if P were Ephorus. Cf. Grenfell and Hunt, ed.pr. p. 137.

between P's careful analysis of the outbreak of the Corinthian War and Ephorus' famous record of the causes of the Peloponnesian War (*F.Gr.Hist.* 70 F 196), and the probability that P's history began with the events of 411 B.C.

De Sanctis[1] proposed the identification of P with Androtion, but the insertion of the name of the eponymous archon in the form ἔτος ὄγδοον ἐνειστήκει [ἐν ᾧ Φορμίων ἦρξεν (as restored by De Sanctis; Lond.pap. IV, 1) has been shown by Bloch[2] to be not at all the method employed by Androtion. Nor did the Atthidographers employ the chronological system of summers and winters as found in P. Again, Plutarch[3] states that Androtion wrote his *Atthis* while in exile in Megara, i.e. later than 344/3 B.C., thus presenting another insuperable obstacle to the identification of P with Androtion.[4] A further minor point is that Androtion (F 39) exaggerates the devastation caused to Attica by the Peloponnesians in the Archidamian War, whereas P (XII, 5) tends to minimize it.

A case has been made by Jacoby[5] for the association of P with Daimachus of Plataea. It rests on the statement of Porphyry (*ap.* Euseb. *Praep. Evang.* p. 464 B=*F.Gr.Hist.* 65 T 1 *a*) that Ephorus plagiarized from Daimachus. We know that Ephorus used P for the years of the extant fragments, but not exactly that he plagiarized. We do not know for certain that Daimachus even covered the same period as P. If Jacoby's thesis cannot be disproved, it is equally true that it cannot be proved. We simply do not know from the evidence at our disposal whether it is a reasonable hypothesis or not.

There remain two possibilities, that P is Cratippus, or that P is not known to us by name at all.[6]

Of Cratippus we know[7] that he was a younger contemporary of

1 *Atti Accad. Torino* XLIII (1908), 331–56; supported by Momigliano, *Atti Accad. Torino* LXVI (1931), 29–49.

2 Art. cit. pp. 329–30.

3 *Mor.* 605 C.

4 On this point see Gigante, pp. li–liii.

5 *Nachr. Ges. Wiss. zu Göttingen*, 1924, pp. 13–18, and *CQ* XLIV (1950), 1–8.

6 I am in agreement with Bartoletti (p. xxi) that one of these alternatives provides the answer to the problem. All the evidence concerning Cratippus is reproduced by Bartoletti, pp. xxi–xxv; cf. *F.Gr.Hist.* 64. See also Gomme, 'Who was Kratippos?', *CQ* XLVIII (1954), 53–5.

7 Cf. Plut. *Mor.* 345 D: ἄνελε τὰ περὶ Ἑλλήσποντον Ἀλκιβιάδου νεανιεύματα καὶ τὰ πρὸς Λέσβον Θρασύλλου καὶ τὴν ὑπὸ Θηραμένους τῆς

Thucydides and wrote a continuation of Thucydides' history. So he *could* be the author of the *Hellenica Oxyrhynchia*; unfortunately that is all we can say. Mention must be made, however, of Bloch's argument[1] from Dionysius of Halicarnassus, *De Thuc.* 9 (which passage I have quoted on page 20), that Dionysius did not know the work of P since he states that *no* historian subsequent to Thucydides made use of the Thucydidean *diairesis* by summers and winters. In view of the fact that Dionysius did know Cratippus, whom he mentions in *De Thuc.* 16, it follows, or appears to follow, that P cannot be Cratippus. This seems logical enough, but, on reflection, if we accept the argument, we are almost bound to conclude that Dionysius did not know the early books of Xenophon's *Hellenica* either, for the parts dealing with the years 410–405 retain distinct signs of the Thucydidean method.[2] This would be a most improbable, if not absurd, supposition and the possibility must be allowed, I think, that Dionysius is in error at *De Thuc.* 9, either momentarily forgetting P, or not intending his statement to be taken absolutely literally;[3] one may therefore suspect that Bloch's argument does not categorically refute the attribution of the work to Cratippus.

The vital question in reaching a personal decision on the authorship is whether one can believe that the author of a work of the length and quality of the *Hellenica Oxyrhynchia* could be completely unknown to us by name. This I find intrinsically unlikely,[4] and hence I am not prepared to exclude the possibility that the Oxyrhynchus history is that of Cratippus. Bloch, however, argues forcibly for an anonymous author,[5] quoting a number of papyrus discoveries for which we are unable even to suggest a possible

ὀλιγαρχίας κατάλυσιν καὶ Θρασύβουλον καὶ Ἀρχῖνον καὶ τοὺς ἀπὸ Φυλῆς ἑβδομήκοντα κατὰ τῆς Σπαρτιατῶν ἡγεμονίας ἀνισταμένους καὶ Κόνωνα πάλιν ἐμβιβάζοντα τὰς Ἀθήνας εἰς τὴν θάλατταν, καὶ Κράτιππος ἀνῄρηται. Dionys. Hal. *De Thuc.* 16: ὧν προνοούμενος ἔοικεν ἀτελῆ τὴν ἱστορίαν καταλιπεῖν (Θουκυδίδης), ὡς καὶ Κράτιππος ὁ συνακμάσας αὐτῷ καὶ τὰ παραλειφθέντα ὑπ' αὐτοῦ συναγαγὼν γέγραφεν...

1 Art. cit. p. 313.

2 E.g. at I, 1. 2; 2. 14; 3. 1; 4. 2; II, 1. 1.

3 Griffith, *loc. cit.*, and Bartoletti, *loc. cit.*, do not consider the argument from Dionysius to be conclusive, and both admit the possibility that P may be Cratippus.

4 Cf. Lipsius, praef. p. 4.

5 Art. cit. pp. 334ff. Gigante also takes this view; cf. p. lv.

author. Yet none of these has the appearance of being part of a work of the magnitude of the *Hellenica Oxyrhynchia*, and not everyone has been convinced by the analogy.

To come to a conclusion is difficult. The argument for anonymity is probably the strongest positive argument; yet I feel that basically it is unlikely that we do not know the author's name, and if we do, it is more probably Cratippus than Daimachus. These exhaust the possibilities.

COMMENTARY ON THE FLORENCE PAPYRUS

I, 1 (=Fragment A, column i, 1–19)

Fragment A, column i, concerns the battle fought between the Athenians and Megarians near the hills called τὰ Κέρατα, 'the Horns', which lie opposite Salamis on the border of Megara and Attica (cf. Strabo IX, 1. 11; also mentioned by Acestodorus, *ap.* Plut. *Them.* XIII, as the vantage-point from which Xerxes watched the battle of Salamis). The battle followed the recovery by the Megarians of the port of Nisaea, which had been held by an Athenian garrison since 424, and thus may perhaps have taken place in 410 since Xenophon (*Hell.* I, 1. 36) implies that Nisaea, as the port of the Megarians, was again available to the Spartans in that year. (Cf. Beloch, *Gr.Gesch.* II, 1^2, 402 n. 2; Xenophon does not actually mention the battle.) Diodorus (XIII, 65. 1–2) provides our only other account of this engagement, based, there can be little doubt, upon that of P, which, however, was clearly much richer in detail. Diodorus dates the battle to 409, placing it and the preceding capture of Nisaea by the Megarians in the same year as the Spartan recovery of Pylos.

An Athenian force under the command of Leotrophides and Timarchus was despatched against the Megarians, who gave battle *en masse*, but despite gaining a notable victory the Athenians did not recapture Nisaea.

Cf. Diod. XIII, 65. 1–2: τούτων δὲ πραττομένων Μεγαρεῖς μὲν Νίσαιαν ὑπ' Ἀθηναίους οὖσαν εἷλον, Ἀθηναῖοι δ' ἐπ' αὐτοὺς ἀπέστειλαν Λεωτροφίδην καὶ Τίμαρχον μετὰ μὲν πεζῶν χιλίων, ἱππέων δὲ τετρακοσίων. οἷς οἱ Μεγαρεῖς ἀπαντήσαντες μετὰ τῶν ὅπλων πανδημεὶ καὶ παραλαβόντες τινὰς τῶν ἐκ Σικελίας, παρετάξαντο πρὸς τοῖς λόφοις τοῖς Κέρασι καλουμένοις. 2 τῶν δ' Ἀθηναίων λαμπρῶς ἀγωνισαμένων, καὶ πολλαπλασίους ὄντας τοὺς πολεμίους τρεψαμένων, Μεγαρέων ἔπεσον μὲν πολλοί, τῶν δὲ Λακεδαιμονίων εἴκοσι μόνον· οἱ γὰρ Ἀθηναῖοι βαρέως φέροντες ἐπὶ τῷ τὴν Νίσαιαν κατειλῆφθαι τοὺς μὲν Λακεδαιμονίους οὐκ ἐδίωξαν, πρὸς δὲ τοὺς Μεγαρεῖς χαλεπῶς διακείμενοι παμπληθεῖς ἀνεῖλον.

The present battle is possibly that referred to by Plato, *Republic* II, 368 A.

τετραϰ[οσι...

It is highly probable that P specified the numbers of Athenian troops since Diodorus (*loc. cit.*) does so. Bartoletti in ed.pr. suggested here ἱππέω]ν̣ [δὲ] τετρακ[οσίων (coll. Diod. μετὰ μὲν πεζῶν χιλίων, ἱππέων δὲ τετρακοσίων). If τετρακ[οσι... here does refer to the number of Athenian cavalry, it is noteworthy that P would be giving the figure after his account of the actual battle, the conclusion of which is recorded in the extant fragment, whereas Diodorus gives his figures before the description of the battle.

]ν̣ προτρο[πάδ]η̣ν̣ ἐ̣[τράπησαν, οἱ δὲ] Λακεδαιμό[νιοι.]ωρι.[..... ......]ν̣ ὑ[π]εχώρου[ν ἐν] τάξει [πρὸς τοὺς λόφο]υ̣ς.

χ]ωρὶς [τῶν συμμάχω]ν̣?: Bartoletti, Teubner, in apparatus. See ed.pr. p. 78: 'Una ricostruzione attendibile, in questi righi, appare ardua. Forse vi si diceva che i Megaresi si dettero alla fuga προτροπάδην, gli Spartani si ritirarono ordinatamente.' The mention of Λακεδαιμό[νιοι as taking part in the battle vindicates the readings Λακεδαιμονίων and Λακεδαιμονίους in the MSS of Diodorus XIII, 65. 2, which Vogel (ed. Teubner, Leipzig, 1893) had proposed to emend to Σικελιωτῶν and Σικελιώτας respectively, on the grounds that Diodorus had only mentioned τινὰς τῶν ἐκ Σικελίας, XIII, 65. 1, but no Lacedaemonians, as joining the Megarians who marched out to give battle.

το]ύ̣τ̣ο̣υ̣ς μὲν οὐκ ἐδίωξαν

Cf. Diod., *loc. cit.*, τοὺς μὲν Λακεδαιμονίους οὐκ ἐδίωξαν. P thus supports Diodorus' statement that the Athenians did not pursue the Spartans, of whom only twenty were killed, but killed great numbers of the Megarians, being angered by their seizure of Nisaea.

καταβάλλουσιν αὐτῶν [ἀριθμὸν πολύ]ν

[ἀριθμὸν πολύ]ν is due to Maas. Cf. Diod., *loc. cit.*, Μεγαρέων ἔπεσον μὲν πολλοί and παμπληθεῖς ἀνεῖλον (*sc.* 'Αθηναῖοι).

μετὰ δὲ ταῦτα καταδρα[μόντες τὴν χ]ώραν καὶ τοὺς νεκροὺς [ἀποδόντες ὑπο]σπόνδους τῶν Μεγαρέ[ων] κα[ὶ τοὺς τῶ]ν Λακεδ[α]ιμονίων (ἀ̣π̣έ̣[θα]νον [δὲ το]ύ̣των ὡς εἴκοσιν) ἱστᾶσιν [τρ]οπαῖ[ον·

τῶν Μεγαρέ[ων ἑ]κα[τόν (ed.pr., Maas, Gigante) is rejected in the Teubner edition by Bartoletti as 'longius spatio'. 100 dead would not, in any case, be as great a number as both P and Diodorus suggest. The details in this passage are not provided by Diodorus, except that he agrees on the number of Spartan dead: τῶν δὲ Λακεδαιμονίων εἴκοσι μόνον (*sc.* ἔπεσον). For the expression καταδρα[μόντες τὴν χ]ώραν cf. Lond.pap. XIII, 5; for τοὺς νεκροὺς [ἀποδόντες ὑπο]σπόνδους cf. Lond.pap. VII, 1 and XVI, 3.

ἱστᾶσιν [τρ]οπαῖ[ον

The passage of Pausanias (below) quoted by Gigante in his *testimonia* does not, of course, refer to the present Athenian victory, but probably to the recapture of Nisaea by the Megarians a little earlier (cf. Diod. XIII, 65. 1). Paus. X, 15. 1: τὸ δὲ αὐτῶν (*sc.* ἀγαλμάτων τοῦ 'Απόλλωνος) Μεγαρεῖς ἀνέθεσαν 'Αθηναίους μάχῃ πρὸς Νισαίᾳ κρατήσαντες.

ἀνεχώ[ρ]ησαν πάλιν

Cf. Lond.pap. XIII, 4 and XIII, 5 πάλιν ἀνεχώρησαν.

I, 2 (= Fragment A, column i, 19–28)

The observations in this section on the reactions of the Athenians to the victory do not find a place in Diodorus' shorter account.

τοῖς [στ]ρατηγοῖς

Leotrophides and Timarchus (cf. Diod. XIII, 65. 1). The suggestion that the Athenians, who supposed the generals to have taken an unnecessary risk, were therefore angry with them, despite their pleasure at the victory, may appear a little inconsistent with the statement of Diodorus that Leotrophides and Timarchus had been expressly despatched against the Megarians, for, if so, they must either have intended to join battle or have realized that an engagement might be forced upon them. The indignation of the Athenian *demos* may simply be yet another expression of its own unpredictable nature. Some doubt may also be cast upon the further inference of certain historians (e.g. Grote, pt. II, ch. LXIII) that the intention of the Athenians was the recovery of Nisaea, for it may be pertinent to ask why neither Diodorus nor P mentions such an attempt, and why the Athenians, after so complete a victory, did not actually make an assault upon Nisaea, which they may have had a good chance, in the circumstances, of retaking.

χαλεπῶς εἶ[χο]ν

Cf. Lond.pap. II, 2; XIII, 2; XIV, 3; XV, 1.

ἀνελέσθαι τὸν κίνδ[υ]νον

Cf. Lond.pap. I, 2 μέγαν ⟨ἀν⟩αιροῦνται κίνδυνον.

περὶ Π[ύλο]ṿ

[ἀπὸ τῆς] περὶ Π[ύλο]ṿ ọτ̣[ρ]α[τεία]ṣ ed. pr. [ἐξ ὅτου] περὶ Π[ύλον Theiler, *ap.* Bartoletti, in *Gnomon* XXII (1950), 382.

The sense appears to be that the present battle was the first in which the Lacedaemonians had been defeated since the Athenian victory at Pylos in 425 B.C. (cf. Thuc. IV, 3ff.).

II (= Fragment A, column ii, plus fragment originally published as E)

Of this column only the initial letters of thirty-six lines have survived. Its content, which is not apparent from the extant scraps of text, has been established fairly securely by the following argument: column i of fragment A seems to bring to a conclusion the account of the Athenian victory over the Megarians, also described in Diodorus XIII, 65. 1–2. The only reasonable guess which could be made about the subject-matter of column ii of the same fragment would be that found in the following sections of Diodorus (XIII, 65. 3–4), namely the exploits at Chios of Cratesippidas, the Spartan nauarch. The question is whether this appears likely from the scant remnants of text. We find, in fact, two references to Pedaritus, the Spartan, whose activity at Chios was described in some detail by Thucydides (VIII, 28ff.), and that P mentioned Pedaritus in connection with Chios seems certain since he actually cites Thucydides. Now the only reason for such references to Pedaritus in a passage relating to events of a few years after his death would be that P digressed from a narrative of later happenings at Chios (probably the activity there of Cratesippidas) to recall what Pedaritus had done for the island. For further discussion of the nature of this digression on Pedaritus see my article 'Chios and P.S.I. 1304', in *Phoenix* XVIII (1964), 272–82.

Diodorus XIII, 65. 3–4: Λακεδαιμόνιοι δὲ Κρατησιππίδαν ἑλόμενοι ναύαρχον, καὶ παρὰ τῶν συμμάχων ναῦς αὐτῶν πληρώσαντες εἴκοσι πέντε, προσέταξαν παραβοηθεῖν τοῖς συμμάχοις. οὗτος δὲ χρόνον μέν τινα περὶ τὴν Ἰωνίαν διέτριψεν οὐθὲν ἄξιον λόγου πράξας· μετὰ δὲ ταῦτα παρὰ τῶν ἐκ Χίου φυγάδων λαβὼν χρήματα κατήγαγεν αὐτοὺς καὶ τὴν ἀκρόπολιν τῶν Χίων κατελάβετο. 4 οἱ δὲ κατελθόντες τῶν Χίων τῶν ἀντιπολιτευομένων αὐτοῖς καὶ τῆς ἐκπτώσεως ⟨αἰτίους ὄντας⟩ εἰς ἑξακοσίους τὸν ἀριθμὸν ὄντας ἐφυγάδευσαν. οὗτοι δὲ τῆς ἀντιπέραν ἠπείρου χωρίον Ἀταρνέα καλούμενον κατελάβοντο, σφόδρα τῇ φύσει καθεστηκὸς ὀχυρόν, καὶ τὸ λοιπὸν ἐκ τούτου τὰς ἀφορμὰς ἔχοντες ἐπολέμουν τοῖς Χίον ἔχουσιν. Cf. Xen. *Hell.* I, 1. 32:...Πασιππίδας ὁ Λάκων ἔφυγεν ἐκ Σπάρτης· ἐπὶ δὲ τὸ ναυτικόν, ὃ ἐκεῖνος ἠθροίκει ἀπὸ τῶν συμμάχων, ἐξεπέμφθη Κρατησιππίδας, καὶ παρέλαβεν ἐν Χίῳ.

The fragment which in ed.pr. was labelled E has been attributed by Bartoletti (ed. Teubner) to lines 1–11 of this column. The three lines in which the addition of fragment E forms reasonable groupings of words are (fragment E in bold type): line 6 τυχ[.]**ν ἰδιωτ**[--; line 7 οὐδ[ἑ]**ν ἧττον** [--; line 10 ἐξ [αὐτ]**ῆς τῆς** [--.

χ]ρήματα (line 4)

Cf., perhaps, Diod. XIII, 65. 3: παρὰ τῶν ἐκ Χίου φυγάδων λαβὼν χρήματα (*sc.* Κρατησιππίδας).

ὁ Πεδάρι[τος

πεδαρει[p. Pedaritus, the son of Leon, had been sent from Sparta in the summer of 412 to take the command at Chios (Thuc. VIII, 28. 5), which he defended with resolution during the succeeding winter under pressure from the Athenians by both sea and land. His difficulties were exacerbated by the persistent refusal of Astyochus to come to his aid, and by a measure of disunity among the Chians which resulted in the execution by Pedaritus of some supporters of Tydeus, the son of Ion, on a charge of being pro-Athenian (Thuc. VIII, 32. 2–3; 33. 3–4; 38. 3–4; 39. 2; 40. 1). Pedaritus met his death when, after a rash attack on the fortifications protecting the Athenian ships, the Chians were routed by an Athenian counter-attack (Thuc. VIII, 55. 2–3).

The form of the name Πεδάριτος is attested by Thucydides (*locc. citt.*), Isocrates VI, 53, and Harpocration, *s.v.* Suidas has Παιδάριτος, and Plutarch, *Mor.* 241 D, Παιδάρητος. See further Wackernagel, in *Philol.* LXXXVI (1930), 140.

It is interesting that Theopompus, like P, also mentioned Pedaritus in the context of a narrative of events later than his death—cf. Harpocration *s.v.* Πεδάριτος: τῶν ἐκ Λακεδαίμονος ἐκπεμφθέντων ἐστὶν οὗτος, ἁρμοστὴς ἀνήρ, τῶν γεγονότων καλῶν, ὥς φησι Θεόπομπος ἐν β̅ Ἑλληνικῶν. Cf. *F.Gr.Hist.* 115 F 8. This can no longer be seriously considered an additional argument for the identification of P with Theopompus.

On Pedaritus, see *P.Lak.* 599.

Lines 25–7 **οὔθ' οἵτινες ἐ.**[---**δυ**]|**ναστείαν, οὐδ**[---**φι**]|**λοτιμίας**

Perhaps P contrasts Pedaritus favourably with other Spartans who held positions of authority abroad.

Line 28 **διέσωσαν**

The subject could well be 'Pedaritus and his troops'; cf. Isoc. VI, 53: Πεδάριτος μὲν γὰρ εἰς Χίον εἰσπλεύσας τὴν πόλιν αὐτῶν διέσωσεν.

Lines 30–1 **ατη γενομένῃ [---πε]|ρὶ ἧς καὶ Θουκ[υδίδης---**

Maas suggested ἄτη, *calamitas*, but it seems improbable that a word so predominantly poetical was used by P. The citation of Thucydides is hardly surprising, but does confirm that P knew his work, as was inferred from his historical method—particularly his chronological system—which appears to have been influenced by Thucydides. It had also been suggested by Hardy, in *CP* XXI (1926), 355, that Thuc. VII, 27 may have been a source of London papyrus XII, 5 (see note *ad loc.*).

Line 32 **Πε{ρι}δαριτọ[**

περιδαρειτọ[p, corrected by Maas, who suggested that the error might result from a reading π$\overset{\alpha\iota}{\varepsilon}$δαρειτο. Confusion with πε]ρὶ ἧς at the beginning of the previous line could also explain the scribe's mistake. Ed.pr. also proposed περὶ ⟨Πε⟩δ.

III (= Fragment B, column i)

Of fragment B, column i, only the final letters of thirty-one lines have survived. One can, however, make a reasonable conjecture as to the subject-matter of the column, for column ii of the same fragment concerns the battle of Notium and the immediate antecedents of it would probably have been recorded here as in Diodorus XIII, 71. 1: 'Αλκιβιάδης δέ, πυθόμενος ἐν 'Εφέσῳ τὸν Λύσανδρον ἐξαρτύειν τὸν στόλον, ἀνήχθη μετὰ πασῶν τῶν νεῶν εἰς Ἔφεσον. ἐπιπλεύσας δὲ τοῖς λιμέσιν, ὡς οὐδεὶς ἀντανήγετο, τὰς μὲν πολλὰς ναῦς καθώρμισε περὶ τὸ Νότιον, τὴν ἡγεμονίαν αὐτῶν παραδοὺς 'Αντιόχῳ τῷ ἰδίῳ κυβερνήτῃ, διακελευσάμενος αὐτῷ μὴ ναυμαχεῖν, ἕως ἂν αὐτὸς παραγένηται, τὰς δὲ στρατιώτιδας ναῦς ἀνέλαβε καὶ κατὰ σπουδὴν ἔπλευσεν εἰς Κλαζομενάς· αὕτη γὰρ ἡ πόλις σύμμαχος 'Αθηναίων οὖσα κακῶς ἔπασχεν ὑπό τινων φυγάδων πορθουμένη. This conjecture may be substantiated to some degree by the one really acceptable restoration of much significance, ταῖς Κλα[ζομεναῖς in ll. 22–3, which could well refer to Alcibiades' visit to that city in 407 at a time when its citizens were being harassed by certain oligarchic exiles (cf. Diod. *loc. cit.*). (Diodorus dates the visit, along with the battle of Notium, to 408. However, since this date is almost certainly too early for the battle of Notium, and as Alcibiades' visit to Clazomenae obviously took place about the time of the battle or not very long before it, I prefer to take the autumn of 407 as the most likely date, although the spring of 406 is also possible. On the date of the battle of Notium, see my note to chapter IV.) Such a reconstruction would once again identify P as the originator of a tradition entirely independent of Xenophon, who passes in silence over the voyage of Alcibiades to Clazomenae; cf. *Hell.* I, 5. 11, which records only that Alcibiades went to the assistance of Thrasybulus at Phocaea just before Antiochus gave battle at Notium.

Although it is, of course, very probable that P mentioned Alcibiades in this chapter, I cannot accept Gigante's speculative restoration of Ἀλκιβ]ιάδης in l. 3 (cf. Gigante, p. lxvii). τ, where Gigante wishes to read δ, is tolerably clear in the papyrus, and Bartoletti, who read]δ̣ι̣ατησε in ed.pr., may well be on the right lines in the Teubner edition, where he proposes (in the apparatus) ἐ]κ̣ρ̣άτησε.

Lines 18–19 βασιλέ|[ως

It may be noteworthy that Diodorus XIII, 70. 3–4, the sections immediately preceding that which I have quoted as a likely parallel to the present passage, concern the decision of Darius to send his son, Cyrus, to Sardis with instructions to assist the Lacedaemonians, and the meeting of Lysander and the Persian prince. In view of the scale of P's work relative to that of Diodorus, the present reference to the King could not occur in a similar narrative to that of Diodorus (it would have appeared somewhat earlier), but might, at a guess, refer back to the events in question.

Line 20 νήσοις

Gigante (p. lxviii) thinks that there is a reference here to the devastation of Cos and Rhodes by Alcibiades (cf. Diod. XIII, 69. 5). Yet in view of Gigante's acceptance of the mention of Clazomenae in l. 22 as corresponding to Diodorus XIII, 71. 1, the inclusion of the events relating to Cos and Rhodes only two lines earlier would give the impression that P's account was much more succinct than that of Diodorus, whereas the reverse is true, that Diodorus, through the intermediary Ephorus, summarized P's work for this period. The same objection may be made to the more general suggestion of Gigante (p. lxvii) that this column contained an account of the naval operations recorded by Diodorus XIII, 66–9. In particular Gigante's opinion (which rests on no evidence) that Coppola (in *Il Popolo d'Italia*, 19 Aug. 1939), when he expressed the view that one of the columns of the Florence papyrus contained mention 'dell'attività di Alcibiade a Bisanzio', meant this column and not fragment C, seems highly improbable. Cf. notes on frag. C = ch. V; also ed.pr. p. 69 n. 1, Maas, in *CQ* XLIV (1950), in a note to his text of frag. C, and Fuks, in *CQ* XLV (1951), 155.

IV (=Fragment B, column ii)

The Battle of Notium

The discovery of this fragment with its account of the battle of Notium confirmed the view expressed by De Sanctis ('La battaglia di Notion', *Riv.Fil.* IX (1931), 222–9; now also in *Studi di storia della storiografia greca* (Florence, 1951), pp. 163–71) that Diodorus' version of the battle must have derived from that of P, and was therefore worthy of greater attention than it had received from modern historians, who tended to accept without question the version of Xenophon. The respective accounts of Diodorus and Xenophon are as follows:

Diod. XIII, 71. 2–4: ὁ δ' Ἀντίοχος ὢν τῇ φύσει πρόχειρος, καὶ σπεύδων δι' ἑαυτοῦ τι πρᾶξαι λαμπρόν, τῶν μὲν Ἀλκιβιάδου λόγων ἠμέλησε, δέκα δὲ ναῦς ⟨τὰς⟩ ἀρίστας πληρώσας, καὶ τὰς ἄλλας τοῖς τριηράρχοις παραγγείλας ἑτοίμας ἔχειν, ἂν ᾖ χρεία ναυμαχεῖν, ἐπέπλευσε τοῖς πολεμίοις, προκαλεσόμενος εἰς ναυμαχίαν. 3 ὁ δὲ Λύσανδρος πεπυσμένος παρά τινων αὐτομόλων τὴν ἄφοδον Ἀλκιβιάδου καὶ τῶν ἀρίστων μετ' αὐτοῦ στρατιωτῶν, καιρὸν εἶναι διέλαβε πρᾶξαί τι τῆς Σπάρτης ἄξιον. διόπερ πάσαις ταῖς ναυσὶν ἀνταναχθεὶς μίαν μὲν τὴν προπλέουσαν τῶν δέκα, καθ' ἣν Ἀντίοχος ἦν ἀντιτεταγμένος, κατέδυσε, τὰς δ' ἄλλας τρεψάμενος ἐδίωξε, μέχρις οὗ τὰς ἄλλας πληρώσαντες οἱ τριήραρχοι τῶν Ἀθηναίων παρεβοήθησαν ἐν οὐδεμιᾷ τάξει. 4 γενομένης δὲ ναυμαχίας ἀθρόαις ταῖς ναυσὶν οὐ μακρὰν τῆς γῆς, Ἀθηναῖοι διὰ τὴν ἀταξίαν ἠλαττώθησαν καὶ ναῦς ἀπέβαλον δύο πρὸς ταῖς εἴκοσι· τῶν δ' ἐν αὐταῖς ἀνδρῶν ὀλίγοι μὲν ἐζωγρήθησαν, οἱ δὲ λοιποὶ πρὸς τὴν γῆν διενήξαντο. Ἀλκιβιάδης δὲ πυθόμενος τὸ γεγενημένον διὰ σπουδῆς ἀνέκαμψεν εἰς τὸ Νότιον καὶ πάσας τὰς τριήρεις πληρώσας ἐπέπλευσε τοῖς λιμέσι τῶν πολεμίων· οὐ τολμῶντος δ' ἀνταναχθῆναι τοῦ Λυσάνδρου τὸν πλοῦν εἰς Σάμον ἐποιήσατο.

Xen. *Hell.* I, 5. 12–14: ὁ δὲ Ἀντίοχος τῇ τε αὑτοῦ νηὶ καὶ ἄλλῃ ἐκ Νοτίου εἰς τὸν λιμένα τῶν Ἐφεσίων εἰσπλεύσας παρ' αὐτὰς τὰς πρῴρας τῶν Λυσάνδρου νεῶν παρέπλει. 13 ὁ δὲ Λύσανδρος τὸ μὲν πρῶτον ὀλίγας τῶν νεῶν καθελκύσας ἐδίωκεν αὐτόν, ἐπεὶ δὲ οἱ Ἀθηναῖοι τῷ Ἀντιόχῳ ἐβοήθουν πλείοσι ναυσί, τότε δὴ καὶ πάσας συντάξας ἐπέπλει. μετὰ δὲ ταῦτα καὶ οἱ Ἀθηναῖοι ἐκ τοῦ Νοτίου καθελκύσαντες τὰς λοιπὰς τριήρεις ἀνήχθησαν, ὡς ἕκαστος ἤνοιξεν. 14 ἐκ τούτου δ' ἐναυμάχησαν οἱ μὲν ἐν τάξει, οἱ δὲ Ἀθηναῖοι διεσπαρμέναις ταῖς ναυσί, μέχρι οὗ ἔφυγον ἀπολέσαντες πεντεκαίδεκα τριήρεις. τῶν δὲ ἀνδρῶν οἱ μὲν πλεῖστοι ἐξέφυγον, οἱ δ' ἐζωγρήθησαν. Λύσανδρος δὲ τάς τε ναῦς ἀναλαβὼν καὶ τροπαῖον στήσας ἐπὶ τοῦ Νοτίου διέπλευσεν εἰς Ἔφεσον, οἱ δὲ Ἀθηναῖοι εἰς Σάμον.

Of course the two versions have much in common as regards the broad outline: both had previously mentioned that Alcibiades, on his departure from Notium, had left in command his helmsman, Antiochus—rather irregularly in preference to the trierarchs—with instructions to avoid battle until his return (and we may assume that P also gave this information somewhere in column i of this fragment, i.e. chapter III). Both narrate Antiochus' disobedience and his provocative action in sailing to the harbour of Ephesus, where the Peloponnesian fleet was moored. Both indicate that eventually Lysander joined battle with all his ships; that the Athenians, being in disorder, were defeated with the loss of a number of ships; and that some Athenians were taken prisoner, but that the majority escaped.

In point of detail, however, there are serious differences between the two accounts, and on these details the agreements between Diodorus and P are striking. According to Xenophon, Antiochus, in the first instance, sailed into the harbour of Ephesus with his own ship and one other; Diodorus indicates that he took ten ships. The restorations πληρώσας τρ[ιήρεις δέκα and αὐτὸς δὲ ταῖς δέκα προ]έπλει in Bartoletti's text of IV, 1, which bring P into agreement with Diodorus on this point, are sound, being based on the mention in IV, 3 of the δεκαναΐα[ν] of the Athenians. Maas (*ap.* ed.pr.) made the interesting proposal [αὐτὸς δὲ σὺν μιᾷ νηῒ προ]έπλει which combines the statements of Diodorus and Xenophon to suggest that only one ship other than that of Antiochus himself actually entered the harbour of Ephesus, whereas ten had set out from Notium. While this view has a certain attraction, and while it seems to me to provide a very reasonable explanation of the difference between Diodorus and Xenophon on this point, it is on the whole more probable, in view of the other disagreements between the P–Diodorus version and Xenophon, that P here too was the source of Diodorus and differed from Xenophon. The reading was not incorporated in Maas's own text.

Lysander, in Xenophon's account, pursued Antiochus at first with only a few ships. Diodorus states that he put to sea with his entire fleet, having been informed of the absence of Alcibiades. P, however, reveals that on this point Diodorus has simply omitted one stage of the proceedings in the cause of brevity, for in IV, 2 three is specified as the number of ships first launched by Lysander. Diodorus and P mention the sinking of Antiochus' own ship at this juncture and the subsequent flight of the remaining Athenian vessels; Xenophon omits the detail. In P and Diodorus the Athenian trierarchs put out from Notium after Lysander brought his whole fleet to the pursuit of the ships which had accompanied Antiochus. Xenophon reverses the order, making Lysander bring out all his ships on seeing 'more' Athenian vessels coming to assist Antiochus. The discrepancy here may be resolved if the 'more' ships to which Xenophon refers are in fact the rest of the ten mentioned by P and

Diodorus, but of which Xenophon had no knowledge. This point may be taken, perhaps, as confirmation of De Sanctis' view (to which I return presently) that Xenophon's version was based on a Spartan source.

In the sea-battle which ensued P and Diodorus give twenty-two as the number of Athenian ships lost; Xenophon gives fifteen. Diodorus does not mention that Lysander set up a trophy before returning to Ephesus, but both P and Xenophon do. After the battle, in Diodorus' account, Alcibiades returned to Notium, sailed against the enemy fleet in harbour at Ephesus, but finding that Lysander now refused to give battle withdrew to Samos. P also indicates that the Athenians were shut up in Notium after the battle. Xenophon, on the other hand, states that the Athenian fleet withdrew to Samos immediately after the battle and, therefore, that it was to Samos, not Notium, that Alcibiades came before attempting to draw Lysander out for a second engagement. Cf. Xen. *Hell.* I, 5. 15: μετὰ δὲ ταῦτα Ἀλκιβιάδης ἐλθὼν εἰς Σάμον ἀνήχθη ταῖς ναυσὶν ἁπάσαις ἐπὶ τὸν λιμένα τῶν Ἐφεσίων, καὶ πρὸ τοῦ στόματος παρέταξεν, εἴ τις βούλοιτο ναυμαχεῖν.

Two phrases in Diodorus' account which have no parallel in P, and in matter of style are alien to P, σπεύδων δι' ἑαυτοῦ τι πρᾶξαι λαμπρόν, and καιρὸν εἶναι διέλαβε πρᾶξαί τι τῆς Σπάρτης ἄξιον, may well derive from Ephorus. The detail that, after the sinking of Antiochus' ship and the pursuit of those with him by Lysander, the Athenian trierarchs were unable to get all the remaining ships out of harbour in time, but only joined battle with the majority of them (ταῖς πλείσταις αὐτῶν), is found only in P (IV, 3). P also provides the detail that the Athenians remained in Notium for three days after the battle (IV, 4).

The argument of De Sanctis that Diodorus' account (and that, of course, means P's account) suggests an Athenian source, whereas Xenophon probably made use of a Spartan source, is quite acceptable; he would go further and suggest (*Studi di storia della storiografia greca*, p. 171) that the Athenian tradition preserved through P in Diodorus derived from reports sent to the boule by the generals. If this should be so it would, of course, be more likely that P is correct on such details as the number of ships lost by the Athenians than that Xenophon is. It is certainly true, moreover, that the precision and coherence of P's account strike the reader as authoritative and render it worthy of at least equal consideration with that of Xenophon in any modern reconstruction of the event. The almost universal acceptance, before the publication of the Florence papyrus, by modern historians of Xenophon's version in preference to Diodorus' was probably, as claimed by De Sanctis, no more than prejudice, even if understandable. De Sanctis' argument that Diodorus should here be taken more seriously, and even preferred to Xenophon since his account was based on P (a hypothesis now substantiated), has recently been upheld by Giannelli, *Trattato di storia greca* (Rome, 1948—still before the publication of P.S.I. 1304), p. 307, and Hammond, *A History of Greece* (Oxford, 1959), p. 414, has accepted from P and Diodorus the details that Antiochus first put out from Notium with ten ships, that his own ship was sunk, and that the number of Athenian vessels lost was twenty-two.

Plutarch (*Alcib.* xxxv, 6–7; *Lys.* v, 1) narrates the battle in substantially the same form as Xenophon, who was probably his source. Two details in the account in the *Alcibiades*—that Antiochus had been instructed not to give battle even if the enemy should take the initiative in sailing against him, μηδ' ἂν ἐπιπλέωσιν οἱ πολέμιοι διαναυμαχεῖν, and the death of Antiochus, αὐτόν τε διέφθειρε τὸν 'Αντίοχον—are not found in Xenophon's version, and may perhaps derive from Theopompus, along with a certain tendency to moralize, as, for instance, in the remark that Antiochus ἀγαθὸς μὲν ἦν κυβερνήτης, ἀνόητος δὲ τὰ ἄλλα καὶ φορτικός (*Alcib.* xxxv, 6).

There is a brief notice of the battle in Pausanias ix, 32. 6 which raises no points of interest except, perhaps, that Lysander is credited with having led Antiochus to believe that he was capable of victory in a sea-battle against the Spartans: τηνικαῦτα τὸν 'Αντίοχον ἐπηγάγετο ἐς ἐλπίδα ὡς ὄντα ἀξιόμαχον ναυμαχῆσαι Λακεδαιμονίοις.

On the date of the battle of Notium the fragment of P provides no new evidence, and Diodorus places the event in the year 408, which is probably too early. It is, therefore, from Xenophon's *Hellenica* that one must attempt to establish the date, but here too accuracy is hardly attainable, as may be seen from the varying opinions held by modern scholars. Keil (*RE* xvii, 1, col. 1,075, *s.v.* 'Notion'), Giannelli (*Trattato di storia greca*) and Bartoletti (ed.pr.) take spring 407; Toepffer (*RE* i, 2, col. 1,530) places the battle within the year 407; and Grote (*A History of Greece*, pt. II, ch. lxiv) and Bury (*A History of Greece*, ch. xi) give autumn 407, but Meiggs, in his revision of Bury's work, alters the date to spring 406. In this he follows Beloch (*Gr.Gesch.* ii, 1^2, 417) and Ferguson (*CAH* v, 353). Hammond (*A History of Greece*, p. 414) also dates the battle to the early part of 406, while Ferrabino (*L'impero ateniese*, p. 401) gives as late a date as summer 406.

There is general agreement that Xenophon, *Hell.* i, 4. 2 (ἀρχομένου τοῦ ἔαρος) refers to spring 407, and *Hell.* i, 6. 1 (τῷ δ' ἐπιόντι ἔτει ᾧ ἡ σελήνη ἐξέλιπεν ἑσπέρας) provides a chronological anchor in mentioning the eclipse of the moon, calculated to have occurred on 15 April 406. Spring 406 must therefore appear as the *terminus ad quem* for the battle of Notium (reported in *Hell.* i, 5. 11–14). Now, at i, 5. 1 Xenophon departs from a chronological sequence of events to recall the arrival of Lysander in Asia (πρότερον τούτων οὐ πολλῷ χρόνῳ, i.e. before the return of Alcibiades to Athens and his subsequent success at Andros, I, 4. 8–22). In other words Xenophon returns to events of spring 407. Thus the attribution of the battle of Notium to spring 407 depends upon the assumption that Xenophon's excursus beginning at I, 5. I continues until I, 5. 15, the end of his account of the battle. This does not seem to me to be the case. Rather, it seems natural that, having brought the reader up to date with the movements of Lysander, Xenophon returns at I, 5. 11 to the activity of Alcibiades after his acquisition of Samos as a base (recorded at I, 4. 23). The alternative dates for Notium, then, are autumn 407 and spring 406, and between these one cannot decide with certainty. It is worthy of note, however, that Xenophon's mention of the election of ten new generals at Athens (at I, 5. 16; that is, before his transition to the year 406) need not refer to the normal election which would take place in spring 406 (in which case his chronology would be faulty, and, further, spring 406 would almost certainly be the date of the battle of Notium, which the election immediately follows). The election in question was probably of an extraordinary nature, resulting from the deposition of Alcibiades after the battle (on this see Hatzfeld, *REA* XXXIII (1931), 111). My own inclination is to date the battle to autumn 407, but a date early in 406 must also be considered possible.

IV, I (=Fragment B, column ii, 1–9)

-]νησιῳ̣[.

'num Πελοπον]νησίω[ν?', Bartoletti. Maas reads -]νησιδ̣[.

πληρώσας τρ[ιήρεις δέκα τὰς ἄριστα] πλεούσας

The subject is obviously Antiochus, the pilot of Alcibiades, who must have been mentioned earlier as having been entrusted with the command for the duration of Alcibiades' absence. For δέκα cf. IV, 3 δεκαναΐα[ν, also Diod. XIII, 71. 2.

τὰς μὲν ἑτ̣[έρας ἐκέλευσε ναυ]λοχεῖν ἕως ἂν ἀπάρω[σιν αἱ τῶν πολεμί]ων πόρρω τῆς γῆς

This remark provides a further indication that the intention of Antiochus was to provoke a full-scale engagement. The meaning of ναυλοχεῖν here would not be merely 'to lie in harbour', but 'to lie in wait in order to sally out on passing ships'; cf. L.–S.–J. *s.v.*

πρὸς τὴν Ἔφεσ[ον

Where Lysander had arrived in spring 407 (Xen. *Hell.* I, 5. I). Xenophon does not actually mention the move of the Athenian fleet from Samos to

Notium, whence, no doubt, a closer watch could be kept on the Spartans at Ephesus; cf. Diod. XIII, 71. 1. Parallel to the present passage of P, cf. Xen. *Hell.* I, 5. 12: εἰς τὸν λιμένα τῶν Ἐφεσίων εἰσπλεύσας (*sc.* Ἀντίοχος). The reference is not to the harbour of the Hellenistic period, to which there was access from the sea only through a narrow entrance, but to that harbour at the foot of the hill of Ayasolouk which was wide open to the sea. The hill was in the centre of the city of Ephesus in the fifth century B.C. See plan in *RE*, *s.v.* 'Ephesos'.

..............] προσαξόμενος αὐτά[ς. (*sc.* τὰς τῶν πολεμίων ναῦς)

εἰς τὸ ναυμαχῆσαι] προ{σ}αξόμενος Maas; εἰς τὴν εὐρυχωρίαν] Wade-Gery, *ap.* Bartoletti. Cf. Diod. XIII, 71. 2: προκαλεσόμενος εἰς ναυμαχίαν. εἰς ναυμαχίαν might also be appropriate to the lacuna in P, but seems a little too short for the space.

IV, 2 (= Fragment B, column ii, 9–18)

Λύσανδρος δὲ κατι]δὼν α[ὐ]τοὺς τρεῖς να̣[ῦς] εὐθὺς καθεῖλκεν·

That Lysander at first deployed three ships is a detail known only from P. Xenophon (*Hell.* I, 5. 13) says ὀλίγας τῶν νεῶν; cf. Plutarch, *Alcib.* XXXV, 7 ὀλίγαις ναυσίν and *Lys.* V, 1 οὐ πολλὰς τῶν τριήρων.

αἵ]περ κα[ὶ] πρότερον αὐ[τ.............] καταδύ[ο]υσι τὸν Ἀ[ν]τ̣[ίοχον...

Despite the poor state in which these lines have been preserved, it seems certain that καταδύ[ο]υσι refers to the sinking of Antiochus' ship; cf. Diod. XIII, 71. 3. πρότερον may well, as Bartoletti suggests, contain some reference to Antiochus, or to his ship, which Diodorus (*loc. cit.*) says was τὴν προπλέουσαν τῶν δέκα. Gigante's idea that it may refer back to some previous activity of Lysander is most improbable, because (*a*) there is hardly sufficient space for such a reference, and (*b*), as Gigante himself admits (pp. 49–50), it is difficult to suggest any appropriate event to which P might have referred.

διαφθείρου[σιν...........τῶν] μὲν Ἀθηναίων κτλ.

Probably a reference to the death of Antiochus. Bartoletti proposed in ed.pr. διαφθείρου[σιν αὐτόν. διόπερ τῶν]. The only other account which specifically mentions the death of Antiochus, as distinct from the loss of his ship, is that of Plutarch, *Alcib.* XXXV, 7: αὐτόν τε διέφθειρε τὸν Ἀντίοχον. There may, however, be some difficulty in making Antiochus the object of both verbs καταδύ[ο]υσι and διαφθείρου[σιν. Accame (*Riv.Fil.* XXVIII

(1950), 35 n. 2) is too dogmatic in stating that the same object for the two verbs 'non ha senso', but his suggestion '*exempli gratia*' καταδύ[ο]υσι τὸν 'Α[ν]τ̣[ίοχον μετὰ τῆς αὐτοῦ νε]ὼς καὶ διαφθείρου[σι δύο ἄλλας. διόπερ τῶν]... could be on the right lines, although it cannot be precisely right since it exceeds the available space in both lacunae by four or five letters.

τῶν] μὲν 'Αθηναίων φ[οβηθέντες οἱ συμπλέον]τες εὐθέως πρὸς τᾰ̣[μπαλιν ἐτράπησαν

Cf. Diod. XIII, 71. 3: τὰς δ' ἄλλας (of the ten ships at first taken by Antiochus; here οἱ συμπλέοντες) τρεψάμενος (*sc*. Λύσανδρος). Maas suggested τῶν] μὲν 'Αθηναίων ο̣[ἱ---ναυλοχοῦν]τες, but, as Bartoletti points out, οἱ ναυλοχοῦντες had not yet left harbour at Notium; cf. IV, 1: τὰς μὲν ἑτ̣[έρας ἐκέλευσε ναυ]λοχεῖν ἕως ἂν ἀπάρω[σιν αἱ τῶν πολεμί]ων πόρρω τῆς γῆς.

Λύσανδρος δὲ ἀ[ν]αλαβ[ὼν πάσας τὰς τρι]ήρεις ἐδίωκε τοὺς [π]ολεμ[ίους.

The mobilization of the entire Peloponnesian fleet based at Ephesus would not be necessary to put to flight the nine Athenian vessels remaining after the destruction of Antiochus' ship, especially as they had already begun a hasty withdrawal. Lysander appears to have been as keen as Antiochus for a major engagement, encouraged by the knowledge (Diod. XIII, 71. 3) that Alcibiades was elsewhere.

IV, 3 (=Fragment B, column ii, 18–35)

οἱ δὲ λοιποὶ] τῶν 'Αθηναίων

I.e. those left in harbour with orders to lie in wait ἕως ἂν ἀπάρω[σιν αἱ τῶν πολεμί]ων πόρρω τῆς γῆς (IV, 1).

δεκαναΐα[ν]

The word is found also in Diod. XIV, 103. 3, Polybius XXII, 7. 4 and XXIV, 6. 1. Cf. the use of πενταναΐα in London papyrus II, 4.

διὰ] ταχέων

Cf. Lond.pap. III, 1; XIII, 5; XVII, 2 and 4.

πάσας μὲν οὐκ ἠ[δύναντο τὰς] τριήρεις φθῆναι π[λ]ηρώ[σαντες, κτλ.

If the discovery of the Florence fragments had preceded the publication of Ferrabino's work *L'impero ateniese* (Turin, 1927), the present passage might have been thought the source of his strange assertion, for which there is no evidence in Xenophon, Diodorus or Plutarch, that 'i trierarchi rimasero incerti fra l'intervenire e il restare; ed il risultato fu che alcuni intervennero, e gli altri no' (*op. cit.* p. 401). P's version of the story does not, however, really lend any support to this hypothesis, since it is clear that the reason for the trierarchs' failure to get all the ships manned in time was the swift action of the enemy fleet, and not indecision as to whether they should obey the orders of Antiochus, now dead, or adhere to the instructions given to him previously by Alcibiades (if, indeed, they knew what these instructions were).

ταῖς δὲ] πλείσταις αὐτῶν μ[ι]κρὸν [ἐκ τοῦ λιμέ]νος ἀναχθέντες το[ῦ τ]ῶν [Κολοφωνίων] τὰς μὲν προπλευ̣[σά]σας [..........,] αὐτοὶ δὲ ταραχθέντες ἀμα[χεὶ.........] καὶ δι' ἀταξίαν ὑπεχώρη[σαν τοῖς πολε]μίοις.

The sense of this passage is a matter of some debate. It seems reasonable to suppose, in the first place (with Bartoletti, ed.pr. p. 80 n. 28), that τὰς προπλευσάσας refers to the ships, now reduced from ten to nine, with which Antiochus had first advanced towards Ephesus (cf. IV, 1: [αὐτὸς δὲ ταῖς δέκα προ]έπλει). Gigante's alternative to this is a little difficult to understand. He suggests in the lacuna which follows ἀ[πέωσαν εἰς τὴν γῆν], for which, incidentally, there is not sufficient space, and interprets the sense (p. 51 n. 28) 'gli Spartani respinsero verso terra quelle che delle navi che sopraggiungevano erano innanzi a tutte'. One would therefore infer that Gigante wishes 'the Spartans' to be the subject of the missing verb, the object of which is τὰς προπλευ̣[σά]σας, yet the sentence construction, ἐπικειμένων τῶν ἐν[αντίων (i.e. the Spartans)...πάσας μὲν οὐκ ἠ[δύναντο (*sc.* οἱ λοιποὶ τῶν 'Αθηναίων above)...ταῖς δὲ] πλείσταις... ἀναχθέντες...τὰς μὲν προπλευ̣[σά]σας [missing verb,] αὐτοὶ δέ..., would surely indicate that the remaining Athenians (i.e. those left at Notium by Antiochus) are the subject of the verb in the lacuna. If, however, the meaning is to be that the Athenians, on sailing out from Notium, forced the leading Peloponnesian ships towards the land (and this is what Gigante's textual restoration would mean, although not, it seems, in accord with his note), this would be a new detail suggesting a limited Athenian success in the first instance, in sharp contrast with the later state of disorder which contributed to their defeat. Gigante does not, however, suggest this in as many words, and it would not, in any case, accord well with the known facts about the engagement.

In the lacuna Maas and Wade-Gery propose ἀπέσωσαν μόλις. Bartoletti (in apparatus) suggests (e.g.) ἐτάραξαν πάνυ. His interpretation thus not only provides a reason for the Athenian disorder, in addition to that of having manned their triremes in great haste, but gives extra emphasis to the Athenian disorder, which is, in fact, stressed by all the sources: 'Atheniensium naves, aliae propere e portu exeuntes, aliae cursu illuc advenientes, eo modo inter se occurrunt invicemque aliae alias perturbant, ut, priusquam cum hostibus celeriter et ipsis supervenientibus pugnam conserant, fugam capere cogantur.' This interpretation I find convincing.

In the second lacuna Bartoletti suggests (e.g.) ἀμα[χεὶ διεσπάρησαν in preference to ἅμα [ἐναυμάχησαν in ed.pr., ἅμα [τε προσέμειξαν Wade-Gery (*ap.* Bartoletti), ἅμα [τε προσέπλευσαν Castiglioni (*Prolegomena* I (1952), 130–2), and ἅμα [διεναυμάχησαν Gigante.

[Κολοφωνίων]

Attributed to Wade-Gery in ed.pr.

Notium was the harbour of Colophon, which was about ten miles inland. After the destruction of Colophon by Lysimachus (Paus. VII, 3. 4) its name came to be applied to Notium. Pliny (V, 116) refers to the disappearance of Notium, meaning that the name had passed out of use and the old Notium was in Roman times called Colophon. Mela (I, 17) also speaks of Colophon, the name by which he knew the former Notium.

Λακεδαιμόνιοι δὲ κα[τιδόντες φεύ]γον[τα]ς τοὺς Ἀθηνα[ί]ους ἐπε[νεχθέντες δι]αφθείρουσιν αὐτῶν καὶ λα[μβάνουσιν εἴ]κοσι καὶ δύο ναῦς, τὰς δὲ λοιπὰ[ς εἰς τὸ Νότιο]ν κατέκλεισαν.

The absence of a separate object for διαφθείρουσιν may present a minor problem. The partitive genitive αὐτῶν alone would not be typical of P; what we do find are expressions like καταβάλλουσιν μὲν [αὐ]τῶν περὶ ἑξακοσίους (Lond.pap. VI, 6) and καταβάλλουσιν αὐτῶν [ἀριθμὸν πολύ]ν (Flor.pap. I, 1). Gigante's restoration ἐπε[δίωκον, τινὰς δι]αφθείρουσιν αὐτῶν is not acceptable, however, since the construction requires a participle for ἐπε[---. There may be a good case for supposing that something has been omitted by the scribe, such as αὐτῶν ⟨οὐ πολλούς⟩, suggested by Castiglioni (*loc. cit.*). P may even have been more specific, but any guess at a number would be worthless.

The other sources do not mention any Athenian dead, but both Xenophon and Diodorus do note that a few were captured and the remainder escaped. This observation evidently did not appear in P, and it may be that Ephorus, the source of Diodorus, obtained this piece of information from Xenophon (cf. ed.pr. p. 80 n. 31–2). The term ἐζωγρήθησαν appears in both Xenophon and Diodorus. Notice should be taken, however, of Accame's observation (*Riv.Fil.* XXVIII (1950), 37) that Diodorus' expression οἱ δὲ λοιποὶ πρὸς τὴν γῆν διενήξαντο seems to reflect an Athenian point of view, and Xenophon's way of putting it οἱ μὲν πλεῖστοι ἐξέφυγον a Spartan one. The implication of this, in Accame's view, is that the occurrence of the statement that some Athenians were captured while most escaped in both Diodorus and Xenophon, but not in P, is quite fortuitous, and that in this detail, as in the rest of the narrative, the two traditions are quite independent.

Diodorus follows P in giving the number of Athenian ships lost as twenty-two; Xenophon and Plutarch (*Lys.*) give fifteen.

IV, 4 (= Fragment B, column ii, 35–40)

τροπαῖον στ[ήσαντες]

This detail is found in Xenophon and Plutarch, but not in Diodorus. For the expression see also Flor.pap. I, 1 and Lond.pap. VII, 1.

τῆς πόλεως

I.e. Notium, unless P wished to be more precise in that Notium was the λιμήν and Colophon the πόλις. See note on IV, 3 above, under Κολοφωνίων.

'Αθηναῖοι δὲ παραυ[τίκα μὲν] ἡ[σ]υχίαν εἶχον, παρελθουσῶ[ν δὲ ......] τριῶν ἡμερῶν θεραπεύσ[αντες.....

Gigante's statement that the sequence δέ...μέν...δέ 'non mi pare accettabile' (p. 51 n. 38–9) would seem to have little justification. There are many near-parallels in the London papyrus, such as, e.g., VI, 6: ἐπακολουθήσαντες δὲ τοῖς πολεμί[ο]ις...καταβάλλουσιν μὲν...ἀποστάντες δὲ τῆς διώ[ξεω]ς ἐβ[ά]δ[ι]ȝον... While it may be true that in the near-parallels in P the first δέ invariably follows a verb and not a noun, there is no cause to regard the construction arising from the restoration of Bartoletti and Maas here as suspect. παραυτίκα is just the sort of temporal adverb which, when used in pairs, or with adverbial expressions of time, tends to appear in the form ...μέν, ...δέ. In support of Bartoletti's reading, I would observe that the only other example of παραυτίκα in P, at Lond.pap. XVI, 4, occurs in the construction παραυτίκα μὲ[ν]... ὕστερον δ[έ]...

τριῶν ἡμερῶν

P is the only authority to mention these days spent at Notium after the battle, although Diodorus agrees that the Athenians returned to Notium, and not directly to Samos as indicated by Xenophon. Maas reads δυεῖν ἢ] τριῶν ἡμερῶν. θεραπεύσ[αντες could, as Gigante notes (p. 51 n. 40), refer to the repair of the fleet; cf. the expression τὸ ναυτικὸν θεραπεύοντας in Thuc. II, 65. 7. An alternative suggestion is made by Accame (*Riv.Fil.* XXVIII (1950), 38): noting that Diodorus' statement that most of the Athenians escaped by swimming, while a few were taken prisoner, probably derives from P, and that this observation does not appear in the surviving fragment of P, he proposes that it may have occurred in parenthesis after θεραπεύσ[αντες τοὺς ναυαγήσαντας (his own restoration) as follows: (τῶν γὰρ ἐν ταῖς ναυσὶν ἀνδρῶν ὀλίγοι μὲν ἐζωγρήθησαν, οἱ δὲ λοιποὶ πρὸς τὴν γῆν διενήξαντο)]. Such a restoration might find support in the fact that Diodorus' notice of this detail appears at the same point in the narrative.

V (= Fragment C)

Content

The correct position of fragment C, relative to A and B, cannot be established with certainty since there is no wide agreement as to what event is here described. The narrative appears to give a very detailed account of a clandestine communication between a representative of a besieging army and one of its accomplices inside the besieged city who happened to be on sentry duty on the walls. The agent of the attacking army (μυνδοσ p), either an exile, by name Μύνδος (or something easily corrupted to that in the text), or a native of Myndus in Caria, if Μύνδ⟨ι⟩ος be read, took advantage of the proximity to the walls of the temple of Demeter and Core to hide in the wood around it, probably part of the *temenos*. When the conspirator within the city assumed guard duty on the wall, he signalled, either by calling or by throwing a stone, and the scout then emerged from the wood. Letters were exchanged between the two men by affixing them to a rope which had been let down over the wall. It seems that the guard on the wall either was an Athenian (if so, probably a deserter) or was betraying his native city and happened to be named Ἀθήναιος. The nature of the episode is thus tolerably clear, but in which city, and on what occasion, is a matter of some dispute. Bartoletti, in ed.pr. p. 69 n. 1, wrote: 'Naturalmente non sarebbe difficile inquadrare questo frammento in qualche situazione storica (come l'occupazione ateniese di Selibria o quella di Bisanzio) vicina agli avvenimenti riferiti in A e B.' Accame (*Riv.Fil.* XXVIII (1950), 30–49) and Pouilloux (*BCH* LXXV (1951), 90–6) argue that the event in question is the siege of Thasos by Thrasybulus in 408 or 407 (cf. Diod. XIII, 72. 1; Xen. *Hell.* I, 4. 9). Maas, in a note to his text in *CQ* XLIV (1950), 11, and Fuks (*CQ* XLV (1951), 155) suggest the capture of Byzantium by Alcibiades in 409 or 408 (cf. Diod. XIII, 66–7; Xen. *Hell.* I, 3. 16–22). Their chief argument is that Dionysius Byzantius, *Anapl.* 13, refers to a temple of Demeter and Core at Byzantium. Gigante makes the rather improbable suggestion (p. lxxv) that this fragment contains part of a digression (from ch. I, i.e. fragment A, column i) on events at Megara in 424 B.C. (cf. Thuc. IV, 66–74; Diod. XII, 66–7). Bartoletti (Teubner, pp. xiii–xiv) puts forward the new theory that this fragment also concerns the events of chapter II (i.e. fragment A, column ii)—the restoration by Cratesippidas of a party of Chian exiles. I have tried to refute Bartoletti's view in *Phoenix* XVIII (1964), 272–82, my own conclusion being that the case for Byzantium is the strongest, although Accame's argument for Thasos is not to be lightly dismissed. If Byzantium or Chios be the place in question the fragment should be placed between A and B; if Thasos, this would also be the correct position chronologically, although Diodorus places his account of the capture of Thasos after that of the battle of Notium, which is described in fragment B, column ii, of P.

V, 1 (= Fragment C, column i, 1–4)

εἰώθει γὰ̣[ρ...

Accame (*loc. cit.*) proposed εἰώθει γὰ̣[ρ πανταχῇ μετὰ τὰς ὁ]μολογίας εὐθέως κ̣[ατάγειν τοὺς φυγ]ά̣δας, on the assumption that Thrasybulus is the subject. A similar restoration might possibly be thought applicable to Alcibiades, if he is the general in question, but if the passage concerns Cratesippidas, as Bartoletti now wishes to suppose, a completely different interpretation would be required.

τοὺς φυγ]ά̣δας

The mention of these exiles, while providing a little more information about the nature of the episode, does nothing to help identify the city concerned. The suggestion that the exiles were Athenians (made by Treu in *Gymnasium* LIX (1952), 311) does not seem at all probable, and, of course, it is true that in practically every city which experienced political dissension during the Peloponnesian War certain persons or factions were banished and, as often as not, sought the aid of foreign arms to reinstate them.

V, 2 (= Fragment C, column i, 4–18)

παρ' αὐτῷ probably refers to the commander of the besieging force. Accame restores παρ' αὐτῷ μὲν [ἦν τις Μύνδος (or φυγάδων) ἐν τῷ ἱερ]ῷ τ̣ῷ τῆς Δήμητρ[ος καὶ Κό]ρης, ὃ [ἐγγ]ὺς τοῖς τείχεσί ἐστι... Acceptable sense is thus provided, although ἦν τις Μύνδος or ἦν τις φυγάδων may be a little too long for the lacuna. On the other hand, it is not easy to think of a suitable restoration if the lacuna contained as few letters as Bartoletti reckons, unless Μύνδος (or its equivalent) had been specifically mentioned in the preceding sentence, which appears unlikely, or even earlier, perhaps, as having been the man to approach the commander in question in the first instance. On Μύνδος as Accame's restoration here, see my note under ὁ δὲ Μύνδ⟨ι⟩ος below.

[τῷ νε]ῳ̣—ὃ̣[ς appears in the Teubner edition of 1959, with the note 'ἱερ]ῷ̣—ὃ (ed.pr.) lacunae minus aptum'.

τῆς Δήμητρ[ος καὶ Κό]ρης

Cf., perhaps, Dionys. Byz., *Anapl.* 13: μικρὸν δ' ὑπὲρ αὐτοῦ (i.e. the τέμενος of Γῆ 'Ανησιδώρα) Δήμητρος καὶ Κόρης παράλληλα. Although Fuks (*CQ* XLV (1951), 155) considers that this passage 'seems to prove beyond reasonable doubt that the city referred to in the fragment is Byzantium', Accame (*Riv.Fil.* XXVIII (1950), 32) points out that the cult of Demeter in Thasos is well attested (cf. *IG* XII, 8. 363; Paus. X, 28. 3; Dionys. Periegeta 523; Avien. 701; Head, *Historia Numorum*², p. 265), and Pouilloux (*BCH* LXXV (1951), 90ff.) seeks to identify the sanctuary of Demeter and Core mentioned by P with the *temenos*, probably of Dionysus, but in which Demeter would be associated, found in 1912 to the south of the city wall of Thasos. On this *temenos* at Thasos, see *CRAI* (1913), pp. 365–8, *BCH* XLV (1921), 165, and *Monuments Piot*, XXXII (1932), 24.

ὃ̣[ς. . . .] γ̣ε τοῖς τείχεσί ἐστι [. . . . .]ου

παρά] γε and [τῆς Χί]ου are suggested by Bartoletti in the apparatus of the Teubner edition in accordance with his hypothesis that the fragment concerns events at Chios. Gigante reads [χωρί]ου; Accame (see next note) changes the construction here, reading [καὶ ἀφ'] οὗ.

διὰ τὴν [. . . .]ν ἐγεγόνει τῇ [ὕλῃ, νύκ]τ̣ωρ̣ [δ]ὲ κατα[στὰς] τ̣ὸν μὲν ⟨ἄλλον⟩ χρόνον [ἡσυ]χίαν εἶχεν [ἐγκρ]ύψας αὐτὸν εἰς τή[ν] ὕλην.

Bartoletti's reading here may be somewhat suspect on account of the need to supply ⟨ἄλλον⟩. Accame (*Riv.Fil.* XXVIII (1950), 30) suggests a different restoration along the following lines: [καὶ ἀφ'] οὗ διὰ τὴν [ὕλη]ν ἐγεγόνει τη[ρεῖν εἴ]σ̣ω. ὁ̣ [δ]ὲ κατὰ [πλεῖσ]τ̣ον μὲν χρόνον [ἡσυ]χίαν εἶχεν κτλ. For the absolute use of τηρεῖν he notes Diod. XIII, 67. 1, Thuc. VII, 80 and Ar. *Nic. Eth.* 1167b13, but this use of ἐγεγόνει is unlikely.

ὁ Ἀθη̣[ναῖο]ς̣ (read as Ἀθ̣[ηναῖο]ς in ed.pr.; as Ἀ̣θ̣[ηναι]ο̣ς by Maas)

It is tempting, but fanciful, to try to fit in one of the names of those Byzantines who betrayed their city to Alcibiades (Xen. *Hell.* I, 3. 18), perhaps Ἀναξίλαος. If Ἀθη̣[ναῖο]ς is right, it may be regarded as a reasonable inference that the besieging army was also Athenian, but why the Athenian would be on sentry duty is a tricky question. Accame (*Riv.Fil.* XXVIII (1950), 30–49) supposes that this man would be an Athenian deserter who, seeing the recent successes of Thrasybulus, and notably the victory he won at Thasos before laying siege to the city, now wished to win the favour of the Athenian general with a view to a return to the Athenian camp. It is well, however, to bear in mind that the use of the article here is no reason to exclude the possibility that Ἀθη̣[ναιο]ς is a proper name. If the article implies a previous mention of the man, it does so whether Ἀθη̣[ναιο]ς is a proper name or the ethnic. Among many examples in P, the construction of London papyrus XVII, 4 provides an exact parallel for this use of the article with a proper name: ἐκεῖ[νον μὲν] ἐκέλευσεν ὁ Ἀγησίλαος. In the case of Thasos, the existence of a proper name Ἀθήναιος is attested by epigraphical evidence. *IG* XII, 8. 277 mentions one Ἀθήναιος Τελεβούλου in the fourth century, and XII, 8. 306 and 354 mention an Ἀθήναιος in the second century B.C.

On grounds of general probability, it must be more likely that ὁ Ἀθη̣[ναῖο]ς is in fact the ethnic. In this case it seems to me to refute the suggestion (not to my knowledge published) that the episode is one in which an Athenian garrison was being besieged. If the agent in the wood waited until 'the Athenian' assumed sentry duty, the implication seems to be clear that all the other sentries were not Athenian.

ἐκεῖνος μέν (i.e. ὁ Ἀθη̣[ναῖο]ς)

Gigante's interpretation, that ἐκεῖνος must refer to the subject of the mutilated opening lines of the fragment and not to Ἀθη̣[ναῖο]ς (p. lxxiv), is not at all convincing and is well criticized by Bartoletti (*Gnomon* XXII (1950), 383).

ὁ δὲ Μύνδ⟨ι⟩ος (μυνδοσ p)

μυνδός, meaning 'dumb' or 'silent', is found in Soph. *fr.* 1072 (ed. Pearson, Cambridge, 1917), Lycophron 1375 (ed. Scheer, Berlin, 1881–1908), and Callimachus, *fr.* 533 (ed. Pfeiffer, Oxford, 1949), but it is improbable that the word used here has that meaning. Maas is most probably right in emending the text to Μύνδ⟨ι⟩ος, which is the ethnic from Μύνδος, a Dorian colony on the coast of Caria, founded by settlers from

Troezen, probably on the site of an older town which continued to exist under the name Palaemyndus. See further *RE* XVI, 1, cols. 1,075 ff., Paus. II, 30. 9, and Strabo XIII, 1. 59. De Sanctis considered Μύνδος as it stands in the papyrus to be a proper name, but no other example of this is known. Pouilloux even suggested that it might be a corruption of Μύλλος, which was a common name at Thasos in the fifth century (cf. Hippocrates, II, 644 L.; *IG* XII, 8. 278, and XII, supp. 390). It may be no more wild, however, to suppose a corruption of the Byzantine name Κύδων (Xen. *Hell.* I, 3. 18), in view of some variants found in P, notably Γύης for Ὦτυς, the Paphlagonian king, but these further suggestions do not seem at all preferable to the reading ὁ Μύνδ⟨ι⟩ος, which one must surely conclude to be the most acceptable proposition.

V, 3 (=Fragment C, column ii)

The few surviving letters in this column are sufficient to suggest that the narrative of the event described in the preceding column is continued here. Cf. τὸ τεῖχ[ος l. 3 and, perhaps, φυλ̣[α-- l. 6 (from φύλαξ, φυλακή, φυλάττειν?).

COMMENTARY ON THE LONDON PAPYRUS

I, 1 (=Column i, 1–7)

In all probability a new book of the history begins here. On the left of column i is a blank margin 4½ cm. wide, whereas the ordinary width of the margin between columns of this papyrus is only 1½ cm.

Ὑπὸ δὲ τοὺ[ς αὐτοὺς χρόνο]υς

This formula indicates that P has adopted Thucydides' method of synchronization of events in different places; cf. Thuc. II, 95. 1 *et passim.* A similar formula appears at IV, 2: κατὰ δὲ τὸν αὐ]τὸν χρόνον. As it is not known with what events P synchronized the adventure of Demaenetus, and the reference to the Spartan, Pharax, as ὁ πρότερον ναύαρχος (II, 1) is the only chronological clue in his account (Pharax's term of office almost certainly ending in the autumn of 397; cf. Xen. *Hell.* III, 2. 12; also note to IV, 1), we can only date the episode by the correct placing of columns i–iv (section A) of the papyrus. It is now generally agreed that the first editors were right in placing columns i–iv before columns v–viii (section B); for their full discussion of this question, see ed.pr. pp. 113–15 and 207–9. Assuming that this problem has been correctly solved, the expedition of Demaenetus could belong either to the winter of 397/6 or to the spring of 396. Of these alternatives, I find the latter preferable for reasons given in my note to IV, 1.

[οὐ μετὰ τῆς τοῦ] δήμου γνώμης

For the expression, cf. I, 3: ο[ὐ με]τὰ τῆς πόλεως, and XV, 3: [οὐ] μετὰ τῆς ἐκείνου γν[ώ]μης.

Δημαίν[ετ]ος

He is also referred to by Aeschines, II, 78, as Δημαίνετος ὁ Βουζύγης: θεῖος δὲ ἡμέτερος Κλεόβουλος ὁ Γλαύκου τοῦ Ἀχαρνέως υἱὸς μετὰ Δημαινέτου τοῦ Βουζύγου συγκατεναυμάχησε Χείλωνα τὸν Λακεδαιμονίων ναύαρχον. That Aeschines' reference is to the same Demaenetus as is mentioned by P appears certain from the reference to the Spartan, Χείλων (the Μίλων of P I, 3; III, 1 and 2), and to the encounter between him and Demaenetus (cf. III, 1–2). It becomes clear from P's account that

Aeschines exaggerated the importance of the 'sea-battle'. Demaenetus is also, probably, identical with the general in Aegina in 388/7 whom Xenophon (*Hell.* v, 1. 10–12) mentions as having defeated the Spartan, Gorgopas. This Demaenetus appears to have been general in 387/6 also, being deceived by the stratagem of Antalcidas, along with his colleagues, Dionysius, Leontichus and Phanias, in the autumn of 387 (cf. Xen. *Hell.* v, 1. 26). See further Kirchner, *PA* 3265 (1, p. 216). As Demaenetus appears to have acted in an entirely private capacity on the present occasion, it is unlikely that he held any official command at the time. Meyer (p. 43) compared the expedition to Crete of Macartatus recorded by Isaeus xi, 48: Μακάρτατον γὰρ ἴστε ὅτι τὸ χωρίον ἀποδόμενος καὶ τριήρη πριάμενος καὶ ταύτην πληρωσάμενος εἰς Κρήτην ἐξέπλευσεν· οὐ γὰρ τὸ ἔργον ἀφανὲς ἐγένετο, ἀλλὰ καὶ λόγον ἐν τῷ δήμῳ παρέσχε, μὴ πόλεμον ἡμῖν ἀντ' εἰρήνης ἐκεῖνος πρὸς Λακεδαιμονίους ποιήσειε. Demaenetus' action differs from that of Macartatus, however, in that Demaenetus was not the owner of the ship, which clearly belonged to the state.

ὁ κ̣ύ̣[ρ]ι̣ος α̣ὐ̣τ̣ῆς

The objection to this reading is that it implies ownership of the trireme by Demaenetus, whereas this was evidently not the case. A single word as a family name would be suitable, but ὁ Βουζύγης 'is inadmissible, though it is possible that the word in the papyrus is a corruption of this' (ed.pr. p. 203). Lipsius, however, read ὁ Βουζύγης. Bury (*ap. OCT*) suggested ὁ Κυνοσάργης(?). If the text is corrupt here, αἴτιος might be substituted for κύριος, with the sense of Thuc. iii, 22. 1; cf. τῆς αἰτίας in 1, 2, dealing with this same episode.

τ[ῶν] πολιτῶν

Cleobulus (Aesch. ii, 78) may well have been one of them.

ἔπλει πρὸ]ς Κόν[ων]α.

Conon, the Athenian (on whom see *PA* 8707 (1, pp. 584–6) and Barbieri, *Conone*) commanding the Persian fleet, had his headquarters at Caunus, or, if the revolt of Rhodes from Sparta had already taken place (cf. ch. x), at Rhodes.

I, 2 (= Column i, 7–18)

καὶ τ[ῶν] Ἀθηναίων ἀγανακτούντω[ν ὅσοι γνώ]ριμ[οι κ]αὶ χαρίεντες ἦσαν κτλ.

Their objection that Demaenetus and his colleagues would give the city a bad name by their act of aggression against Sparta was, no doubt, a valid one (I read δια]βα[λοῦ]σι (ed.pr.) for κατα]βα[λοῦ]σι), although probably many Greeks would applaud such an act; cf. II, 2. The danger of possible retaliation was a more practical consideration. There is no reason to suppose that this party of Athenians was philo-Laconian. They were probably former adherents of the oligarchy, or had tendencies towards favouring an oligarchic form of government, if the common political implications of the terms *gnorimoi* and *charientes* are not to be overlooked. The various political groups in Athens at this time are examined in my article 'Athenian Foreign Policy in 396–395 B.C.' in *CJ* LVIII (1963), 289–95. I conclude that there was no significant pro-Spartan party in Athens at this time, although some of the wealthier citizens were opposed to any disturbance of the *status quo* which might endanger their personal fortunes, while many of the democrats hesitated to provoke a war because Athens was unwalled and lacked a navy.

οἵ τε περὶ Θρασύβουλον καὶ Αἴσιμον καὶ Ἄνυτον

The leaders of the moderate democrats, as distinct from the extreme democrats led by Epicrates and Cephalus (II, 2). P ignores Archinus (*PA* 2526, I, p. 169), who was also prominent at the time, being, along with Thrasybulus, an opponent of the Spartan Empire; cf. Plut. *De glor. Ath.* 345 E: Θρασύβουλον καὶ Ἀρχῖνον καὶ τοὺς ἀπὸ Φυλῆς ἑβδομήκοντα κατὰ τῆς Σπαρτιατῶν ἡγεμονίας ἀνισταμένους...For details of the career of Thrasybulus, son of Lycus, who is well known as general and statesman, see *PA* 7310 (I, pp. 476–9). On Aesimus, see *PA* 311 (I, p. 22): he led the citizens back to Athens from Piraeus in 403, and may have been general at that time (cf. Lysias XIII, 80–2). He served as an ambassador to Chios in 384 (cf. Tod, *GHI* II, 118) and to Methymna in 377 (cf. *GHI* II, 122). On Anytus, see *PA* 1324 (I, p. 91): he was general in 410/9 at Pylos and was subsequently prosecuted on a charge of bribery (Diod. XIII, 64. 6; Ar. *Ath. Pol.* 27. 5; Harpocration, *s.v.* δεκάζων). He was later a supporter of Theramenes, along with Archinus, Cleitophon and Phormisius (Ar. *Ath. Pol.* 34. 3), and was exiled under the Thirty (Xen. *Hell.* II, 3. 42–4). On his return, μέγιστον δυνάμενος ἐν τῇ πόλει (Isoc. XVIII, 23), he brought Socrates to trial in 399 along with Meletus and Lycon, and in the same year he and Cephalus were advocates of Andocides (Andoc. I, 150).

The cautious policy of this section of the Athenian democrats is at first sight in contrast to the unanimous acceptance of the Theban request for an alliance in or about August 395, when Thrasybulus himself spoke in favour of the alliance (cf. Tod, *GHI* II, 101; Xen. *Hell.* III, 5. 16). Their opposition to Demaenetus on this occasion, I suggest, reflects a realization that, as he was sailing in a state warship, the expedition might reasonably be thought by the Spartans to have been authorized by the Athenian people. In this case the Spartans might retaliate by invading Attica while Athens, still unwalled, would be defenceless. By the time of the defensive alliance with Thebes it was already clear that the Spartans would invade Boeotia, and an invasion of Attica too may have seemed a real possibility. The acquisition of strong allies was then the only means of defence. See further my comments in *Emerita* XXVIII (1960), 82ff., and *CJ* LVIII (1963), 293f.

I, 3 (=Column i, 18–27)

τῶν δὲ Ἀθηναίων οἱ μὲν ἐπ⟨ι⟩εικεῖς καὶ τὰς οὐσίας ἔχοντες

These were assumed by Meyer (p. 49) to be identical with the γνώριμοι καὶ χαρίεντες, and in all probability this is the correct view. The terms γνώριμοι, ἐπιεικεῖς and χαρίεντες are little more than political catch-phrases applied to oligarchic or aristocratic groups by writers with some degree of bias in their favour, and these appellations are often coupled with one implying wealth, even if some of the most wealthy men in a city were sometimes leaders of the democrats. There may, however, be a slight distinction, in that the ἐπιεικεῖς καὶ τὰς οὐσίας ἔχοντες were 'moderate' in the sense of having to be careful, since many of them may have been former supporters of the oligarchy who had gained financially at that time and owed their present status in society to the amnesty declared after the restoration of the democracy.

ἔστεργον τὰ παρόντα

The commonly held view is that τὰ παρόντα refers to the 'present situation of peaceful relations with Sparta'. The only objection to this view is that P has not been talking about the peaceful relationship with Sparta, but about an incident which, however trivial, was openly hostile to Sparta. Gigante therefore (p. xviii) takes the view that τὰ παρόντα means the state of unrest occasioned by Demaenetus, saying that the ἐπιεικεῖς καὶ τὰς οὐσίας ἔχοντες were content with 'la torbida situazione'. In this he is quite mistaken, for P indicates that this group was not a 'war-party'—indeed, if identical with the γνώριμοι καὶ χαρίεντες, it was quite the reverse. I have considered the possibility that τὰ παρόντα could refer to the proceedings of the assembly, in other words to the proposal of the party of Thrasybulus, since the sentence immediately preceding the reference to the 'moderate and wealthy' class tells us of the proposal, while in contrast to the reaction of οἱ μ ὲ ν ἐπιεικεῖς καὶ τὰς οὐσίας ἔχοντες we are given the reaction to the same proposal of οἱ δ ὲ πολλοὶ καὶ δημοτικοί. This interpretation, however, may well seek to attach too precise a sequence of thought to P, and, τὰ παρόντα being the sort of word which might well be used more loosely, I accept the common view that the state of peace with Sparta is here indicated.

οἱ δὲ πολλοὶ καὶ δημοτικοί

It may be a safe inference that πολλοί indicates a majority party. Cf. the care with which P refers at II, 3 to the Corinthian democrats, who were a minority group, as οἱ μεταστῆσαι τὰ πράγματα ȝητοῦντες. Xenophon (*Hell.* IV, 4. 1) describes the Corinthian oligarchs at about this time as οἱ πλεῖστοι καὶ βέλτιστοι, πλεῖστοι probably signifying a majority group. Perhaps all the πολλοὶ καὶ δημοτικοί may be called 'extreme' democrats, in so far as they are distinguished from the adherents of Thrasybulus and Aesimus and Anytus, although the friends of Epicrates and Cephalus are singled out as being the chief advocates of war (II, 2).

Μίλωνα

Harmost of Aegina. He is identical with Χείλων in Aeschines II, 78 (cf. note to I, 1); it is not known which form of the name is correct. He is styled nauarch by Aeschines, but inaccurately, since the Spartan nauarchs are now fairly securely established as being the following: Pharax, 398/7; Archelaïdas, 397/6; Pollis, 396/5; Cheiricrates, 395. Cf. notes to IV, 1 and 2. Milon may well be identified with the Χίλων of Xen. *Hell.* VII, 4. 23. Cf. also *P.Lak.* 535.

II, 1 (= Column i, 27–33)

ἀπέπεμπ[ο]ν μὲν γὰρ ὅπλ[α τε καὶ ὑπη]ρεσίας ἐπὶ τὰς ναῦς τὰς μετὰ τοῦ Κ[όνωνος

The sending of arms and sailors to assist Conon is mentioned by Isocrates, *Paneg.* 142: ἐν δὲ τῷ πολέμῳ τῷ περὶ 'Ρόδον...χρώμενος... (*sc.* βασιλεὺς) ταῖς ὑπηρεσίαις ταῖς παρ' ἡμῶν, στρατηγοῦντος δ' αὐτῷ Κόνωνος...

It is not known whether warships had actually been sent to Conon from Athens before. As the assistance must have been secret, or given voluntarily by individuals in a private capacity, for Athens was officially at peace with Sparta, it may have been considered unwise to risk sending a trireme, the presence of which in the Persian fleet might not easily be concealed. Even if an Athenian had bought a trireme as Macartatus later did (cf. note on Demaenetus in I, 1), it would still appear to the Spartans to be a state-owned ship and indicative of state action. Athens would not have had many ships at her disposal at this period in any case. Under the terms of surrender in 405/4 she was allowed to retain only twelve ships

(Xen. *Hell.* II, 2. 20; Plut. *Lys.* XV, 1), or ten according to Diodorus (XIII, 107). On the activities of Conon at this time cf. also Diod. XIV, 39; 79. 5; Plut. *Artax.* XXI; Plato, *Menex.* 244D; Nepos, *Conon* II.

ὡς βασιλέα π̣[....οἱ περὶ..]..κράτη καὶ Ἁγνίαν καὶ Τελε[σήγ]ορον·

Various readings here include π[ρότερον (Meyer), which is 'somewhat too long' (ed.pr. p. 203); π[ρόσθεν (Castiglioni), which is used five times by P, but always in the phrase εἰς τὸ πρόσθεν; π[ρῶτον (Bury), as being the first embassy to the Great King since the Peloponnesian War; π[έντε (Richards), which seems too precise, while it is also, perhaps, hardly appropriate that five men should be described as οἱ περί three others; and π[άλιν (Kalinka), possibly the best reading. Cf. VII, 1, XVI, 2 and XVI, 6, where πάλιν with verbs of motion does not imply a previous visit to the place in question. τ[ινές or π[οτέ could also be possible readings. The name here may well be Ἱπποκράτη or Αὐτοκράτη. Ἐπικράτη ('vestigiis minus aptum', Bartoletti) is unlikely as the author would surely have distinguished him from Epicrates, the democratic leader of II, 2. Ἀριστοκράτη 'seems to be too long' (ed.pr. p. 203), but could be read with π[οτέ, or with τ[ινές, omitting οἱ.

Hagnias is also known from Isaeus XI, 8: Ἁγνίας οὖν, ὅτε ἐκπλεῖν παρεσκευάζετο πρεσβεύσων ἐπὶ ταύτας τὰς πράξεις αἳ τῇ πόλει συμφερόντως εἶχον, οὐκ ἐφ' ἡμῖν τοῖς ἐγγύτατα γένους, εἴ τι πάθοι, τὰ ὄντα κατέλιπεν... Cf. Harpocration, *s.v.* Ἁγνίας: τοῦτον καὶ τοὺς συμπρεσβευτὰς αὐτοῦ φησὶν Ἀνδροτίων ἐν πέμπτῳ τῆς Ἀτθίδος καὶ Φιλόχορος ὡς ἑάλωσάν τε καὶ ἀπέθανον ὑπὸ Λακεδαιμονίων. (= *F.Gr.Hist.* 324 F 18, 328 F 147.) Cf. further Kirchner, *PA* 133 (I, p. 10).

Telesegorus (*PA* 13,512 (II, p. 304)) may perhaps be the father of Λεωμήδης Τελεσηγόρου Κολλυτεύς (*PA* 9098 (II, p. 13); *CIA* II, 1010).

οὓς καὶ συλλαβὼν Φάραξ ὁ πρότερον ναύαρχος

The date of the embassy, formerly unknown, can be fixed within certain limits by the reference to Pharax as ὁ πρότερον ναύαρχος; cf. Xen. *Hell.* III, 2. 12–14, in which Pharax is operating with Dercylidas in the spring and summer of 397. Even if the events of chapters I–III are not correctly dated to the spring of 396 (cf. note to I, 1 on p. 50), our knowledge of Pharax's successors would suggest 398/7 as a more likely date than 397/6 for his nauarchia. For a fuller discussion of the relevance of this mention of Pharax's nauarchia to the chronology of chapters I–III, see note to IV, 1. Cf. also *P.Lak.* 717.

ἀπέστειλε πρὸς τοὺς Λ[α]κεδαιμονίους, οἱ δ' [ἀ]πέκτειναν αὐτούς

If it is a fair argument from silence that the Athenians made no protest about the execution of these envoys, the reason may well be that responsibility for their mission had to be disclaimed by the state since it might be construed as collaboration with Sparta's enemies. Cf. the terms of the peace: τὸν αὐτὸν ἐχθρὸν καὶ φίλον νομίζοντας Λακεδαιμονίοις ἕπεσθαι (Xen. *Hell.* II, 2. 20).

II, 2 (= Column i, 33–column ii, 14)

παροξυνόντων τῶν περὶ τὸν Ἐπικράτη καὶ Κέφαλον

παροξύνειν occurs also at XIII, 3 and 4, and possibly at IV, 2 (παροξυνό]ν-των ed.pr.).

On Epicrates, see *PA* 4859 (I, p. 321 and addendum II, p. 457). He was one of the democrats of the Piraeus in 403; cf. Dem. XIX, 277: σπουδαῖος καὶ πολλὰ χρήσιμος τῇ πόλει, καὶ τῶν ἐκ Πειραιῶς καταγαγόντων τὸν δῆμον, καὶ ἄλλως δημοτικός. He is described as ῥήτωρ καὶ δημαγωγός (schol. to Ar. *Eccles.* 71), and Lysias (XXVII, 5–6) testifies to his great influence with the people. He was a man of some wealth, and this may have been accumulated during the period of the Corinthian War; cf. Lys. XXVII, 9–10. Being appointed συλλογεύς, he was accused of fraud, and this was the occasion of Lysias' speech (XXVII) against him. He had previously been tried on a charge of receiving bribes (δώρων κριθείς, Lys. XXVII, 3) but was acquitted (Lys. XXVII, 4). He served as an envoy to the Great King with Phormisius, and on this occasion appears to have accepted bribes; cf. Plato com. *fr.* 119: κᾆτ' ἔλαβον Ἐπικράτης τε καὶ Φορμίσιος | παρὰ τοῦ βασιλέως πλεῖστα δωροδοκήματα. It seems from Philochorus F 149*a* (Jacoby) that Epicrates was one of Andocides' colleagues on the embassy to Sparta in 391, and that he subsequently went into exile, but Aristeides, *Panathen.* I, 283 (Dindorf) and the scholion (III, 277) suggest that he persuaded the Athenians to accept the Peace of Antalcidas. Dem. XIX, 277 indicates that he was condemned to death for failure to perform his duties as ambassador satisfactorily. See also note on Timocrates, below.

On Cephalus, see *PA* 8277 (I, p. 549). He was as well-known and influential a democratic leader as Epicrates. He too was ῥήτωρ καὶ δημαγωγός (Suidas, *s.v.*), and is described as ῥήτωρ ἔνδοξος καὶ μέγας (Dem. XVIII, 219) and as ὁ δοκῶν δημοτικώτατος γεγονέναι (Aeschines III, 194). He was an advocate of Andocides in 399 (Andoc. I, 115 and 150) along with Anytus. In 386 he was the mover of a rider to the decree rewarding Phanocritus of Parium, by which the status and title of πρόξενος were added (Tod, *GHI* II, 116). In 384 he served as an envoy to Chios on the occasion of an alliance between the Athenians and Chians (*GHI* II, 118). As a supporter of the Theban cause in 378 ἔγραψεν ἐξιέναι βοηθήσοντας Ἀθηναίους τοῖς κατειληφόσι τῶν φυγάδων Θήβας (Deinarchus I, 39). He was a counsellor of the Athenians during the times of Conon, Iphicrates, Chabrias and Timotheus (Deinarchus I, 76ff.), and, like Epicrates, he was ridiculed by Aristophanes (*Eccles.* 248f.) and Plato comicus (*fr.* 185). See also note on Timocrates, below.

While Epicrates and Cephalus were undoubtedly leaders of the democrats as were Thrasybulus, Aesimus and Anytus, this passage indicates that in foreign policy the two groups of leaders may be distinguished as representing, if not different attitudes to Sparta, certainly different ideas as to what action should be taken. The more belligerent policy of Epicrates and Cephalus would appear to have been rather irresponsible in view of the weaknesses of Athens in 396, and in this connection there may be some significance in the references to both men as 'demagogues'. (By this I do not mean to imply that statesmen whom we know as demagogues were necessarily irresponsible—on this see Finley, *Past and Present* XXI (1962), 3–24—but that the authors who describe Epicrates and Cephalus as such probably intended the word to carry that implication.) We may perhaps infer that Epicrates and Cephalus also stood for a more extreme democracy in domestic politics. Cf. Aesch. III, 194: Κέφαλος ὁ παλαιὸς ἐκεῖνος ὁ δοκῶν δημοτικώτατος...λέγων, ὅτι πλεῖστα πάντων γεγραφὼς ψηφίσματα οὐδεμίαν πώποτε γραφὴν πέφυγε παρανόμων.

If the followers of Epicrates and Cephalus (οἱ πολλοὶ καὶ δημοτικοί, I, 3) commanded a majority of the citizen body, we should ask why their policy of active anti-Laconism had not become the policy implemented by the assembly between 403 and 396. The support for Epicrates and Cephalus would presumably have been, in the first instance, on the ground of domestic politics; the majority of the democrats, however, may well have been afraid to risk an open breach with Sparta at this time, and this supposition, if correct, would help to explain the apparent ease with which they were won over to the cautious policy of Thrasybulus on the occasion of the adventure of Demaenetus (I, 2–3). The actual acts of hostility to Sparta (i.e. acts of assistance to Conon; II, 1) were instigated or carried out by οἱ περὶ τὸν Ἐπικράτη καὶ Κέφαλον (II, 2), and P may be referring to a few extremist friends of Epicrates and Cephalus, rather than to the mass of their followers, whom he earlier described as οἱ πολλοὶ καὶ δημοτικοί (I, 3). For further discussion of the foreign policy of the various factions in Athens in 396 see my comments in *CJ* LVIII (1963), 289ff.

Τιμοκράτει διελέχθησαν καὶ [τ]ὸ χρυσίον [ἔλαβον, κτλ.
Epicrates and Cephalus are said to have been desirous of bringing Athens into conflict with Sparta long before they spoke with Timocrates and accepted the gold which he offered. Although Xenophon explicitly states that the Athenians did not take the bribes brought by Timocrates (Ἀθηναῖοι δὲ καὶ οὐ μεταλαβόντες τούτου τοῦ χρυσίου ὅμως πρόθυμοι ἦσαν εἰς τὸν πόλεμον, *Hell.* III, 5. 2), the view of P, who is supported by Pausanias (III, 9. 8), that Epicrates and Cephalus did, seems more probable, for that it was widely believed in the fourth century B.C. is shown by the reference in this passage to certain unnamed persons (τινές) who thought that the Persian gold was the cause of antipathy to Sparta in Athens, as well as in Boeotia and the other cities visited by Timocrates. ταῖς ἄλλαις πόλεσι ταῖς προειρημέναις, i.e. Corinth and Argos, probably refers back to the main account of Timocrates' visit which was probably narrated shortly before the point at which the London papyrus begins.

The following table may show clearly the persons in the various cities reputed to have accepted money from Timocrates (cf. Meyer, p. 46):

City	P	Pausanias (III, 9. 8)	Xenophon (*Hell.* III, 5. 1)
Thebes	Ismenias Antitheus Androcleidas (XII, 1)	Ismenias Amphithemis Androcleidas	Ismenias Galaxidorus Androcleidas
Corinth	Timolaus and others (II, 3)	Timolaus Polyanthes	Timolaus Polyanthes
Argos	unknown	Cylon Sodamas	Cylon 'and those with him'
Athens	Epicrates Cephalus (II, 2)	Epicrates Cephalus	—

The mention of Timolaus and Polyanthes in Pausanias' account as ὅσοι Κορινθίων ἐφρόνουν τὰ Ἀργείων may be a hint that the union of Corinth and Argos (on which see Griffith, *Historia* I (1950), 236–56) was already projected.

'On the question of the date of Timocrates' mission and the Persian who inspired it, P is certainly right as against Xenophon' (ed.pr. p. 205). Xenophon (*Hell.* III, 5. 1) attributes the mission of Timocrates to Tithraustes, and proceeds to narrate the outbreak of the Corinthian War, which he takes to be the direct result of the visit of Timocrates to Greece.

Pausanias (III, 9. 8) also associates the sending of Timocrates with Tithraustes, and regards the event as a cause of the war. The chronological difficulty raised by these accounts is that if Tithraustes, who cannot have reached Sardis before June 395 (cf. ed.pr. p. 204), sent Timocrates, he must have reached the Greek cities after the outbreak of the war and therefore the bribes he brought could not have been, or have been thought, a cause of it. Xenophon and Pausanias place the mission of Timocrates after the battle of Sardis in 395; cf. Plut. *Artax.* XX, 4; *Lys.* XXVII, 1; *Ages.* XV, 8.

P, having almost certainly mentioned the visit of Timocrates in its chronological position before the beginning of the London papyrus, and taking not Tithraustes but Pharnabazus as its sponsor (cf. II, 5: διὰ Φαρνάβαζον καὶ τὸ χρυσίον), thus dates it, in all probability, to 397; cf. ed.pr. p. 205, De Sanctis, *Atti Accad. Torino* LXVI (1931), 169ff., and Gigante, p. xi. Barbieri, *Conone*, pp. 90ff., argues more precisely that the visit of Timocrates must have preceded the capture by Pharax, the Spartan nauarch, of the Athenian ambassadors mentioned in II, 1, in other words that the visit occurred before August/September 397, when Pharax's term of office ended. This argument is based upon the observation of De Sanctis, *loc. cit.*, that the whole passage from the last sentence of I, 3 to the end of chapter II is uninterrupted digression. Consequently, ἠναντιοῦντο δὲ ταῦτα (II, 2) indicates not general opposition to Sparta in 396 by the adherents of Epicrates and Cephalus, but the instigation by these men of the actual acts of hostility mentioned in II, 1, which took place during Pharax's nauarchia. As P is refuting the opinion of some who believed that these acts of opposition to Sparta were caused by Timocrates' bribes, his visit to Greece must have been anterior to the acts themselves.

Polyaenus, I, 48. 3, also associates the mission of Timocrates with Pharnabazus, but adds that Conon was its real instigator: Κόνων Φαρναβάζῳ συμμαχῶν Ἀγησιλάου τὴν Ἀσίαν πορθοῦντος ἔπεισε τὸν Πέρσην χρυσίον πέμψαι τοῖς δημαγωγοῖς τῶν πόλεων τῆς Ἑλλάδος, οἳ λαβόντες πείσουσι τὰς πατρίδας ἐκφέρειν τὸν πρὸς Λακεδαιμονίους πόλεμον. οἱ μὲν δεκασθέντες ἔπεισαν, καὶ συνέστη πόλεμος Κορινθιακός. Jacoby, *F.Gr.Hist.* IIC, 8, observes that Polyaenus here derives from both P and Xenophon (*Hell.* III, 5. 1–2); more precisely, perhaps, as De Sanctis (*loc. cit.*) points out, he derives from P and Theopompus, who in turn derives from Xenophon.

Meyer, pp. 44ff., and Jacoby, *F.Gr.Hist.* IIC, 9, date the visit of Timocrates to winter 396/5 or spring 395. Such dating would seem to be dependent upon their general view of the chronology of P, on which see my note to IV, 1. Against their dating of Timocrates' visit, see De Sanctis, *loc. cit.*

As for Xenophon's version of the sending of Timocrates, Accame, *Ricerche intorno alla guerra corinzia*, pp. 29ff., suggests that, being in Asia with Agesilaus at the time, he had no sufficiently exact information from the mainland of Greece. Barbieri, *Conone*, pp. 90ff., points out that while this might account for the chronological discrepancy, it does not necessarily explain Xenophon's association of the visit of Timocrates with Tithraustes. A more satisfactory explanation might be the following: it appears from XIII, 1 (ὑπολα]μβάνοντες βασιλ[έ]α χρήματα π[α]ρέξε[ιν, ὅπερ ὁ π]αρὰ τοῦ βαρβάρου π[ε]μφθεὶς ἐπηγγέλλετο) that Timocrates had authority not only to distribute money in Greece, but to promise further assistance for the future. He may, then, have received a second grant of funds for distribution in the Greek cities some two years later, that is, after the war had begun, and on this occasion the money may have been provided by Tithraustes. For further details of this argument, see Barbieri, *op. cit.* pp. 95ff. Whether or not this hypothesis is to be accepted, there can be no doubt that the information given by P is preferable to that of Xenophon, which is clearly confused in view of the fact that the bribes, if sent by Tithraustes, could not have been thought a cause of the outbreak of the war since the war would already have been in progress.

οἱ μὲν Ἀργεῖοι καὶ Β̣ο̣ι̣ω̣τ[οὶ. . . .]τ̣ωται̣

']τωται (vel]τωτας) potius quam]γωται (vel]γωτας) p', Bartoletti. Gigante reads Βοιωτ[ῶν προσ]τ⟨ά⟩ται, the restoration of Castiglioni (*Boll.Fil.Class.* XXVII (1921), 146f.), which is by far the best of those attempted. The anti-Spartan party of Ismenias and Androcleidas at Thebes would already have been the dominant party (cf. XII, 2) and its leaders may aptly be called Βοιωτῶν οἱ προστάται. The difficulties of this reading are (i) ω is clear in the papyrus, and must be regarded as the scribe's error, and (ii) Βοιωτοί might be expected in the same case as Ἀργεῖοι; cf. τοῖς Ἀργείοις καὶ τοῖς Βοιωτοῖς a few lines below in II, 3. Other proposed readings include Βοιωτ[οὶ στασι]γῶται, ed.pr. ('but Βοιωτός is not used as an adjective at this period', ed.pr. p. 206); Βοιωτ[οὶ συνεσ]τῶτ⟨ε⟩ς?, *OCT*; Βοιωτ[ῶν οἱ προεσ]τῶτ⟨ε⟩ς, Lipsius (longer than the space); Βοιωτ[ῶν κ' (=καὶ) νησ]ιῶται?, Pfeiffer (but why any isolated reference to islanders?); Βοιωτ[ῶν οἱ ἰδι]ῶται, Kalinka (but what would this mean?).

ὅτι τοῖς ἐναν[τίοι]ς τῶν πολιτῶν αὐτοῖς ἐχρῶντο φίλοις

I have suggested in *Emerita* XXVIII (1960), 79f., that P's interpretation of the causes of anti-Laconism in Argos and Boeotia is incorrect and reflects to some extent a pro-Spartan point of view. In any case Spartan treatment of former allies and enemies alike since 404 had given ample cause for hatred, and Spartan support for the political rivals of the Argive and Boeotian leaders was probably given just because those leaders were already openly anti-Spartan. It is interesting to note here P's assumption that there was at Argos also a party on friendly terms with Sparta. It cannot have been very strong at this time, for some twenty years elapsed before *stasis* broke out at Argos.

[ο]ἱ δ' [ἐ]ν ταῖς 'Αθήναις κτλ.

Anti-Laconism is not identified with internal political rivalry at Athens, and this could be because there was no pro-Spartan group at Athens; cf. my article in *CJ* LVIII (1963), 289ff. The motives attributed to the Athenians by P, described in ed.pr. p. 206 as 'sarcastic and somewhat unfair criticism', may find some support in the case of Epicrates from Lysias XXVII, 9–10: οὗτοι (*sc.* 'Επικράτης καὶ οἱ συμπρεσβευταί) μὲν γὰρ ἐν τῷ πολέμῳ ἐκ πενήτων πλούσιοι γεγόνασιν ἐκ τῶν ὑμετέρων, ὑμεῖς δὲ διὰ τούτους πένητες. Xenophon (*Hell.* III, 5. 2) gives the Athenians the natural motive of wanting to restore their influential position in the Greek world, as must surely be the meaning of the corrupt words: νομίζοντες †τε αὐτῶν ἄρχεσθαι†.

II, 3 (=Column ii, 14–22)

οἱ μεταστῆσαι τὰ πρά[γμ]ατα ζητοῦντες

We may note the precise method of referring to the minority Corinthian democratic party here. They achieved their aim with the establishment of a democracy in or about March 392 (cf. Xen. *Hell.* IV, 4. 1ff.).

Τ[ιμό]λαος δὲ μόνος αὐτοῖς διάφορος γεγονὼς ἰδ[ί]ων ἐγκλημάτων ἕνεκα

It is not known what the ἴδια ἐγκλήματα were. It may be that P did not know and made the inference from Timolaus' past record of friendship with the Spartans. The absence of any specific mention of Polyanthes is noteworthy, since Xenophon (*Hell.* III, 5. 1) and Pausanias (III, 9. 8) name him along with Timolaus as being a recipient of the gold brought by Timocrates. Cf. Jacoby, *F.Gr.Hist.* II C, 9–10.

λακωνίζων implies, perhaps, positive active support for the Spartans (cf. II, 4) as opposed to a mere favourable disposition, as indicated by the expression φρονεῖν τὰ Λακεδαιμονίων (XII, 1).

II, 4 (= Column ii, 22–32)

ἐκεῖνος γὰρ ὁτὲ μὲν πενταναΐαν ἔχων ἐπόρθησε τῶν νήσων τινὰς κτλ.

The plundering of certain islands of the Athenian empire, at some time before the revolt of Thasos, is probably of no very great significance, and is not recorded by Thucydides.

On the term πενταναΐαν, cf. δεκαναΐα[ν] in Flor.pap. IV, 3.

After sailing to Amphipolis with two triremes, and manning four more put at his disposal there, Timolaus defeated an Athenian general in a sea-battle. As the name of the general, σιχιον, p, must be corrupt, it has been corrected to Σίμιχον by Fuhr, *Berl.Phil.Woch.* (1908), cols. 156f., coll. schol. Aeschines II, 31 Σιμίχου (*sic* Sauppe; σιμμιχου, συμβιχου codd.). Cf. *PA* 13,030 (II, p. 279), Σύμβιχος.

It appears to have been a habit of P, when he recalled some event which he had previously described, to draw attention to his former mention of it in some such phrase as ὥσπερ εἴρηκ[ά π]ου καὶ πρότερον. Cf. XII, 1 ὥσπερ καὶ πρότερον εἴρηκα and II, 2 and 5 ταῖς πόλεσι ταῖς προειρημέναις.

That Timolaus' exploit at Amphipolis had been mentioned in an earlier part of the history was taken by the first editors to be an indication that P's work was a continuation of Greek history from the point reached by Thucydides, and this view is substantiated by the subject-matter of the Florence papyrus.

[........] ἔχων τριήρ[εις]

Wilamowitz (*ap.* ed.pr.) restored [τὰς ἕνδεκα], by addition of the two with which Timolaus sailed to Amphipolis, the four he obtained there and the five captured from the enemy. Lipsius read [τὰς (ἁ)πάσας].

The expedition to Thasos must have been towards the end of 411 (cf. Meyer, p. 47 n. 2). Thucydides VIII, 64 relates the overthrow of the democracy in Thasos in 411 and the expectation of assistance from Sparta, which cannot have been long delayed, for in 410 Thasos was under the Spartan harmost, Eteonicus; cf. Xen. *Hell.* I, 1. 32.

II, 5 (= Column ii, 32–5)

διὰ Φαρνάβαζον

Cf. note on II, 2 discussing the mission of Timocrates, the Rhodian, to Greece. Polyaenus I, 48 supports P in stating that Timocrates was sent by Pharnabazus; Xenophon, *Hell.* III, 5. 1 and Pausanias III, 9. 8 associate his mission with Tithraustes.

ἐπηρμένοι μισεῖν ἤ[σ]αν
The strange word order here is probably due to P's desire to avoid hiatus.

III, 1 (= Column ii, 35–40)

Μίλων

Harmost of Aegina; see note on him under I, 3. Cf. also Aeschines II, 78 (quoted in note to Δημαίνετος in I, 1), where his name is given as Χείλων.

μὲν ὢν μένων, ed.pr.; divided by Boissevain (*Berl.Phil.Woch.* (1908), cols. 189f.).

περὶ Θορικὸν τῆς Ἀττικῆς·
Thoricus is on the eastern coast of Attica, opposite the northern part of the island of Helene. Demaenetus would have sailed only some forty sea miles by this time, assuming that he kept fairly close to the coast. If Θορικόν] is to be restored in the lacuna after πρό[ς in III, 2, or alternatively τὴν γῆν], meaning that at or around Thoricus, it would appear that Demaenetus had not long arrived in the area of Thoricus. From this we may infer that the outcry at Athens, the subsequent assembly, and the implementation of the decision to inform Milon of the situation (I, 1–3) had all taken place within a very short period of time (indicating, perhaps, that the Athenians had been brought to realize that this was a crisis demanding prompt action), or that Demaenetus had been in no great haste (anticipating no hindrance to his scheme provided that he could escape the notice of any Spartan harmosts *en route*, of whom Milon was one). The two possible inferences are not, of course, mutually exclusive.

III, 2 (= Column ii, 40–column iii, 7 with fragment 1)

That fragment 1 belongs to the first five lines of column iii is certain because of (*a*) its suitability to the context, (*b*) the suitability of the beginnings of two lines of the land-survey on the recto to the first two lines of the column on the recto of column ii, and (*c*) the colour of the papyrus, which resembles columns i and ii in being lighter than the rest. Cf. ed.pr. p. 206 n. iii, 1–5. The remainder of column iii (ch. III, 2 and ch. IV, 1–3) is on a separate fragment along with the remains of column iv (ch. V), but internal evidence leaves us in no doubt about the correctness of its position following column ii.

The lacunae on either side of fragment 1 (see diagram) are of uncertain width, and pose a number of problems intimately concerned with the determination of the course of events narrated in this section. Bartoletti, aiming at a reliable text, leaves three of these lacunae unfilled, perhaps wisely, as follows: ἐ[πει]δὴ δὲ προσπλεύσας ἐκεῖν[ο]ς πρὸ[ς ......] ἐπεχείρη[σεν.....]ειν, ὥρμησεν ἐπὶ πọλụ[.....]ειν· κρατήσ̣[ας δὲ μιᾶς ν]εὼς αὐτῶν τὴν μὲν ὑ[φ' αὐτῷ] ναῦν, ὅτι χε[ῖρον ἦν τὸ σκ]άφος, αὐτοῦ κατέλ̣[ιπ]ε̣ν̣ κτλ. Ed.pr. reads πρὸ[ς Θορικὸν] ἐπεχείρη[σεν ἐμβαλ]εῖν. Boissevain (*Berl.Phil.Woch.* (1908), cols. 189f.) conjectured πρὸ[ς τὴν

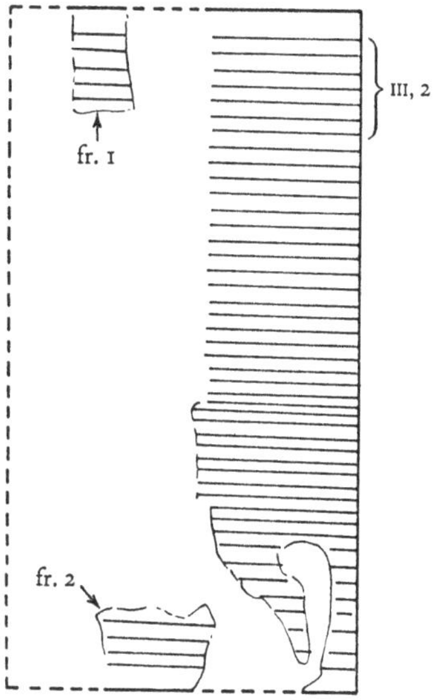

Fig. 1. Col. iii.

γῆν] ἐπεχείρη[σεν ἐξωθ]εῖν (*sc.* τὴν ναῦν, the ship of Demaenetus), for which there are close parallels in Thuc. II, 90. 5; VII, 52. 2; VIII, 104. 4. In the third of these lacunae ed.pr. has ἐπὶ πọλ̣ὺ [προπλ]εῖν, but cf. *OCT*: 'sed litterae ολ incertissimae, et nomen loci latere videtur; πό]λιν tamen pro πλ]εῖν non legendum, de ε enim vix dubitari potest'. Bartoletti rightly marks the υ also of πολύ as uncertain. The name of a town would indeed be in keeping with the precise writing of P, and the following have been proposed: ἐπὶ Π[οταμὸν? πλ]εῖν (Lipsius), ἐπὶ Π[ρασιάς? προπλ]εῖν (Kalinka), ἐπὶ Π[οιᾶσσαν πλ]εῖν (Roos). Gigante adopts the restoration of Lipsius since Potamus is nearer to Thoricus than the other two places; cf. Gigante, p. 56. Clearly the text here cannot be restored with certainty, and it is not impossible that the place referred to is in fact Thoricus.

κρατήσ[ας δὲ μιᾶς ν]εὼς αὐτῶν

μιᾶς (Lipsius), although rejected by the first editors as 'not satisfactory', seems to be the most acceptable of the proposed restorations, in view of a consideration of what ship is here referred to. The first editors gave three very convincing reasons for supposing that this ship belonged to the people of the place mentioned above, be it Thoricus or Potamus or some other place, rather than that it was Milon's own ship, as held by Wilamowitz (*ap.* ed.pr.), whose reading τῆς ν]εὼς is adopted by Gigante: (1) It is not easy to see how Demaenetus obtained possession of Milon's ship without capturing Milon himself, who, it appears from the last sentence in the chapter, returned safely to Aegina. (2) αὐτῶν suits the inhabitants of a place just mentioned better than the Spartans (cf. II, 4: εἰς 'Αμφίπολιν καταπλεύσας καὶ παρ' ἐ[κεί]νων...). One cannot easily be persuaded by Gigante that αὐτῶν and ἐκείνων (just below) refer to Milon '*sensus gratia*'. (3) The remains of the section suggest that Demaenetus took to flight on Milon's approach, rather than that he gave action.

The retention of τῆς ν]εώς, despite these arguments, would mean that the place in question had only one ship, which would not, of course, be impossible, yet, on balance, μιᾶς ν]εώς appears the more probable reading. του ν]εώς, meaning one of the ships which came with Milon, was suggested by Bury, but the argument (3) above serves as an objection to this reading also. We may further note that III, 1 mentions Milon as manning 'a trireme' and following Demaenetus, not as taking a number of ships.

με[τὰ τῆς αὐτοῦ νεὼς ἐπανῆκε.

Bartoletti writes νεώς for τριήρους 'propter lacunae spatium'. The restoration otherwise is due to Castiglioni (*Boll.Fil.Class.* XXVII (1921), 146f.), and is preferable to με[τὰ τῶν ἄλλων νεῶν ἔπλευσε (Gigante), which implies that Demaenetus captured Milon's ship or one of those with him. III, 1 (συμπληρωσάμενος τριήρη) makes no mention of any accompanying ships.

The course of events, then, appears to be the following: when Milon came in pursuit of Demaenetus and tried to force him ashore, the latter made for some town (perhaps Thoricus), where he obtained a new ship, embarked his crew, abandoning his own ship which had some defect in the hull, and sailed away to join Conon. Milon gave up the pursuit and returned to Aegina.

IV, 1 (= Column iii, 7–19)

τὰ μ]ὲν οὖν ἁδρότατα τῶν [κατὰ τὴν Ἑλλάδα τῷ χειμῶν]ι τούτῳ συμβάντων [οὕτως ἐγένετο· ἀρχομένου] δ̣ὲ τοῦ [θ]έρους τῇ μὲν [......................] ἔτος ὄγδοον ἐνειστήκει [.............. ....]αρος κτλ.

χειμῶν]ι	*supplevit* Bartoletti
ἔτε]ι	De Sanctis
θέρε]ι	Fuhr; Lipsius
ἀρχομένου	Wilcken, *ap.* Meyer
ἀπὸ τούτου	Grenfell and Hunt, *OCT*
ἐπιγιγνομένου *vel* μεσοῦντος	De Sanctis
τελευτῶντος	Pareti; Lipsius
ἐπιόντος	Underhill
alii alia	
τῇ μὲν [εἰρήνῃ τῇ πρὸς Ἀθηναίους]	*dubitanter* ed.pr.
[τῶν Λακεδαιμονίων ἀρχῇ]	Meyer
[πόλει μετὰ τὴν ἀναρχίαν]	De Sanctis
[πόλει πάλιν δημοκρατουμένῃ]	Pareti
[Ἑλλάδι τῆς κοινῆς εἰρήνης]	Keil
[μετὰ τὸν πόλεμον εἰρήνῃ]?	Jacoby
[κατὰ τὴν Ἑλλάδα εἰρήνῃ]	Lipsius
alii aliter	

The chronological problem

The lacunae in this important section have given rise to much argument about the chronological system used by the historian, and about the dating of the events recorded in the early part of the London papyrus. The various restorations of these lacunae represent attempts to harmonize the text with one or another of the views proposed regarding the author's chronological arrangement. The problem is complex, yet one may attempt to clarify the various questions it presents as follows:

(1) What year is the ἔτος ὄγδοον?

(2) From what point or event is the numbering of the years reckoned?

(3) Does [θ]έρους indicate spring or midsummer?

(4) With these questions is intimately connected the date of the assumption by Pollis of the Spartan nauarchia, recorded in IV, 2.

Grenfell and Hunt (ed.pr. pp. 207–9) show convincingly that the eighth year cannot be as early as 397/6 from the reference to Pharax as ὁ πρότερον ναύαρχος in II, 1, for he is known from Xenophon (*Hell.* III, 2. 12–14) to have held the office in the spring and summer of 397. They then take the eighth year to be 396/5, and discuss the question of whether the θέρος is spring or midsummer on this assumption. On the possibility of the eighth year being 395/4 they state: 'If the θέρος in [column] iii, 9 refers to 395, there is not the least doubt that cols. v–viii should precede i–iv, not follow them.' No very clear reason is given for this statement. They discuss the results of such a transposition of columns i–iv and v–viii, if the eighth year is 395/4, the first being that the θέρος would have to mean midsummer, and not spring, since the account of Agesilaus' campaign in the spring and early summer of 395 (chs. VI–VII) would have preceded chapter IV. They considered, however, that it was 'not worth while reviewing in detail the consequences that would ensue from the combination of the present arrangement of cols. i–viii [i.e. as accepted in all subsequent editions] with the view that the θέρος belongs to 395, for that hypothesis would remove none of the difficulties which have led us to place cols. i–iv before v–viii, and would not be supported by the chief argument for transposing v–viii before i–iv, the fact that cols. i–iv are in the same hand as that of vi, 27–xxi.'

Yet it is just this combination—the placing of cols. i–iv before v–viii and the equating of the eighth year with 395/4—that has gained much support and, as we shall see, is the only plausible alternative to the view of the first editors. However, two arguments against the theory that the eighth year is 395/4, advanced by the editors in discussing the results of the transposition of cols. i–iv and v–viii, are still valid if the columns are not transposed: (1) The new Spartan nauarch, Pollis, whose assumption of command is recorded in IV, 2, was succeeded by Cheiricrates soon after midsummer 395 (ch. XIV, 1). Whatever the irregularities of the Spartan nauarchia, Pollis would have had a strikingly short term of office if he entered upon it in the spring (not to mention the midsummer!) of 395. (2) It is by no means easy to see why the historian should have chosen to reckon the number of the year from the uneventful year 402/1, which would be the case if the eighth year were 395/4. Nor is it easy to see what might have stood in the lacuna after τῆ μὲν [--. Although Grenfell and Hunt were surely right in thinking that P did not use Attic archons for dating purposes, but reckoned back to some event, the archonship of Eucleides, or the restoration of the Athenian democracy, in 403/2 would seem a far more suitable point to which to reckon back.

While these arguments would seem to me to carry considerable weight, many scholars, whose views we shall consider later, have not found them convincing and have offered alternative explanations in support of the hypothesis that the eighth year is 395/4.

Grenfell and Hunt argue further that if the eighth year is 396/5, it is preferable to suppose that the θέρος, with which the year began according to P's system, refers to midsummer than to spring. On the assumption, which seems to be the indication of the opening part of IV, I, that the events of I–III belong to the end of the seventh year and those of IV, I to the beginning of the eighth, Grenfell and Hunt suggest: (1) that it would be surprising, if the eighth year began in spring, that the narrative should commence with the 'comparatively unimportant' naval war in preference to the expedition of Agesilaus to Asia. (2) The arrival of reinforcements from Phoenicia to Conon (IV, 2) is more likely to have occurred late in 396 than early, since the statements of Isocrates (*Paneg.* 142) would not suggest that these reinforcements were available to Conon throughout the campaign of 396. (3) If the nauarch Pollis assumed his duties in spring he would have held the office for considerably more than a year in view of his replacement by Cheiricrates in the late summer of 395 (XIV, I). This, if not impossible, would be rather unusual.

Although no one of these arguments alone is very strong, together they may outweigh the natural inclination to assume that P must have followed the example of Thucydides in reckoning in years beginning with the spring.

De Sanctis (*Atti Accad. Scienze Torino* LXVI (1931), 157ff.) is in agreement with Grenfell and Hunt that the eighth year is 396/5, holding the view that P takes as his epoch year 403/2, that of the restoration of the Athenian democracy. De Sanctis further agrees with the first editors that the θέρος with which the year begins is midsummer, but he believes that this is because P based his chronological system upon the Attic archon-year. This accords with De Sanctis' dubious view that Androtion was the author of the *Hellenica Oxyrhynchia*, in consequence of which he restored in the lacuna after ἐνειστήκει [ἐν ᾧ Φορμίων ἦρξεν... Of more recent writers on the subject, the Italian scholars Gigante (in his edition) and Barbieri (*Conone*) accept the conclusions of De Sanctis regarding the identification of the eighth year as 396/5 and the θέρος as midsummer.

Bartoletti, on the other hand, supports the view that the eighth year is 395/4 and that the θέρος is not midsummer, but spring. He does not argue the case in detail, but states in his preface (p. xv) that he is convinced by the arguments of Meyer (pp. 58ff.), Jacoby (*F.Gr.Hist.* IIC, 10–11) and Bloch (*HSCP*, supp. vol. I (1940), pp. 331–4). It may be appropriate to attempt here a summary of the views of these scholars, and also of Underhill (*JHS* XXVIII (1908), 279–82). In order of publication, Underhill's paper was the first to attack Grenfell and Hunt's view that if the eighth year was 395/4, columns v–viii should precede i–iv. Favouring the view that the eighth year is 395/4, Underhill sought to refute the arguments of the first editors for taking that year as 396/5 as follows: (1) The first editors' list of Spartan nauarchs contains certain irregularities. The list is:

398–397 (autumn) Pharax; 397 (autumn)–396 (autumn) unknown (now known to be Archelaïdas); 396 (autumn)–395 (summer) Pollis; 395 (summer–winter) Cheiricrates; 394 Peisander. To suppose that Pollis came in spring 395 and was replaced later in the same summer makes the list 'but little more irregular'. (2) The editors' argument for 403/2 as the epoch year, on the grounds that the restoration of the democracy at Athens would be a suitable event from which to reckon, is irrelevant to the issue. The theory proposed by Underhill was that P reckoned not from any particular event, but from the beginning of his work, and he thought that the dative τῇ μέν (cf. Thuc. IV, 51, etc.) after ἐνειστήκει might support this view. In this particular Underhill has, of course, been proved wrong by the discovery of the Florence papyrus, which reveals that the work began with events much earlier than those of 402/1, probably with those of the year 411/10.

To support his contention that the θέρος referred to spring, Underhill cited Thucydides' and Xenophon's use of the beginning of summer (being the beginning of the campaigning season) as the starting point for the narrative of each year. That P did likewise is a presumption which, as Grenfell and Hunt pointed out, may or may not be correct. Underhill saw in XI, 1 and XVII, 2 and 4 implications of such a system of reference to the seasons from a military standpoint. He further tried to show, from rather insubstantial evidence, that no columns are lost between columns iv and v. The view that the eighth year is 396/5 would then involve the unlikely appearance that P dismissed the year 396 in two columns (or four, if θέρος refers to midsummer, plus any before column i which may have dealt with the very early part of 396), while the year 395 takes up at least seventeen columns. The suggestion that nothing is lost between columns iv and v, although supported by Meyer, is rejected by most editors, including Grenfell and Hunt and Bartoletti. The latter (p. xvi) admits that Grenfell and Hunt were right in asserting from the evidence of the recto that at least one column is missing (*OCT*, p. v). Although thinking that the number of lost columns must be small because in his view IV, 1 already concerns the year 395, Bartoletti also mentions the possibility of 193 lines being lost between columns iv and v if the letter δ̄ which appears in the left margin opposite column v, line 45 signifies the 400th line of the book, since from col. i, 1 to col. v, 45 there are 207 lines extant. Four or five columns would thus be lost here, and this might be an attractive hypothesis to those who hold that the eighth year is 396/5. However, Grenfell and Hunt also recognized that the narrative of 396 would not be expected to take up as much space as that of 395, for apart from the activity of Agesilaus in Asia there were not many events of much importance in 396.

The final argument of Underhill is that the visit of Timocrates to

Greece must have occurred very shortly before the summer campaign of 395 in Greece, thus suggesting 395/4 for the ἔτος ὄγδοον. His logic here appears to me to be at fault, however, and this whole question of the visit of Timocrates is admirably discussed by De Sanctis, art. cit. pp. 169ff., Barbieri, *op. cit.* pp. 90–100, and Accame, *Ricerche intorno alla guerra corinzia*, pp. 27ff. Cf. also my note to II, 2.

Meyer (p. 61) rejected Underhill's mistaken view that the work of P began with 402/1 and reaffirmed the first editors' belief that it was a continuation of Thucydides' history. But Meyer also took the view that the eighth year was 395/4 and the θέρος spring. His chief contribution to the discussion on the chronology is an argument intended to show that spring 402/1, contrary to the objections of Grenfell and Hunt, would be a most suitable date from which to reckon the numbers of subsequent years. Although the length of the Peloponnesian War down to the surrender of Athens in spring 404, if we follow Thucydides' numbering of the years, would be twenty-seven years, Xenophon, *Hellenica* II, 3. 9 reads τελευτῶντος τοῦ θέρους [εἰς ὃ ἑξάμηνος καὶ ὀκτὼ καὶ εἴκοσιν ἔτη τῷ πολέμῳ ἐτελεύτα] (εἰς ὃ...ἐτελεύτα *del.* Brückner). Xenophon thus considered the war to have lasted 28½ years, i.e. until autumn 403, and P might therefore be expected to have done the same. As he seems, in Thucydidean manner, to have divided his years by summers and winters (Meyer assumed that, like Thucydides, P reckoned in summers beginning with the spring), the historian would have no choice but to commence his post-Peloponnesian-War narrative with the spring of the following year, that is 402/1. This view is strongly supported by Jacoby (*F.Gr.Hist.* II C, 11), who also quotes, as evidence that the war was thought to include the period of anarchy before the archonship of Eucleides, Dion. Hal. *Ad Pomp.* 3. 10. In holding that the θέρος refers to spring, Jacoby asserts that in P's formula θέρος indicates not a particular season, but the first half of the military year, the years being campaigning seasons and these divided into 'summer' and 'winter'.

Jacoby further argues that if the eighth year were 396/5 and the notice of the transition to the ninth year occurred in the lacuna between chapters IV and VI, then, since chapters VI–VIII narrate events of March–June 395, the new year (i.e. the θέρος) would have to begin in spring, not midsummer. Consequently, if IV, 1 refers to spring 396, there is insufficient room for the events of 396, and the chronological problems concerning the mission of Timocrates become insoluble. But as the first editors pointed out, if the θέρος of IV, 1 is midsummer 396 the transition to the ninth year, if noted at all, would occur in the gap before chapter X, and on this assumption De Sanctis and Barbieri (*locc. citt.*) have provided plausible solutions to the problems of Timocrates.

On the question of the Spartan nauarchs, Jacoby accepts that the series Pharax 398/7, Archelaïdas 397/6, Pollis 396/5, Cheiricrates, is certain, but rightly states that the official duration of each term of office is uncertain. There are two dates to contend with, the official election to office in the autumn (the beginning of the Spartan year) and the actual assumption of duties (decided in each case by the ephors). The implication is that the argument about the short period of Pollis' nauarchia, which Grenfell and Hunt stated, becomes irrelevant to the chronological questions. This view is upheld by Bloch in his excellent study (cited above), and he is severely critical of the attempts of Pareti (*Mem. Accad. Torino* LIX (1909), 71–160) to establish a uniform date for the assumption of actual command by the Spartan nauarchs.

Most of Bloch's comments on chronology appear under the heading 'Androtion and the Hellenica of Oxyrhynchus', in which section he successfully refutes De Sanctis' view that P is Androtion. He is perhaps too dogmatic, however, in his rejection of De Sanctis' opinion that the eighth year is 396/5. Bloch's main argument, and a completely original one, is that if the beginnings of the ναυαρχίαι of Pollis and Cheiricrates had both been in August, the one in 396 and the other in 395, we should expect the notice of the latter to appear, on the example of IV, I, immediately after the supposed *Jahresformel* of the ninth year (which, if it occurs, must fall in the lacuna before chapter X), not in chapter XIV after the long descriptions of the Rhodian revolution and the situation in Boeotia. Further, the dispute between Phocis and Locris (ch. XIII) took place, according to Pausanias III, 9. 9, τοῦ σίτου ἀκμάζοντος (i.e. May or June 395) and before the beginning of the Attic year in July. If P were part of an Atthis, as De Sanctis had argued, the *Jahresformel* of 395/4 would have occurred between chapter XIII (May–June) and XIV (the arrival of Cheiricrates in August). However, if P is not the author of an Atthis, and assuredly he is not, we must not disregard the opinion of Grenfell and Hunt that 'there is no reason to think that P's arrangement of facts was so strictly annalistic as to prevent his grouping together an intimately connected series of events belonging to the conclusion of the eighth and the beginning of the ninth year'. I would add also that Bloch's argument, while a strong one, rests on the assumption that P did note the beginning of each year by reference to his epoch year in Thucydidean manner, and however probable this may appear to some, it remains an assumption.

All this, then, is the evidence. We are faced with two alternatives: the θέρος of the ὄγδοον ἔτος is either midsummer 396 or spring 395. Neither view can claim to be conclusive, although this claim has been made for both. The reader's own view will depend on which parts of the evidence strike him as most convincing. For my own part, I incline to the former view, and my notes on the date of the adventure of Demaenetus and the mission of Timocrates are based upon this view. I have preferred to date the expedition of Demaenetus to spring 396 rather than winter 397/6 (which would be the case if IV, 1 concerned spring 396) or winter 396/5 (which would hold if the θέρος of IV, 1 were spring 395). On the dating of Timocrates' visit, a rather more complex question, see my note to II, 2.

IV, 1 continued

[.......................]**αρος** (-δρος cannot be read, ed.pr.)

Grenfell and Hunt assumed that -αρος was the name of a man, probably a Persian commander (cf. their note, ed.pr. p. 210, iii, 11 ff.), and this would appear to be the view of most of those who have attempted restorations of the lacuna: ὁ δὲ ...]αρος De Sanctis; [ἐν δὲ τῇ 'Ασίᾳ--]αρος Judeich; [κατὰ δὲ τὴν 'Ασίαν τότε...]αρος Lipsius; [τοῦ δ' ἀρχομένου χειμῶνος..]-αρος Pareti. Bartoletti, assuming that the θέρος of IV, 1 refers to the spring, conjectures (e.g.) [Κόνων δὲ ἐπιγιγνομένου τοῦ ἔ]αρος. If -αρος is a person he would become the subject of ἀπα[γαγών? (Fuhr) or καταπλεύσας. He might appear to have negotiated with Pharnabazus about the sailors' pay (καὶ μισθὸν ἀπολα[βεῖν), and is possibly mentioned twice more in IV, 2; cf. ed.pr. *ad loc.*

ἐ]κεῖ

Perhaps Caunus, the headquarters of the Persian fleet before the revolt of Rhodes from Sparta, or Rhodes, which subsequently became the headquarters. Grenfell and Hunt thought the former, but see my note to IV, 2 under Φοινίκων [καὶ Κιλίκων ἧκον ἐνενήκοντ]α νῆες εἰς Καῦνον κτλ.

βουλό[μενος...................]αι καὶ μισθὸν ἀπολα[βεῖν

βουλό[μενος τῷ Φαρναβάζῳ συμμεῖξ]αι, ed.pr., coll. XIV, 1, is the most acceptable restoration proposed here.

IV, 2 (=Column iii, 19–31)

..].ος --α]ρος, ed.pr., coll. IV, 1.

'].ος vel]τος p. Num αὐ]τός? οὖ]τος?', Bartoletti.

αὐτοῦ διε[......

διέ[τριβεν (Grenfell and Hunt) seems quite appropriate to the context and adequately fills the space left by the restoration [......ἐπὶ δὲ τὰς ναῦς τῶν Λακ]εδαιμονίων καὶ τῶν [συμμάχων ἀφικνεῖται Πόλλις] ναύαρχος ἐκ Λακε[δαίμονος εἰς τὴν ναυαρχίαν τὴ]ν 'Αρχελαΐδα κατα[στὰς διάδοχος. This excellent restoration is due to W. L. Newman (*ap. OCT*) and has been applauded by all subsequent editors. For the existence of such a proper name at Sparta, cf. Polyaenus II, 8, 'Αρξιλαΐδας ὁ Λάκων (on whom see Poralla, *P.Lak.* p. 30). For διάδοχος and Πόλλις cf. XIV, 1. On the date of the assumption of command by Pollis, see note on the chronological problem under IV, 1. We can be sure of the following list of Spartan nauarchs, but not of the exact date at which each took over the command (as opposed to the official date of their election): Pharax 398/7, Archelaïdas 397/6, Pollis 396/5, Cheiricrates 395. In ed.pr., Grenfell and Hunt, taking 'Αρχελαΐδα to be the name of a ship, substituted 'unknown' for 397/6. For detailed studies of the problems concerning the Spartan nauarchs, although with none too convincing conclusions, see Bauer, *Wiener Studien* XXXII (1910), 296–314 and Pareti, *Mem. Accad. Torino* LIX (1909), 71–160. Pareti attempted to establish a consistent date for the actual assumption of duties by the Spartan nauarchs, that of the beginning of the Spartan year in the autumn. Bauer suggested 397/6 as the date of Pharax's nauarchia, with both Pollis and Cheiricrates in the year 395/4.

Archelaïdas may also be mentioned in fragments 19 and 20 (see notes to chs. V and IX). Jacoby in his text places fragments 17–20 between columns iii and iv (chs. IV and V); Grenfell and Hunt had tentatively assigned these fragments to column iv. Cf. *P.Lak.* 146 (Archelaïdas) and 621 (Pollis).

κατὰ δὲ τὸν αὐ]τὸν χρόνον Φοινίκων [καὶ Κιλίκων ἧκον ἐνενήκοντ]α νῆες εἰς Καῦνον, ὧν [δέκα μὲν ἔπλευσαν ἀπὸ Κιλι]κίας, αἱ δὲ λείπουσαι [...

Cf. Diod. XIV, 79. 8: παρεγενήθησαν δὲ τῷ Κόνωνι τριήρεις ἐνενήκοντα, δέκα μὲν ἀπὸ Κιλικίας, ὀγδοήκοντα δ' ἀπὸ Φοινίκης, ὧν ὁ Σιδωνίων δυνάστης εἶχε τὴν ἡγεμονίαν.

For a detailed discussion of some of the problems concerning the naval war, see ed.pr. pp. 211–13. On the question of the agreement of P and Diodorus as to the chronological order of the main events of this part of the war, I would suggest the following alternative to the argument of Grenfell and Hunt:

Chapters 79–81 of Diodorus XIV are assigned to 396/5, but as he deals only with Sicilian history in his narrative of the preceding two years it is not unlikely that these chapters include the events of three years. In sections 4–8 of chapter 79, Diodorus lists four episodes of the naval war: (1) Pharax, the Spartan nauarch, put out from Rhodes with 120 ships and besieged Conon with the King's fleet of forty ships in Caunus.

(2) Artaphernes and Pharnabazus came to the assistance of Conon and the Caunians with a large force, and Pharax retired to Rhodes. (3) After this, Conon sailed to the Chersonese of Cnidus with eighty ships. The people of Rhodes revolted from Sparta, expelling the Spartan fleet. Conon was then admitted to Rhodes with the King's fleet. (4) Ninety ships came from Cilicia and Phoenicia to assist Conon.

That these events were recorded in chronological order was doubted by Grenfell and Hunt in their note on event (4) above, which is also recorded in *Hell.Oxy.* IV, 2. I accept Grenfell and Hunt's dating of the much discussed θέρος of the ὄγδοον ἔτος in IV, 1, and, in particular, I accept their date for event (4) above, late summer or early autumn of 396. Events (1) and (2) above are dated to 397 by the nauarchia of Pharax (398/7) and the improbability of the naval war having started in 398. On the date of event (3), the revolt of Rhodes, we know only that it preceded the democratic revolution in that city in the summer of 395 (cf. ch. X). Grenfell and Hunt therefore took autumn or winter 396 as the latest reasonable date for the revolt. Assuming that this was in fact the date, they found it necessary to suppose that event (3) followed event (4), the order of events in Diodorus' account being incorrect, and the account of the revolt of Rhodes in P being lost between columns iii and v of the papyrus. That the reinforcements from Phoenicia helped the Rhodians to expel the Spartan fleet (or the part of it which was in Rhodes at the time) would not, in itself, be unlikely, but so far from giving that impression Diodorus indicates that they arrived after the revolt, and gave assistance to Conon, who had not, apparently, co-operated in the expulsion of the Spartans. The statement of P that the reinforcements came to Conon at Caunus does not of necessity mean that Conon had not by this time moved his headquarters from Caunus to Rhodes, for, as we see from X, 1 and XIV, 1, Conon was in the habit of visiting Caunus with some of his fleet from time to time after his admission to Rhodes.

For some reason Grenfell and Hunt did not consider a date earlier than the *terminus ad quem* for the revolt of Rhodes. The longer the interval between the revolt and the democratic revolution (summer 395), the more understandable is the murder of the Diagoreans by the democratic conspirators (X, 2). The Diagoreans must have taken a lead in expelling the Spartans; if not it would be improbable that they could have assumed the government of the city subsequently. As liberators of Rhodes they would have enjoyed popular esteem, at least until they had had some time in office in which to incur resentment. According to Diodorus' chronology, the date for the revolt would be winter 397 or spring 396. The account of this event in P would then have occurred before the beginning of the London papyrus. The result of this hypothesis is that the apparent discrepancy between P and Diodorus disappears, and Diodorus' sequence of events is confirmed. A second consequence of my conclusion is that the suggestion of Meyer (*ap.* ed.pr.), that if 'Αρταφέ]ρνη[ς] ἀνὴρ Πέρσης be read in IV, 3 P is there referring to event (2) above from Diodorus, becomes quite unacceptable, as that event, being dated with some certainty to 397, must have appeared at some point before the beginning of the London papyrus.

]ας αὐτῶν ὁ Σιδώνιος [δυνάστης...

Cf. Diod. XIV, 79. 8. Grenfell and Hunt (and others) read "Ακτων ὁ Σιδώνιος, although the name "Ακτων is not known. Bartoletti has no doubts about his reading αὐτῶν, and suggests tentatively τὰς δὲ πλείστ]ας αὐτῶν (*sc.* τῶν νεῶν).

.].αρος

ὁ μὲν οὖν....].αρος, ed.pr., coll. IV, 1, on the supposition that -αρος was a Persian naval commander. Bartoletti comments 'ante αροσ vestigium unius litterae incertissimum (γ, ε, κ, σ, τ, υ, χ legi potest)'. If Grenfell and Hunt were right in thinking that -αρος was a Persian commander, the context here may indicate a change of command in the Persian navy, for although it appears from Diodorus that Conon was in sole command of the fleet from the beginning of the naval war until the battle of Cnidus, Xenophon (*Hell.* IV, 3. 11) does refer to Pharnabazus as ναύαρχος at the battle of Cnidus, and it is a possibility that while Conon was actually directing operations at the time to which the present passage refers, some Persian other than Pharnabazus may have been the nominal commander-in-chief. It must be admitted, however, that the complete absence of any mention by Diodorus of this man, if he held such a position, would be rather surprising.

IV, 3 (=Column iii, 31–43, with fragment 2)

ποταμ[ὸ]ν τὸν Καύ[νιον καλούμενον εἰς λίμνη]ν τὴν Κ̣[α]υνίαν εἰσέπλευ[σε

The river is to be identified with the Calbis, which flowed for some five miles from the Caunian Lake to the sea. Caunus itself was situated a little to the west of the river, about midway between the Lake and the coast. The Caunian Lake is the modern Köyceğiz Gölü. Cf. Strabo XIV, 2. 2: Καῦνος καὶ ποταμὸς πλησίον Κάλβις βαθύς, ἔχων εἰσαγωγήν.

....**φέ]ρνη[ς] ἀνὴρ Πέρσης**

Perhaps Πασιφέ]ρνη[ς]; cf. XIV, 3: Τιθραύστης...καταστήσας στρατηγοὺς ἐπὶ τῶν πραγμάτων Ἀριαῖον καὶ Πασιφέρνη...

The name is not known from the other sources. Diod. XIV, 79. 5, referring to the siege of Caunus, mentions a certain Artaphernes, who might also be the ἀνὴρ Πέρσης of this passage: Ἀρταφέρνου⟨ς⟩ δὲ καὶ Φαρναβάζου μετὰ πολλῆς δυνάμεως παραβοηθήσαντος τοῖς Καυνίοις. Grenfell and Hunt mentioned the possibility that the name Artaphernes in Diodorus' account might be an error, the Pasiphernes of P XIV, 3 being the man in question.

Fragment 2

On the position of *fr.* 2 in lines 40–3 of column iii see diagram in my note to III, 2. Ed.pr., p. 214, comments: 'Fr. 2, containing the letters]υφιλ],]ασ[,]ηλθ[, and]εασα[, is placed here chiefly on the evidence of colour; the recto is blank at this point, and the proposed arrangement is by no means certain.'

V (= Column iv)

Of column iv only the beginnings of lines 28–42 remain, and in these lines there are never more than seven letters legible. A few words of no particular significance can be distinguished in lines 35–42.

Fragments 17 and 18, which both contain a few letters from the opening lines of a column, may belong to column iv (cf. ed.pr. pp. 195 and 242, and Lipsius, *ad loc.*). Fragments 19 and 20 may also belong to this column (cf. ed.pr., *loc. cit.*, and Meyer, pp. 174f.). That the early part of column iv, at least, dealt with the naval war is apparent from the end of column iii.

φε[, in line 29, might possibly contain a name such as Τισσαφέρνης, Πασιφέρνης, or Ἀρταφέρνης, and if so the reference could be to the -]ρνη[ς] ἀνὴρ Πέρσης of IV, 3. Although it is unlikely that the name in IV, 3 is Τισσαφέρνης, ed.pr. p. 242 suggested as a reason for attributing *fr.* 17 to column iv the apparent references to Tissaphernes in this fragment, Τι]σσαφ[έρν.. and Τισσα]φέρ[ν (?). As the form Τι]σσαφ[έρν.. in *fr.* 17 would occur in line 1 of column iv, and there does not seem to be any mention of Tissaphernes in column iii, the narrative of which extends at least into the opening lines of column iv, the appearance of his name in *fr.* 17 might rather suggest that the fragment belongs elsewhere, perhaps to a missing column between iv and v (i.e. sections A and B of the papyrus), or even to column v.

The apparent reference to Archelaïdas in *fr.* 20 (Ἀρχελ[αΐδ..), and possibly also in *fr.* 19 ('Αρχε[λαΐδ..), would suit the context of the naval war, but would not be particularly appropriate to column iv since Pollis had already superseded Archelaïdas as Spartan nauarch (cf. IV, 2).

Kalinka suggests Σ?]άμο. in *fr.* 17 and Σά[μο?]υ as the last word of the last line (43) of column iii, but the possible circumstances of a reference to Samos are not known.

VI, 1 (= Column v, 1–6)

We now come to P's detailed account of the campaigns of Agesilaus in Asia. Chapters VI and VII concern the spring campaign of 395 in Lydia, and P's narrative is of special interest in that it is based on entirely different sources from that of Xenophon. For a most excellent analysis of this campaign, and also that of autumn 395 in Phrygia (chs. XVI–XVII), reference should be made to Dugas, 'La campagne d'Agésilas en Asie Mineure', in *BCH* XXXIV (1910), 58–95.

We can only guess at the subject-matter of section 1, which is severely mutilated. It is not unreasonable to suppose, however, that P made some mention of the preparations of Agesilaus at Ephesus (cf. Xen. *Hell.* III, 4. 16–19) before setting out on his march from that city to the valley of the Hermus and the region of Sardis. The itinerary of Agesilaus is outlined in sections 2 and 3.

VI, 2–3 (= Column v, 6–13 and 13–47)

On the march of the Greeks from Ephesus to the site of the battle of Sardis (VI, 4–6), cf. Diodorus XIV, 80. 1–2: μετὰ δὲ ταῦτα 'Αγησίλαος μὲν ἐξαγαγὼν τὴν δύναμιν εἰς τὸ Καΰστρου πεδίον καὶ τὴν περὶ Σίπυλον χώραν, ἐδῄωσε τὰς τῶν ἐγχωρίων κτήσεις· Τισσαφέρνης δὲ μυρίους μὲν ἱππεῖς, πεντακισμυρίους δὲ πεζοὺς ἀθροίσας, ἐπηκολούθει τοῖς Λακεδαιμονίοις καὶ τοὺς ἀποσπωμένους τῆς τάξεως ἐν ταῖς προνομαῖς ἀνῄρει. 'Αγησίλαος δὲ εἰς πλινθίον συντάξας τοὺς στρατιώτας ἀντείχετο τῆς παρὰ τὸν Σίπυλον παρωρείας, ἐπιτηρῶν καιρὸν εὔθετον εἰς τὴν τῶν πολεμίων ἐπίθεσιν. 2 ἐπελθὼν δὲ τὴν χώραν μέχρι Σάρδεων ἔφθειρε τούς τε κήπους καὶ τὸν παράδεισον τὸν Τισσαφέρνους, φυτοῖς καὶ τοῖς ἄλλοις πολυτελῶς πεφιλοτεχνημένον εἰς τρυφὴν καὶ τὴν ἐν εἰρήνῃ τῶν ἀγαθῶν ἀπόλαυσιν.

Cf. Xen. *Hell.* III, 4. 20–1: (ὁ 'Αγησίλαος) προεῖπεν αὐτοῖς ὡς εὐθὺς ἡγήσοιτο τὴν συντομωτάτην ἐπὶ τὰ κράτιστα τῆς χώρας, ὅπως αὐτόθεν οὕτω τὰ σώματα καὶ τὴν γνώμην παρασκευάζοιντο ὡς ἀγωνιούμενοι. ὁ μέντοι Τισσαφέρνης ταῦτα μὲν ἐνόμισε λέγειν αὐτὸν πάλιν βουλόμενον ἐξαπατῆσαι, εἰς Καρίαν δὲ νῦν τῷ ὄντι ἐμβαλεῖν, καὶ τό τε πεζὸν καθάπερ τὸ πρόσθεν εἰς Καρίαν διεβίβασε καὶ τὸ ἱππικὸν εἰς τὸ Μαιάνδρου πεδίον κατέστησεν. ὁ δ' Ἀγησίλαος οὐκ ἐψεύσατο, ἀλλ' ὥσπερ προεῖπεν εὐθὺς εἰς τὸν Σαρδιανὸν τόπον ἐνέβαλε. See also Xen. *Agesilaus* I, 28–9; Plutarch, *Ages.* X, 1 and Nepos, *Ages.* III, 4–5, who summarize Xenophon; Paus. III, 9. 5; Polyaen. II, 1. 9; Frontin. I, 8. 12.

The general agreement between the fragmentary narrative of P and that of Diodorus may be seen from the following points:

Col. v, 8 **Κ̣α[ΰσ]τ̣ρι[ον πεδίον**

Diodorus specifies that Agesilaus first led his army from Ephesus to the plain of the Cayster. Xenophon, however, relates that Agesilaus gave notice of his intention to advance by the shortest route (τὴν συντομωτάτην) against the chief positions of the country, and indeed did so, invading τὸν Σαρδιανὸν τόπον. The route implied by these remarks of Xenophon is discussed later in this section of commentary.

Col. v, 9 **τὰ ὄρη**

The reference may well be to the vicinity of Sipylus, which is the next location on the march to be mentioned by Diodorus. Agesilaus plundered the possessions of the inhabitants of this area.

Col. v, 13–14 **Τισσαφέρ[ν]ης [.......................ἐπηκο]λούθει τοῖς Ἕλλη[σ]ιν**

Cf. Diodorus, *loc. cit.*, Τισσαφέρνης...ἐπηκολούθει τοῖς Λακεδαιμονίοις. Xenophon, on the other hand, indicates that Tissaphernes, believing Agesilaus to have announced his intention of marching straight towards Sardis in order to deceive him, had transferred his infantry into Caria and stationed his cavalry in the plain of the Maeander. Tissaphernes had previously been deceived by the Spartan king when he made open preparations for a drive into Caria (Xen. *Hell.* III, 4. 11–12), but on this occasion, while Tissaphernes led his infantry into Caria, Agesilaus began to march in the opposite direction.

Col. v, 15–16 **[...............ἱππέας μὲν...α]κισχιλίους κα[ὶ] μυ[ρίους, πεζοὺς δὲ........μυρίων ο]ὐκ ἐλάττους.**

The restoration of the first editors, retained by Bartoletti, which indicates that the number of ἱππεῖς was given before that of πεζοί, is based on Diodorus, *loc. cit.* One may note also that P, at XVII, 2, in giving numbers of ἱππεῖς and πεζοί, places the ἱππεῖς first. This order is reversed in VIII, 1 (τῶν [πε]ζῶ[ν] καὶ τῶν ἱππέω[ν...]), but here no numbers appear to be specified. Diodorus mentions 10,000 cavalry and 50,000 infantry. πεντακισμυρίων ο]ὐκ ἐλάττους might therefore be suggested for the number of infantry in the present passage, so as to make P agree with Diodorus. However, P would seem not to be in concord with Diodorus on the number of cavalry. Such a discrepancy is not unique; in VI, 6, for instance, P reads ἑξακοσίους while Diodorus has ἑξακισχιλίους (XIV, 80. 4). Grenfell and Hunt (ed.pr. p. 211) quote two other such instances, in IV, 2, concerning the number of ships from Phoenicia and Cilicia, and VI, 4, but in these places the fragmentary nature of P gives no room for certainty as to whether P and Diodorus agree or not. If the discrepancy between the two historians in VI, 6 is due to a corruption in the MSS of Diodorus, as Grenfell and Hunt suggested, the possibility of a similar occurrence in the passage under review might lend support to the restoration of Wilamowitz (*ap.* ed.pr.), πεζοὺς μὲν πεντα]κισχιλίους κα[ὶ] μυ[ρίους ἔχων, ἱππέας δὲ μυρίων ο]ὐκ ἐλάττους, and his emendation in the parallel passage of Diodorus of πεντακισμυρίους to πεντακισ⟨χιλίους καὶ⟩ μυρίους. On the other hand, if we reject Wilamowitz's emendation, the remarkably high figure given by Diodorus for the Persian infantry would appear to be supported by the remark of Pausanias (III, 9. 6) to the effect that this was the greatest concentration of Persian infantry since the time of Xerxes: καὶ τὸ πεζὸν τότε πλεῖστον ἀθροισθὲν μετά γε τὸν Ξέρξου...στρατόν. One might add, of course, that Pausanias' source is unknown, and his statement may have been an observation based on such figures as those quoted by Diodorus.

Col. V, 34–5 **τοῦ πλιν[θίου**

Cf. Diod. *loc. cit.*, Ἀγησίλαος δὲ εἰς πλινθίον συντάξας τοὺς στρατιώτας κτλ. The πλινθίον was probably mentioned earlier in P's account, but the proposed reading ταξάμε[νος εἰς πλινθίον in col. V, lines 9–10 (ed.pr. p. 214) seems improbable since it would occur before the arrival of Tissaphernes' troops (lines 13 ff.). As was pointed out by Busolt (*Hermes* XLIII (1908), 262), the formation into the πλινθίον would probably have taken place after the passage of the Karabel since such a manœuvre would be dangerous tactics in mountainous country.

Of the ravaging of the plain of Sardis and the gardens of Tissaphernes, mentioned by Diodorus, there is no trace in P's account. Dugas (art. cit.) aptly observes that such activity would be highly dangerous, if not impossible, in view of the proximity of Tissaphernes' troops in so large numbers. Remarking that Diodorus XIV, 80. 4 mentions only the plundering of the Persian camp after the battle near Sardis (contrast P VII, 1), he suggests that one is led to suppose a transposition in Diodorus' account of the plundering which occurred after the battle to this point in the narrative previous to the battle.

From the fragmentary remains of P's account, and from the version of Diodorus, visibly dependent upon P, we may reconstruct the main points of P's narrative as follows: (1) Agesilaus leads his army from Ephesus to the plain of the Cayster. Dugas (art. cit.) suggests that φθά[σας in VI, 2 (col. V, 11) indicates that Agesilaus was at this time in advance of Tissaphernes. (2) Tissaphernes pursues the Greeks with both cavalry and infantry. (3) Being overtaken by the Persians, Agesilaus forms his troops into squared column and continues his march from the region of Sipylus. (4) With the Persians in attendance the Greeks reach the valley of the Hermus.

Any announcement by Agesilaus of his plans (as in Xenophon's account) does not appear to have been mentioned by P, unless in a missing column before col. V, and if these plans included a direct march to Sardis they were certainly not carried out in P's version. The chief differences between the accounts of P and Xenophon lie in the itinerary of Agesilaus and the location at which he first encountered Persian troops. Xenophon gives no details of the route by which the Greeks reached the plain of Sardis, but implies that they took the shortest route. For three days they met no enemy, but on the fourth day the Persian cavalry arrived: καὶ τρεῖς μὲν ἡμέρας δι' ἐρημίας πολεμίων πορευόμενος πολλὰ τὰ ἐπιτήδεια τῇ στρατιᾷ εἶχε, τῇ δὲ τετάρτῃ ἧκον οἱ τῶν πολεμίων ἱππεῖς (*Hell.* III, 4. 21). It appears from the next sentence, concerning the battle which ensued, that their arrival occurred when the Greeks had reached the river Pactolus. We know from Herodotus V, 54, and Xenophon, *Hell.* III, 2. 11, that the journey from Ephesus to Sardis by the ordinary route was of three days' duration, and this would seem to be the route indicated by Xenophon on the present occasion, if we suppose that an army might take a little longer than an individual. This route followed the Cayster valley for some way to Hypaepa, then turned towards the north, and passing by Mount Tmolus followed the Pactolus to Sardis (cf. Radet, *La Lydie*, pp. 31, 102; Cousin, *Kyros le Jeune en Asie Mineure*, p. 85; Haussoullier, in *Revue de Philologie* XXIII (1899), 293).

As for the itinerary given by P and Diodorus, the reconstruction of Dugas (art. cit.) is highly convincing. Agesilaus followed the main route from Ephesus to Smyrna for a little way, perhaps as far as Metropolis, whence he turned north-east and, by way of the Karabel pass and Sipylus, joined the main route from Smyrna to Sardis along the Hermus valley.

It is not always easy to determine which of two so divergent accounts is the more acceptable. In favour of that of P, one might suggest: (1) The route indicated by Xenophon was the normal one; P would not have described another in some detail unless he had good reason to do so. (2) The direct route might have been more dangerous for Agesilaus, whose army was greatly outnumbered by that of Tissaphernes, in view of his apparent unwillingness to risk open battle. He may have hoped to deceive Tissaphernes by taking the route through the Karabel. (3) The region of Sipylus would offer opportunities for plunder as it had not previously been looted by the Greek army, and Agesilaus would be in no hurry to reach Sardis, which he could not hope to storm. Even after winning a battle in the vicinity of the city he made no attempt to take it.

On the other hand, Busolt, *Hermes* XLIII (1908), 255–85, argues that Xenophon's version has the greater appearance of authenticity.

Col. v, 41–2 **μᾶλ|λο[ν**

The combinations (here) μᾶλ|λο[ν and 'Α[γησί]|λα[ος in lines 47–8, and the fact that .ι[-- in the last line of *fr.* 3 is in fact the last line of a column

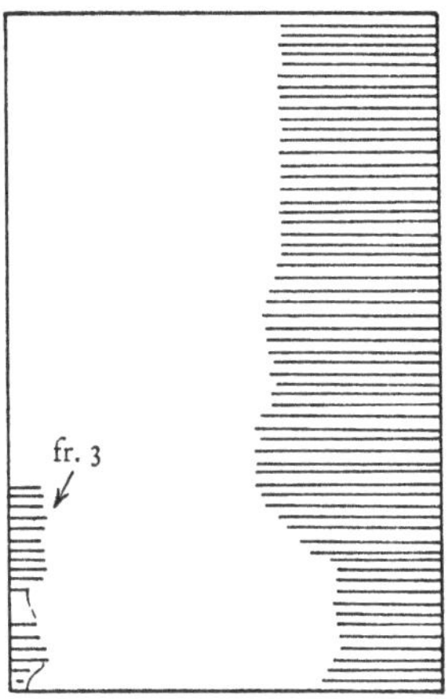

Fig. 2. Col. v.

are the grounds for placing *fr.* 3 in this position so as to provide the beginnings of lines 42–9 and 54–60 of column v. No letter is visible on the fragment for what would be lines 50–3. Ed.pr. cautiously states that this position for the fragment is not certain, and the recto gives no help in establishing its correct position.

Column v, 42–3 **τὸν ποτ[αμόν**

This is thought by Fuhr (*Berl.Phil.Woch.* (1908), cols. 156–8) to be an indication of the place at which the battle of Sardis took place (see Appendix 1). Fuhr took the river to be the Pactolus, in which case P would confirm Xenophon's site for the battle (*Hell.* III, 4. 22). It is equally probable, however, in view of the route taken by Agesilaus in P's account, that the river, while very possibly indicating the site of the battle, is the Hermus.

Column v, 45 δ̄ appears in the left margin opposite this line (see note to IV, 1). If it indicates the 400th line of the papyrus, 193 lines would be lost between sections A and B (i.e. between the columns we designate iv and v).

VI, 4 (= Column v, 47–column vi, 9)

The first editors made section 4 begin at column v, line 59, and did not divide the remainder of the chapter into sections 5 and 6. Sections 4–6 concern the battle fought near Sardis between Agesilaus and Tissaphernes. The discrepancies between the account of P (and of Diodorus XIV, 80. 2–4) and that of Xenophon (*Hell.* III, 4. 22–4; *Ages.* I, 30–2) are very remarkable, and are discussed in some detail in Appendix 1. Cf. Dugas, *BCH* XXXIV (1910), 65–73, and Cornelius, 'Die Schlacht bei Sardes', in *Klio* XXVI (1933), 29–31.

τῆς νυκτ[ὸς].ι[--

Cf. Diod. XIV, 80. 2: ἀπέστειλε Ξενοκλέα τὸν Σπαρτιάτην μετὰ χιλίων καὶ τετρακοσίων στρατιωτῶν ν υ κ τ ὸ ς εἴς τινα δασὺν τόπον. As Grenfell and Hunt remarked, the vestiges of the letter before ι do not suit ε, and εἴς τινα δασὺν τόπον is thus inadmissible in P. The restoration of Kalinka, δ]ι[ὰ δασέων τόπων, however, may be worthy of notice.

--μὲν] ὁπλίτας, [πεν]τακοσίους δ[ὲ ψ]ιλούς

On the number of troops allotted to Xenocles for the ambush, cf. Diod., *loc. cit.* [πεν]τακοσίους 'spatio magis convenit quam [ἑπ]τακοσίους vel [ὀκ]τακοσίους', Bartoletti. Cf. also Dugas, art. cit. p. 67 n. 3. If Diodorus' figure of 1,400 is to be accepted, one might read with Kalinka ἐνακοσίους μὲν] ὁπλίτας.

Ξενοκλέα

Mentioned below in VI, 5 and in Diod. XIV, 80. 2. We know from Xenophon, *Hell.* III, 4. 20, that Xenocles was one of the successors to the thirty Spartans, including Lysander, who returned to Greece from Asia in spring 395. The newcomers are referred to as οἱ περὶ Ἡριππίδαν. Of these Agesilaus Ξενοκλέα μὲν καὶ ἄλλον ἔταξεν ἐπὶ τοὺς ἱππέας. Cf. *P.Lak.* 569.

βαδίζοντε[ς] κατ' αὐτούς [--

The subject of βαδίζοντε[ς] evidently appeared in the lacuna after αὐτούς. Grenfell and Hunt thought it more likely to be Agesilaus' troops than the enemy, and suggested (e.g.) οἱ ἐπὶ τῆς οὐραγίας; cf. Diod. XIV, 80. 3. Similarly Lipsius suggested οἱ τελευταῖοι τῆς στρατιᾶς (for τελευταῖοι cf. XVI, 2). Kalinka, however, restored οἱ πολέμιοι; cf. XVI, 2, in which an account is given of an ambush of the Mysians. The difference between the two ambushes, as Grenfell and Hunt rightly indicated, is that in the present case the party under Xenocles was sent in advance of the army, which would thus have to pass the hiding-place, whereas in the later incident the troops selected for the ambush were left behind the rest of the army, so that only the enemy would pass them.

ἅ[μα τῇ ἡμ]έρᾳ

Cf. Diod. XIV, 80. 3 ἅμ' ἡμέρᾳ. As with τῆς νυκτ[ὸς] (above) the version of P inserts the article, while Diodorus does not. The reading of ed.pr., ἅ[μα ἡμ]έρᾳ, is shorter than the space.

πε[ριίππε]υον

Restored by Boissevain, *Berl.Phil.Woch.* (1908), cols. 189f., and most suitable to the context.

ἀτάκτ[ως

Cf. Diod. XIV, 80. 3 προσπίπτοντες ἀτάκτως.

VI, 5 (= Column vi, 9–18)

καιρ[ὸν ὑπ]έλαβεν

Cf. the use of this phrase in X, 2. In P's account Xenocles has authority to decide for himself the most opportune moment for action; Diodorus XIV, 80. 3 represents Agesilaus as acting first, and the soldiers under Xenocles as joining battle when they had received a signal from Agesilaus.

VI, 6 (= Column vi, 18–27)

περὶ ἑξακοσίους

Diodorus gives the number of Persians killed as ὑπὲρ τοὺς ἑξακισχιλίους (XIV, 80. 4). It is easy to imagine how a copyist's error could have converted 600 to 6,000, since Diodorus is clearly dependent upon P, albeit through the work of Ephorus. It is also a possibility, however, that

Ephorus (or Diodorus) increased the number intentionally, since in view of the size of the Persian force—60,000 men in all according to Diodorus—6,000 may have appeared a more realistic, or more exciting, number of dead. In this connection we may note that while there is no trace of any hard-fought battle in P, Diodorus refers to a καρτερὰ μάχη, and this, as Jacoby observed (*F.Gr.Hist.* II C, 12), is an Ephorean phrase. Dugas (art. cit.) suggests that Ephorus, who 'aimait à introduire des batailles là où n'avait eu lieu aucune rencontre' (p. 68), greatly exaggerated the dimensions of this one.

For further discussion of sections 4–6, see Appendix 1, 'The Battle of Sardis'.

VII, 1 (= Column vi, 27–34)

τ[ῆς] μάχης

I.e. the battle of Sardis (VI, 4–6).

καταπλαγέντες

Cf. Diod. XIV, 80. 5: ἀπὸ δὲ τῆς μάχης Τισσαφέρνης μὲν εἰς Σάρδεις ἀπεχώρησε καταπεπληγμένος τὴν τόλμαν τῶν Λακεδαιμονίων.

ἀπεχώρησ[αν σὺν] τῷ Τισσαφέρνει πρὸς τὰς Σάρδεις·

The contrast between this version and that of Xenophon is noteworthy in that the latter indicates that Tissaphernes was already in Sardis, having taken no part in the battle. Cf. Xen. *Hell.* III, 4. 25: ὅτε δ' αὕτη ἡ μάχη ἐγένετο, Τισσαφέρνης ἐν Σάρδεσιν ἔτυχεν ὤν. Diodorus XIV, 80. 2–4, Pausanias III, 9. 6 and Plutarch (who generally seems to have followed Xenophon's account), *Ages.* X, 2 support P in representing Tissaphernes as having been present at the battle.

τὴν γῆν ἅπασαν ἐ[πόρθ]ησεν

Although in the *Hellenica* Xenophon passes straight from the capture of the Persian camp after the battle of Sardis to the murder of Tissaphernes, he does, in the *Agesilaus*, mention this devastation of the plain of Sardis after the battle: ὡς δ' ἤκουσε τοὺς πολεμίους ταράττεσθαι διὰ τὸ αἰτιᾶσθαι ἀλλήλους τοῦ γεγενημένου, εὐθὺς ἦγεν ἐπὶ Σάρδεις. κἀκεῖ ἅμα μὲν ἔκαιε καὶ ἐπόρθει τὰ περὶ τὸ ἄστυ, ἅμα δὲ καὶ κηρύγματι ἐδήλου τοὺς μὲν ἐλευθερίας δεομένους ὡς πρὸς σύμμαχον αὐτὸν παρεῖναι· εἰ δέ τινες τὴν 'Ασίαν ἑαυτῶν ποιοῦνται, πρὸς τοὺς ἐλευθεροῦντας διακρινουμένους ἐν ὅπλοις παρεῖναι (*Ages.* I, 33–4). For the additional statement of the attempt by Agesilaus to win over some of the local inhabitants, this passage is the only authority. Whatever the extent of such activity by the Spartan king, the reason for the insertion of the information may be found partly in Xenophon's desire to portray the personal character of his hero. On this see further ed.pr. p. 239, n. xviii, 39, and Dugas, *BCH* XXXIV (1910), 73. For πορθεῖν see also II, 4; XIII, 5; XVI, 1 and 5.

προῆγεν τὸ στρ[άτε]υμα εἰς Φρυγίαν πάλιν [τὴν] μεγάλην.

Since the campaign of 396 had been conducted in Phrygia Minor against Pharnabazus (cf. Xen. *Hell.* III, 4. 12–15; Diod. XIV, 79. 3), and not in Phrygia Magna (ἡ μεγάλη), πάλιν can scarcely be interpreted to mean that this was a second invasion of Phrygia Magna. Grenfell and Hunt (ed.pr. p. 218) mentioned the possibility that the somewhat unusual position of the word πάλιν might indicate that it was intended to qualify Φρυγίαν alone, and not [τὴν] μεγάλην. It seems to me much more probable, however, that πάλιν qualifies only προῆγεν: 'he again led forward the army, (this time) into Φρυγίαν τὴν μεγάλην'. For similar uses of πάλιν cf. XVI, 2 ἀνασ[τὰς πρ]οῆγε τὸ στράτευμα πάλιν; XVI, 6 ἀφικόμενος δὲ πάλιν πρὸς Γόρδιον (there is no evidence of a previous visit to Gordium); and VI, 4 [τ]ὸ [στ]ρά[τε]υ[μα πάλιν] ἀνῆγεν εἰς τὸ πρ[όσθεν (if one accepts the restoration).

As it appears (from VII, 4) that Agesilaus did not, in fact, cross the Maeander, which probably constituted the boundary between Lydia and Phrygia (see note to VII, 3), εἰς here might be more accurately rendered 'towards' than 'into', as the first editors translated it. Dugas (art. cit. p. 74 n. 2) makes the same point about the translation of εἰς τὴν Φ[ρυγίαν in VII, 3: 'le mot...a donc le sens de *vers*, non de *dans*'. In this second instance, Grenfell and Hunt's translation reads: 'Agesilaus...brought them down to Phrygia until they reached the river Maeander.'

The march of Agesilaus southwards as far as the Maeander and then, apparently, down the river to Magnesia and the coast, with which the remainder of this chapter is concerned, is not mentioned at all by Xenophon. Diodorus XIV, 80. 5 gives a brief statement which is probably a résumé of P: Ἀγησίλαος δ' ἐπεχείρησε μὲν εἰς τὰς ἄνω σατραπείας, ἐν δὲ τοῖς ἱεροῖς οὐ δυνάμενος καλλιερῆσαι πάλιν ἀπήγαγε τὴν δύναμιν ἐπὶ θάλατταν. The details provided by the discovery of P were thus unknown previously.

VII, 2 (=Column vi, 34–40)

ἐποιεῖτο δὲ [τ]ὴν πορείαν

Cf. uses of the same expression at XVII, 2 and 3.

οὐκέτι συντεταγμένους ἔχων ἐν τῷ πλ[ι]νθίῳ τοὺς στρατιώτας

Cf. VI, 3 and note; Diod. XIV, 80. 1. Agesilaus had adopted this formation while on the march in the region of Sipylus, in order to minimize the danger from the numerically superior forces of Tissaphernes, which were in close pursuit.

(Τισσαφέρνης δὲ...) ἀναλαβὼν αὖθις τοὺς β̣[αρβάρους ἐ]πη[κολο]ύθει κτλ.

Xenophon appears to have been as ignorant of the movements of Tissaphernes as of Agesilaus after the battle of Sardis, for in his brief record of the death of Tissaphernes (which he places immediately after the battle in his narrative) he gives no hint of the place at which the assassination took place. It becomes evident from the detailed versions of Polyaenus VII, 16. 1, Diodorus XIV, 80. 6–8 and P VIII, that Tissaphernes must have returned again to Sardis after giving up his pursuit of Agesilaus (reported in the present passage), since it was from Sardis that he was summoned to Colossae by Ariaeus.

VII, 3 (= Column vi, 40–7)

'Αγ]ησίλ[αος] δὲ διεξελθ[ὼν] τὸ πε[δ]ίον τὸ τῶν Λυδῶν

Agesilaus probably took the same route from Sardis to the Maeander as did Cyrus a few years earlier. Cf. Xen. *Anab.* I, 2. 5: Κῦρος δὲ...ὡρμᾶτο ἀπὸ Σάρδεων· καὶ ἐξελαύνει διὰ τῆς Λυδίας σταθμοὺς τρεῖς παρασάγγας εἴκοσι καὶ δύο ἐπὶ τὸν Μαίανδρον ποταμόν. After marching up the valley of the Cogamus, he crossed the mountains to the north of the Maeander and thus reached the river, which, as has been noted above, probably formed the boundary between Lydia and Phrygia. Cf. Strabo XII, 8. 15: ἐντεῦθεν δ' ἤδη γενόμενος Μαίανδρος τέως μὲν διὰ τῆς Φρυγίας φέρεται, ἔπειτα διορίζει τὴν Καρίαν καὶ τὴν Λυδίαν κατὰ τὸ Μαιάνδρου καλούμενον πεδίον.

[ἦγε τὴν στρ]ατιὰν [......] διὰ τῶ[ν] ὀρῶν τῶν διὰ μέσου κε[ιμένων τῆ]ς̣ τ[ε Λυδίας] καὶ τῆς Φρυγίας.

The most suitable restoration proposed for the lacuna is [ἀμαχεί] (Wilamowitz, *ap.* ed.pr.). On the description of the mountains as being between Lydia and Phrygia, Dugas (*BCH* XXXIV (1910), 74 n. 2) argues that while the Maeander would form the official boundary, the more effective natural barrier was the mountain range which lies along the north side of the river. If P were writing in more precise terms, in that he referred to Phrygia as distinct from Caria, the mountains in question would be those in the small area between the source of the Cogamus and the Maeander, and, of course, this region would be exactly that in which Agesilaus had to cross the mountain chain.

εἰς τὴν Φ[ρυγίαν

Cf. note to VII, 1, suggesting that both there and here εἰς might be better translated 'towards' than 'into'.

Μαίανδρον ποταμόν, ὃ[ς ἔχει μὲν τὰς πηγὰς ἀπὸ Κελαι]νῶν, ἣ τῶν ἐν Φρυγίᾳ μεγίστη [πόλις ἐστίν, ἐκδίδωσι δ'] εἰς θάλατταν παρὰ Πριήνην κ[αὶ........

Cf. Strabo XII, 8. 15: καὶ μεταξὺ Μιλήτου καὶ Πριήνης ποιεῖται (Μαίανδρος) τὰς ἐκβολάς. ἄρχεται δὲ ἀπὸ Κελαινῶν, λόφου τινός, ἐν ᾧ πόλις ἦν ὁμώνυμος τῷ λόφῳ.

Various attempts have been made to fill the lacuna after παρὰ Πριήνην κ[αί. Fuhr proposed Μίλητον, citing Strabo (above), Livy XXXVIII, 13. 7 and Pliny *NH* V, 113. Wilamowitz proposed Μυοῦντα, and Wilcken Μυκάλην. Jacoby, *F.Gr.Hist.* IIC, 13, quotes Strabo XIV, 1. 12 against Wilcken: μετὰ δὲ τὰς ἐκβολὰς τοῦ Μαιάνδρου ὁ κατὰ Πριήνην ἐστὶν αἰγιαλός· ὑπὲρ δ' αὐτοῦ ἡ Πριήνη καὶ Μυκάλη τὸ ὄρος. On Fuhr's restoration, Jacoby comments: 'aber Μίλητον erscheint zu kurz'. Gigante accepts Μυοῦντα in his text.

VII, 4 (=Column vi, 47–column vii, 4)

ἐθύετο πότ[ερ]α χ[ρὴ] δ[ι]αβ[αίνειν τὸν ποτ]αμὸν ἢ μή, κτλ.

Certain more practical considerations than the divine answer to the sacrifices are suggested by Dugas (*BCH* XXXIV (1910), 74–5) as leading Agesilaus to the decision not to cross the Maeander or march on Celaenae, but to return to the coast along the north bank of the river. While the penetration into Phrygia Magna might be a spectacular enterprise, it would also expose the Greeks to the danger of being cut off from the sea by the very considerable forces of Tissaphernes, whose impending fate could not by this time have been known to Agesilaus. On the other hand, the valley of the Maeander, between the point at which Agesilaus reached the river and the coast, would provide greater opportunities for plunder than the more mountainous and less fertile country upstream, and, furthermore, had escaped previous depredation, being defended by the Persian cavalry (Xen. *Hell.* III, 4. 12 and 21). We may note that in the campaign of 396 the auspices had also proved unfavourable for an advance inland, and Agesilaus had in consequence returned to the coast. Cf. Xen. *Hell.* III, 4. 15: θυομένῳ τῷ 'Αγησιλάῳ τῇ ὑστεραίᾳ ἐπὶ προόδῳ ἄλοβα γίγνεται τὰ ἱερά. τούτου μέντοι φανέντος στρέψας ἐπορεύετο ἐπὶ θάλατταν.

ἀπῆγ]εν τὸν [στρατὸν.............

Kalinka restored πάλιν εἰς Λυδίαν. Gigante argues that this is not sufficiently precise (cf. βαδίζειν ἐπὶ Κελαινάς, above) and proposes πρὸς τὴν Ἔφεσον. It appears from VIII, 1 that Agesilaus made an extended halt at Magnesia on his way to Ephesus ('Αγησιλά]ου κα[θ]ημένου περὶ [τ]ὴν Μαγν[η]σ̣[ί]α̣ν̣). I therefore suggest that ἐπὶ Μαγνησίαν would be as suitable as Gigante's restoration, and has the advantage that Magnesia was, like Celaenae, but unlike Ephesus, on (or very near) the Maeander. Bartoletti tentatively suggests 'an ἐπὶ θάλατταν?', coll. Diod. XIV, 80. 5.

Αγησί]λαος μὲν οὖ[ν..............τὸ πεδίον τὸ Μαιάν]δρου καλούμενο[ν] δ̣[.........................].νέμονται Λυδ[οὶ] κ̣[αὶ...

μὲν οὖ[ν παρὰ τὴν Μεσωγίδα κτλ. δ̣[ιεξελθὼν Lipsius. μὲν οὖ[ν διαπορευθεὶς κτλ. δ̣[ιεξῆλθεν παρὰ τὴν Μεσωγίδα, ἣν] νέμονται κτλ. Kalinka.

Either of these restorations provides what must have been the general sense of the passage. In view of the route clearly taken by Agesilaus to Magnesia and Ephesus, it is highly probable that some mention would be made by P of the Mesogis. If the restoration of something like παρὰ τὴν Μεσωγίδα is accepted, in one or other of the lacunae, there is some weight to be attached to the proposition of Wilamowitz that the last sentence of the chapter should read νέμονται Λυδ[οὶ] κ̣[αὶ Μυσοί, Κᾶρές τε καὶ Ἴωνες (cf. Strabo XIII, 4. 12: ἡ δὲ Μεσωγὶς εἰς τὸ ἀντικείμενον μέρος διατείνει μέχρι Μυκάλης ἀπὸ Κελαινῶν ἀρξάμενον, ὥς φησι Θεόπομπος, ὥστε τὰ μὲν αὐτοῦ Φρύγες κατέχουσι τὰ πρὸς ταῖς Κελαιναῖς καὶ τῇ 'Απαμείᾳ, τὰ δὲ Μυσοὶ καὶ Λυδοί, τὰ δὲ Κᾶρες καὶ Ἴωνες). However, Wilamowitz based his restoration on the hypothesis, now discredited, that P is Theopompus, and that the present passage of P is that referred to by Strabo. Against the restoration, the remarks of Grenfell and Hunt (ed.pr. p. 219) are worthy of note: 'This restoration and identification seem to us very doubtful, even if P is Theopompus; for ἀπὸ Κελαι]νῶν in [column] vi, 45 apparently refers to the Maeander not to the Mesogis, about which Theopompus was speaking, and there is no room for anything corresponding to ὥστε τὰ μὲν αὐτοῦ Φρύγες---'Απαμείᾳ.' The case is strong against the identification of the passage with that of Theopompus (it is, of course, not the same passage), but presents no very valid argument against Wilamowitz's restoration as such.

Lipsius restored κ[αὶ Κᾶρες, κατῆρεν εἰς Μαγνησίαν.

VIII, 1 (= Col. vii, 4ff. and fragments 4, 5, 6, and 7, col. i)
VIII, 2 (= Col. viii, i.e. column ii of fragment 7)

Figure 3 indicates the position of *frr.* 4–7. Fragment 7, in addition to the final letters of three lines in column vii, contains all that remains of column viii. The correctness of the place assigned to *fr.* 4, to quote ed.pr. p. 219, 'is guaranteed (1) by internal evidence, since it clearly contains the

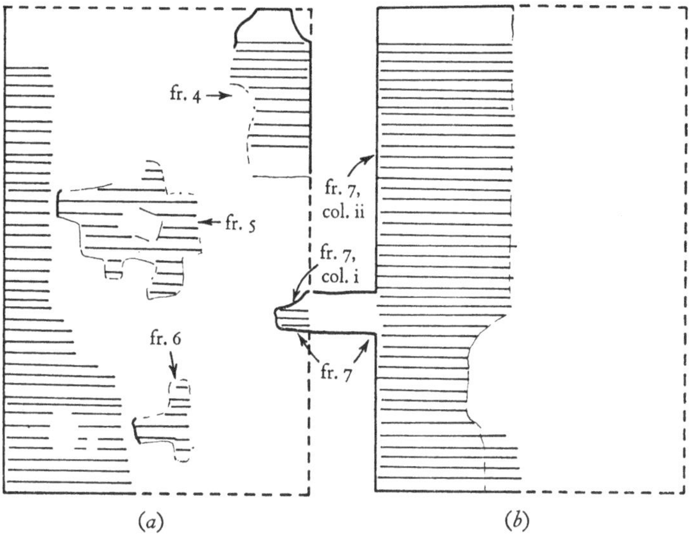

Fig. 3. (*a*) Column vii. (*b*) Column viii (= fragment 7, column ii).

transition from Agesilaus' campaign to the arrangements for the removal of Tissaphernes, (2) by the suitable combination μᾶλ|λο[ν in lines 9–10 (of col. vii), (3) by the evidence of the recto, which has ends of lines at the right point, (4) by the colour and texture of the papyrus, which agree with those of fragment 7, containing column viii'. The position of *frr.* 5 and 6 in column vii is virtually certain because of the suitability of the recto, and in the case of *fr.* 5 because of appropriate references to ἐπιστ]ο-λάς and Τι]σσαφ[έ]ρνη[.; see further ed.pr. p. 220. On the placing of *fr.* 7, which contains the endings of three lines of column vii and all that remains of column viii, the first editors wrote (ed.pr. p. 221): 'That Fr. 7...is correctly placed admits of no doubt; for although the ends of a few lines of the preceding column preserved in it do not provide any certain combination with the rest of column vii, the mentions of Ariaeus,

Tithraustes, and Tissaphernes and of the ἐπιστολαί establish its near connexion with column vii, and the texture and colour of Fr. 7 closely resemble those of Fr. 4, while the white stains found on the recto of both Frs. 5 and 6 and the rest of column vii are also present on the recto of Fr. 7.' The rather insignificant fragments 21 and 22 probably also belong to column vii or viii.

Columns vii–viii (chapter VIII) clearly contained an account, at considerable length, of the execution of Tissaphernes after his supersession by Tithraustes. For other accounts of the death of Tissaphernes, see Diod. XIV, 80. 6–8; Xen. *Hell.* III, 4. 25; Polyaenus VII, 16. 1; Plut. *Ages.* X, 5; *Artax.* XXIII, 1. Cf. also Nepos, *Conon* III–IV, 1.

The execution of Tissaphernes is dealt with only briefly by Xenophon, who states that as Tissaphernes was in Sardis when the battle took place nearby he was accused by the Persians of betraying their cause. The King decided that Tissaphernes was responsible for his recent adverse fortunes, transferred his command to Tithraustes, and had his head cut off. Ὅτε δ' αὕτη ἡ μάχη ἐγένετο, Τισσαφέρνης ἐν Σάρδεσιν ἔτυχεν ὤν· ὥστε ᾐτιῶντο οἱ Πέρσαι προδεδόσθαι ὑπ' αὐτοῦ. γνοὺς δὲ καὶ αὐτὸς ὁ Περσῶν βασιλεὺς Τισσαφέρνην αἴτιον εἶναι τοῦ κακῶς φέρεσθαι τὰ ἑαυτοῦ, Τιθραύστην καταπέμψας ἀποτέμνει αὐτοῦ τὴν κεφαλήν (*Hell.* III, 4. 25). The version of Diodorus, which is longer than Xenophon's, and that of Polyaenus, which contains a great deal of detail about the actual capture and execution of Tissaphernes, both appear to derive from P so far as may be judged from the fragmentary remains in the papyrus. The length of P's account would suggest that it was even more detailed than that of Polyaenus. According to Diodorus, after the Persian defeat in the battle of Sardis Artaxerxes, alarmed at the course of the war with the Greeks, turned his anger upon Tissaphernes as being responsible for its outbreak. As in Xenophon's account, and we may assume in P's also, the connection with the battle of Sardis is clear. Urged by Parysatis, the King appointed Tithraustes commander-in-chief and gave him instructions to arrest Tissaphernes. The charges against Tissaphernes, the King's decision to punish him, and the sending of Tithraustes would be narrated in VIII, 1 of P (column vii, 1–22 approx.). There may be, in line 15 of col. vii, a reference to Parysatis (]απαρ[), but it is rather bold to establish the text with Meyer as Παρ[ύσατις?. Then there is an interesting reference to certain letters sent by the King (col. vii, 22): ἀνέπεμψ[εν ἐπιστ]ολὰς ἃς ἔφερ[ε.........]ρα[......]ι πρὸς 'Αρι[αῖον. Cf. Polyaenus VII, 16. 1: 'Αρταξέρξης ἐπὶ τὴν Τισσαφέρνους σύλληψιν κατέπεμψε Τιθραύστην δύο ἐπιστολὰς κομίζοντα, τὴν μὲν πρὸς αὐτὸν περὶ τοῦ πολέμου τοῦ πρὸς τοὺς Ἕλληνας, ἐπιτρέπων αὐτῷ τὰ πάντα, τὴν δὲ πρὸς 'Αριαῖον, ὅπως αὐτὸν συλλάβοι μετὰ Τιθραύστου. Diodorus XIV, 80. 7, however, gives rather a different impression of the destination and content of the King's letters: πρὸς δὲ τὰς πόλεις καὶ τοὺς σατράπας ἔπεμψεν ἐπιστολὰς ὅπως {ἂν} πάντες τούτῳ (Τιθραύστῃ) ποιῶσι τὸ προσταττόμενον. It is possible that the King sent other letters to this effect to the cities and satraps after the removal of Tissaphernes, for there are references to ἐπιστολαί later in P's account (col. viii, 18 and 36). Otherwise the considerable detail of Polyaenus' version suggests reliability. Diodorus' statement that Tithraustes came to Colossae in Phrygia and captured Tissaphernes, through the agency of Ariaeus, while he was bathing is clearly a condensed version of the more detailed story which was followed by Polyaenus. The common source is almost certainly P. The details in Polyaenus' account are the following (VII, 16. 1): 'Αριαῖος ἀναγνοὺς τὴν ἐπιστολὴν ἐν Κολοσσαῖς τῆς Φρυγίας καλεῖ Τισαφέρνην ὡς ὁμοῦ βουλεύσασθαι δέον τά τε ἄλλα καὶ περὶ τῶν Ἑλλήνων. ὁ δὲ μηδὲν ὑπιδόμενος τὸ μὲν στρατόπεδον κατέλιπεν ἐν Σάρδεσιν, αὐτὸς δὲ μετὰ τριακοσίων λογάδων 'Αρκάδων καὶ Μιλησίων ἀφικόμενος ἐν 'Αριαίου κατέλυεν· ἤδη δὲ περὶ λουτρὸν ἔχων τὸν ἀκινάκην ἀπέθετο. 'Αριαῖος μετὰ τῶν θεραπευτήρων συναρπάσας αὐτόν, καθείρξας εἰς ἁρμάμαξαν κατερραμμένην ἄγειν Τιθραύστῃ παρέδωκεν. ὁ δὲ μέχρι μὲν Κελαινῶν ἐγκατερραμμένον ἤγαγεν, ἐνταῦθα δὲ ἀποτεμὼν αὐτοῦ τὴν κεφαλὴν ἀνεκόμισε βασιλεῖ. βασιλεὺς δὲ ἔπεμψε τῇ μητρὶ Παρυσάτιδι, ἣ μάλιστα ἐσπουδάκει τίσασθαι Τισαφέρνην ἐπὶ τῇ Κύρου τελευτῇ. With this story we may compare isolated words or phrases in P. Col. vii, 34ff. appears to tell of the message sent by Ariaeus to Tissaphernes at Sardis requesting him to come to Colossae in order to discuss matters relating to the war. Cf. Τισσα]φέρνη[ν ἀ]πέστειλεν; 'Αρ[ι]α[ῖ]ος εἰς Σάρδεις; and possibly connected with the alleged reasons for the meeting βέλτιστοι τῶν στρ[ατη]γῶ[ν; ἀκιν]δυν[ότ]ερον ἕξειν τ[ὰ κ]ατὰ τὴ[ν] σα[τ]ραπία[ν 'Αγησιλά]ου κα[θ]ημένου περὶ [τ]ὴν Μαγν[η]σ[ί]αν; τῶν [πε]ζῶ[ν] καὶ τῶν ἱππέω[ν. Col. viii, 20ff. may have recorded the arrival of Tissaphernes at Colossae and his arrest there. Cf. Μιλη[σι---] with the 'Αρκάδων καὶ Μιλησίων in Polyaenus' version; there is mention of 'Αριαῖον; διατρίβω[ν and ἱμάτια and συναρ[πα-- may well refer to the seizure of Tissaphernes while bathing.

It is noteworthy that there is no hint in P (or Diodorus or Polyaenus) that Conon was in any way concerned with the downfall of Tissaphernes, as is suggested by Nepos, *Conon* III, 2 (*Huius* (sc. *Tissaphernis*) *accusandi gratia Conon a Pharnabazo ad regem missus*...). The further implication of Pharnabazus in Nepos' account suggests, in fact, that he has confused the present episode with the mission of Conon which is related in XIV, 1 of P, and which took place in the late summer of 395, some time after the death of Tissaphernes.

The brief remarks of Plutarch (*locc. citt.*) about the death of Tissaphernes may well derive from Xenophon, although Plutarch in addition makes a point of stressing the hatred felt towards Tissaphernes by the Greeks.

VIII, 1–2

ADDITIONAL NOTES

Column vii, 4–10 was restored by Kalinka, following Diodorus, as follows: τότε] δὲ βασιλεὺς [πυθόμενος τὰ γενόμενα..........π]ερὶ τούτους Τ[ιθραύστην........κατέστησε στρ]ατηγόν, ἅμα δὲ---Τισσαφέρνῃ, ἔτ[ι δὲ.....τὸν πόλεμον τὸν πρὸς το]ὺς Ἕλληνας, οἳ---.νον, καὶ μᾶλλο[ν κατορρωδῶν]...The inclusion of all these points within so short a space does not seem to me at all compatible with the obvious length of P's account, in which the actual departure of Tithraustes appears to occur about line 22. In lines 18–25 Kalinka restores, following Diodorus and Polyaenus: ὥς] τε βασιλεὺς ὁμολογούντ[ως] μάλιστ[α θυμωθεὶς] δι[ὰ Τισ]σαφέρνην καὶ πα[ύ]ων ἐκεῖνον [τῶν πραγμάτων] πάντων, καθ' ἃ Τιθρα[ύστης α]ὐτὸν κα[κῶς εἶπε καὶ 'Αριαῖ]ος, ἐπειδὴ καταφ[θεῖραι Φρυ]γίαν καὶ Λυδ[ίαν ἐλέγε]το, [τέως? μ]ὲν ἀνέπεμψ[εν ἐπιστ]ολάς, ἃς ἔφερ[εν ἐκεῖνος ἑτέ]ρα[ν μὲν ἤδ]η πρὸς 'Αρι[αῖον, ἣ Τι]σσαφ[έ]ρνη[ν, ὃς μεταξὺ δι]επ[ορεύετ]ο πρὸς Με...αῖον ὡς ἀ[πορῶν φίλων, ὡς τάχι]στ[α δὴ συλ]λαβεῖν ἐκέ[λευσε]· αἱ δ[ὲ ἕτεραι...For some criticisms of these readings, see Gigante, pp. 62–3.

Column vii, 23]**ρα**[, as Grenfell and Hunt commented (ed.pr. p. 220), might well be πα]ρά, but it is difficult to make a guess at the next word [......]ι. The ι could be η or even σ, but the lacuna is not long enough to admit βασιλέω]ς. ἔφερ[εν αὐτὸς ὁ Τιθ]ρα[ύστης might be read, but cf. Kalinka: 'ρα ineunte in versu, qua re cave legas Τιθραύστης'.

Col. vii, 23 and 36; col. viii, 24. Ariaeus

A friend of Cyrus, he commanded the left wing of his army at Cunaxa in 401 (Xen. *Anab.* I, 8. 5; Diod. XIV, 22). On the death of Cyrus he joined the Greeks (Xen. *Anab.* II, 1–4), but later changed sides again and was pardoned by Artaxerxes after giving assistance to Tissaphernes against the Greek generals (Xen. *Anab.* II, 5. 35 ff.; Plut. *Artax.* XVIII). After his part in the assassination of Tissaphernes, we hear of him as being entrusted, along with Pasiphernes, with the command at Sardis when Tithraustes left to visit the King in the late summer of 395 (P XIV, 3). In the winter of 395/4 he was joined there by Spithridates (Xen. *Hell.* IV, 1. 27).

Column vii, 24 **Μ̣ε.[..]αιον** 'is probably a proper name, perhaps that of another general' (ed.pr. p. 220 n. 21–5). The fact that Polyaenus' informed account states that there were two letters and names the recipients of both, and the absence of any other reference to such another general, may suggest that the name of a place is more suitable, yet the objections to the introduction of an otherwise unknown place-name are probably equally strong.

Column vii, 39–40 **'Αγησιλά]ου** Cf. ed.pr. p. 220 n. 36–41. As Tissaphernes remained at Sardis (Polyaen. VII, 16. 1, Xen. *Hell.* III, 4. 25), the general at Magnesia was probably Agesilaus, since Magnesia would lie on his route down the Maeander to the coast. Cf. also my note to VII, 4, under ἀπῆγ]εν τὸν [στρατὸν...

Column viii, 28 **]νον** may very well be the end of λουόμενον (cf. Diod. XIV, 80. 8), or, as Grenfell and Hunt suggested, γυμνόν.

IX (= Columns ix–x)

Subject-matter

Grenfell and Hunt commented (ed.pr. p. 221 n. ix, 16ff.): 'The subject here (in column x) seems to be a favourable character-sketch of some general or politician, but the fragments are unfortunately not sufficiently intelligible to allow of his identity being determined.' Various attempts have been made to establish the identity of this man, although some rest on very meagre, if any, evidence. Fuhr, *Berl.Phil.Woch.* (1908), col. 157, proposed Evagoras of Cyprus, Meyer, p. 60, suggested Agesilaus, and Bury, *The Ancient Greek Historians*, p. 158 n. 1, Dionysius, the tyrant of Syracuse, although there is really no evidence that P included Sicilian history in his work.

It is remarkable that before Bartoletti (pp. xvi–xvii) no one had proposed Cyrus the Younger. In the first place, the words of col. x, 19ff., οὐ γὰρ ὥσπερ ο[ἱ πλεῖστοι τῶν πρὸ τοῦ δυ]ναστευόντων ὥρμησεν ἐ[πὶ τὰς τῶν χρημάτων ἁρπα]γάς, καὶ δη[μο]τικώτα̣[τ]ο̣ς̣..., would be highly appropriate to a character-sketch of Cyrus; furthermore, Bartoletti argues, one may discern, despite the mutilation of the papyrus, that P, after narrating the victory of Agesilaus over Tissaphernes at Sardis (cols. v–vi = chs. VI, VII), recorded successively the anger of King Artaxerxes against Tissaphernes (col. vii, 4ff. = ch. VIII, 1), the appointment of Tithraustes as commander-in-chief for the war, the sending of messages to that effect to the cities and satraps (col. vii, 20ff. = ch. VIII, 1) and the death of Tissaphernes at the hand of Tithraustes, after his capture by Ariaeus (col. viii, 9ff. = ch. VIII, 2). If support is required for this reconstruction of the content of chs. VI–VIII, it may be found in the accounts of Diodorus (especially XIV, 80. 6–8) and Polyaenus (especially VII, 16. 1), both of which are widely agreed to have derived from P. At this point in the narrative Polyaenus states that Tithraustes brought the head of Tissaphernes to the King, and βασιλεὺς δὲ ἔπεμψε τῇ μητρὶ Παρυσάτιδι, ἣ μάλιστα ἐσπουδάκει τίσασθαι Τισαφέρνην ἐπὶ τῇ Κύρου τελευτῇ. Cf. Diodorus XIV, 80. 6: καὶ ὑπὸ τῆς μητρὸς δὲ Παρυσάτιδος ἦν ἠξιωμένος (*sc.* 'Αρταξέρξης) τιμωρήσασθαι τὸν Τισσαφέρνην· εἶχε γὰρ αὕτη διαφόρως πρὸς αὐτὸν ἐκ τοῦ διαβεβληκέναι τὸν υἱὸν αὐτῆς Κῦρον, ὅτε τὴν ἐπὶ τὸν ἀδελφὸν στρατείαν ἐποιεῖτο. Bartoletti's thesis, then, is that these brief references to Cyrus by Polyaenus and Diodorus were derived from P, who, in accordance with his custom, had written at greater length than the other two historians, and had digressed on the character of Cyrus. We are, of course, left to speculate what P may have written in an earlier book about the expedition of Cyrus against his brother and of his death at Cunaxa, but a full account of the military operations on that occasion need not necessarily have prevented P from inserting a character-study here by way of a digression. That the present passage appears to view the man in question favourably was observed in ed.pr. p. 221, and P comments favourably on Cyrus the Younger at XIV, 2: διὰ τὴν Κύρου προθυμίαν.

A similar argument could, of course, be adduced in support of Meyer's view that Agesilaus is the subject of column x. Diodorus XIV, 80. 8 records that, immediately after the sending of Tissaphernes' head to Artaxerxes, αὐτὸς (*sc.* Τιθραύστης)...τὸν 'Αγησίλαον πείσας εἰς λόγους ἐλθεῖν ἑξαμηνιαίους ἀνοχὰς ἐποιήσατο. Meyer thought that column ix was concerned with the negotiations for this armistice and that column x contained a digression on the character of Agesilaus. The probable reading of *fr.* 10, lines 3–4, Λα]κεδα[ιμον.., might conceivably lend support, if slight, to this view. On the other hand, *fr.* 11, line 9, τῶν] ἄ̣λλ̣ω̣ν βαρβάρω[ν, might suggest that the man in question was himself a βάρβαρος, in which case the mutilated fragment would seem to support the argument for Cyrus.

On grounds of general probability, it seems to me more likely that a reference to the expedition of Cyrus against his brother would be taken by the historian as an opportunity to write a note on his character—especially as his death was a fairly recent event—than that a reference to the truce between Agesilaus and Tithraustes would seem an appropriate occasion for a digression on the Spartan king. That P was at this point in his work writing in some detail about Persian internal affairs may be seen from the fragmentary remains of chapter VIII.

However, Bartoletti's hypothesis has not appeared persuasive or even probable to everyone; Westlake, *CR* n.s. X (1960), 209, for example, considers it 'no more convincing than earlier suggestions'.

It is a necessary corollary of Bartoletti's argument for Cyrus, if correct, that columns ix–x (ch. IX) follow columns v–viii (chs. VI–VIII). Assuming that Bartoletti's view is to be accepted (as being, in my view, if not conclusive, more probable than previous theories), we may observe that Grenfell and Hunt did, as it happens, place columns ix–x correctly, although commenting (ed.pr. p. 221 n. ix, 16ff.): 'Whether cols. ix–x precede or follow v–viii is quite uncertain.' Bartoletti, however, would go further and place columns ix–x *immediately* after columns v–viii, whereas the first editors assumed that there would be a number of missing columns between viii and ix.

For other favourable character-sketches of Cyrus the Younger, see Xenophon, *Anab.* I, 9 and *Oeconomicus* IV, 18–19.

The fragments assigned to columns ix and x

Fragments 8 and 9 were assigned to column ix by the first editors 'owing to the similarity of the script, which is here somewhat smaller than usual, and the colour of the ink, which is exceptionally black'. Their judgement has been generally accepted. With more hesitation they thought *fr.* 33 might also belong to column ix. The opinion of the first editors that fragments 10–15 inclusive probably belong to column x has also been generally accepted. Fragments 23, 24 and 25, which only contain a few letters, may also be assigned to column x (cf. ed.pr. p. 196). Fragments 19 and 20, which were doubtfully assigned to column iv by Grenfell and Hunt, are thought by Barns, *ap.* Bartoletti, to belong to column x on account of the colour of the ink and of the papyrus.

A number of words appearing in these fragments give rise to certain problems on the question of subject-matter. Of these the chief is the reference in *fr.* 9 to Macedonia (]Μακεδο---). If the fragment is correctly placed, as all the editors agree, the occasion for the reference defies identification. Gigante, p. 63, argues from this reference to Macedonia in *fr.* 9 that *fr.* 19, line 8 ('Αρχε[---) and *fr.* 20, line 11 ('Αρχελ[---) may concern King Archelaus (a possibility already noticed by Grenfell and Hunt, ed.pr. p. 242). However, by placing *frr.* 19 and 20 in column iv (ch. V), he seems to decrease the likelihood of there being any connection between the passages. Indeed there would appear to be some inconsistency between Gigante's note on p. 63: 'Nel fr. 9...vi è l'accenno alla

Macedonia, che i primi editori collegano col fr. 19 (l. 8), ove è probabile si accenni al ré Archelao...' and his text of *fr.* 19, line 8, 'Αρχε[λαΐδ? (also of *fr.* 20, line 11, 'Αρχελ[αΐδ?). It is, in fact, much more probable that *frr.* 19 and 20 do contain references to Archelaïdas, the Spartan nauarch (cf. IV, 2), in which case they might be more appropriately placed in column iv (to which the first editors hesitantly attributed them) than in column x, as suggested by Barns. It should be noted, however, that the attribution of these fragments to column iv, if they do contain references to Archelaïdas, would still give them a position chronologically later than the replacement of Archelaïdas by Pollis as nauarch, recorded in column iii (IV, 2). Mention of a former nauarch would not, on the other hand, be out of character, for the historian is prone to enlarge to some extent on past events when they are noted in the course of his narrative, and there is, of course, a reference to Pharax as ὁ πρότερον ναύαρχος at II, 1. That P was in fact discussing Spartan operations at this point may appear more likely if the restoration Λυσαν[δρ.. (*fr.* 20, line 6) is accepted as a possibility. It is also true, however, that a reference to Lysander might not be inappropriate to a résumé of the career of Cyrus the Younger, if *fr.* 20 is placed, as by Barns, in column x, for Cyrus had entrusted his satrapy and revenues to Lysander when on a visit to Darius, his father, in 405 (Xen. *Hell.* II, 1. 14; Plut. *Lys.* IX).

The mention of Λα]κεδα[ιμον.. in *fr.* 10, lines 3–4, does not really help to identify the subject of the character-sketch in column x, and might just as easily occur in a discussion of Cyrus as of Agesilaus (the latter being thought by Meyer to be the man in question). Some interesting words in *fr.* 33, which Grenfell and Hunt thought might belong to column ix, would be highly suitable to a narrative of Persian affairs: Δ]αρεικο[ῖς (Wilcken, *ap. OCT*) in line 3; βασιλ[ε.. in line 4 and σ]τρατο[in line 6. One should note, however, the caution of the first editors, who wrote (ed.pr. p. 242): 'But it is not certain it [i.e. *fr.* 33] belongs to [P.Oxy.] 842 at all. The recto is blank.' Finally, if Cyrus is the subject of column x, there is a temptation to restore, if with some audacity, Παρυσά]τιδα in *fr.* 14, line 4.

IX, 2

ADDITIONAL NOTES

Column x, 16 **.τέρους 'Ελ[λ]ῃ[ν---]**, Grenfell and Hunt remarked, cannot be restored as ἑτέρους Ἕλ[λ]η[νας since the first letter of the line may be α, ο or ω, but hardly ε. The mention of Greeks here could conceivably indicate a brief reference to those who joined Cyrus in the march against his brother.

Column x, 18 ..]νος δὲ τὴν [ἡ]σ̣[υ]χ[ί]αν ἄριστα τ[οῖς πράγμασι φαίνεται] κεχρημέν[ος]

Bartoletti's reading ἡσυχίαν seems more appropriate than ἀτυχίαν, the only possible alternative; cf. ed.pr. p. 221. For ἄριστα cf. Xen. *Oecon.* IV, 18: Κῦρός γε, εἰ ἐβίωσεν, ἄριστος ἂν δοκεῖ ἄρχων γενέσθαι.

Column x, 19 ο[ἱ πλεῖστοι τῶν πρὸ τοῦ δυ]ναστευόντω[ν]

πρὸ τοῦ is added by Bartoletti to fill the available space better. That P uses δυναστεύειν in a non-technical sense, meaning simply 'to be in authority', may be seen from XII, 3.

X, 1 (=Column xi, 1–12)

For a discussion of the events narrated in this chapter, see my article 'The Democratic Revolution at Rhodes', in *CQ* n.s. XI (1961), 166–70. At some time during the years 398–395 the Rhodians revolted from Sparta and admitted Conon and his fleet into their harbour. This episode was overlooked by Xenophon, but was recorded by Diodorus (XIV, 79. 6) and Pausanias (VI, 7. 6), who quotes Androtion. The democratic revolution reported by P took place in the summer of 395, for we know (from XI, 1) that the outbreak of war between Boeotia and Phocis occurred τούτου τοῦ θέρους, i.e. the summer in which the democratic revolution was effected at Rhodes.

ἐξήτ[αζε

A technical term; cf., e.g., Thuc. VI, 97. 1; VII, 33. 6; VII, 35. 1. On the purpose of these daily parades, see *CQ* n.s. XI (1961), 169f.

προφασιζόμενος μὲ]ν κτλ.

In view of the procedure on the day of the *coup d'état* (π[αρόντων ἐπὶ] τὸν ἐξετα[σμὸ]ν τῇ ὑστεραίᾳ τῶν στρατι[ωτῶν καθά]περ εἰώθε[σαν], τοὺς μὲν αὐτῶν παρῆγα[γον ἐν τοῖ]ς ὅπλοις εἰς [τὸ]ν λιμένα, τ[ο]ὺς δὲ μικρὸν [ἔξω τῆ]ς ἀγορᾶς, X, 2) I was at first attracted by the possibility of restoring, in place of προφασιζόμενος μέ]ν, καὶ κατὰ τὴν ἀγορά]ν. Thus the daily parades would bring the troops to the region of the agora, where some of them were stationed on the day of the *coup*. In consequence of such a restoration, however, it became necessary to regard βου[λόμε]νος δὲ παρασκε[υάζειν... as introductory, beginning a new sentence, and to replace the subordinate clause [ὡς δὲ σύνηθες] κτλ. by a main clause. My restoration, therefore, with a speculative attempt to reproduce also the sense of the opening lines, read as follows: [τῶν ἐν τῇ ʽΡόδῳ τινές...τὸν Κόνωνα ἔπεισαν | αὐτοῖ]ς β̣ο[ήθειαν παρέχειν εἴ τι δέοι. ὁ δ]ὲ̣ καθ' ἑκά[στην] ἡ̣μ̣έ̣[ρ]α̣ν̣ ἐξήτ[αζε τ̣οὺς στρατιώτας] σὺν τοῖς ὅ[πλοις] ἐν τῷ λιμέν[ι καὶ κατὰ τὴν ἀγορὰ]ν ἵνα μὴ ῥα̣[θυμο]ῦντες χείρους [γένωνται πρὸς τὸν] πόλεμον. βου[λόμε]νος δὲ παρασκε[υάζεσθαι τούτους] τοὺς ʽΡοδίους [ὅταν ἴ]δωσιν ἐν τοῖς ὅ[πλοις τοὺς στρατιώ]τας τηνικαῦ[τα τοῖ]ς ἔργοις ἐπιχειρε[ῖν, ἀεὶ φανερὸν ἅ]πασιν ἐποι[εῖτο] ὁρᾶν τὸν ἐξετα[σμόν. ἔπειτα εἴ]κοσι λαβὼν [τῶν] τριήρων ἐξέπλευ[σεν εἰς Καῦνον...

'Certain of those in Rhodes...persuaded Conon to give them assistance if the need should arise. Now, every day he used to parade his soldiers under arms at the harbour and in the market-place, so that they should not, through their inactivity, deteriorate in war. Wishing to put these Rhodians in a position to carry out their task at such a time as they should see the soldiers under arms, he always made the parade plain for all to see. Then, taking twenty triremes, he sailed for Caunus...'

The sense provided by this rendering of the text I find attractive, but, having been persuaded by certain objections to it on linguistic grounds brought to my notice by the editors of *CQ*, I conclude that P was perhaps less explicit than I had wanted him to appear. The objections are the following: (1) Grenfell and Hunt's restoration αὐτὸς μὲν εἴ]κοσι λαβὼν κτλ. is certainly right since it provides the required antithesis to ʽΙερωνύμῳ [δὲ κ]αὶ Νικοφήμῳ κτλ., below. If this reading is to be accepted, it must have been preceded by a subordinate clause introducing it, such as ὡς δὲ σύνηθες ἅ]πασιν κτλ. (2) Further, if such a subordinate clause be admitted, βου[λόμε]νος δὲ παρασκε[υάζε.... cannot be introductory but must be the second of a pair of participles, in fact must follow something like προφασιζόμενος μέ]ν.

ἐξέπλευ[σεν εἰς Καῦνον, βου]λόμενος [μὴ π]αρεῖναι τῇ διαφθο[ρᾷ τῶν ἀρχόντω]ν̣

For εἰς Καῦνον, cf. πάλιν ἐκ Καύνου in x, 3.

τῶν ἀρχόντω]ν̣: an excellent restoration by Bartoletti; cf. συν[έ]δρια τῶν ἀρχόντων in x, 2. τῶν Διαγορείω]ν (ed.pr.) is a little too long for the space.

The government of Rhodes, after the expulsion of the Spartans, had been assumed by the family of Diagoras (cf. x, 2 τοὺς Διαγορείους), the son of Damagetus, king of Ialysus (cf. H. van Gelder, *Gesch. der alten Rhodier*, pp. 77 ff.). The Diagoreans were particularly famous for their athletic successes. Pindar, *Olymp.* VII, celebrates the victory of Diagoras in the boxing contest at Olympia in 464 B.C. His sons, Acusilaus, Damagetus and Dorieus, were all renowned athletes, Dorieus winning the *pancration* at Olympia on three successive occasions. Dorieus led a contingent of ships from Thurii, where he had settled, to assist the Spartans in 412 (Thuc. VIII, 35. 1; 84, 2), and in 407 was taken prisoner by the Athenians, but released as a mark of admiration (Xen. *Hell.* I, 1. 2ff.; I, 5. 19). He was later put to death by the Spartans (Paus. VI, 7. 6), perhaps at the time of the revolt of Rhodes (Diod. XIV, 79. 6).

Conon's unwillingness to be present at the murder of the Diagoreans, against whom the democratic revolution was directed, may be due in some measure to his personal regard for them, and possibly also to gratitude for the support they clearly gave him in allowing him to make Rhodes his headquarters. That he did not wish his troops to be openly associated with the democratic rising is indicated not only by his own departure from Rhodes, but by the fact that his men took no active part in it. The taking of twenty triremes on his brief visit to Caunus (apparently on no urgent business, since he returned as soon as the Rhodian conspirators had carried out their plans) may have been intended to weaken any future allegation that the fleet was implicated in the revolution, in the event of its failure.

῾Ιερωνύμῳ [δὲ κ]αὶ Νικοφήμῳ

Cf. Diod. XIV, 81. 4, where they are left in command of the fleet while Conon is on a visit to the Great King. (P XIV, 1 suggests that Conon did not on this occasion meet the King in person, but communicated with him by letter through the agency of Tithraustes.)

On Hieronymus, see *PA* 7552 (I, p. 494). Cf. Harpocration, *s.v.*: ῾Ιερωνύμου τοῦ στρατηγήσαντος ᾽Αθηναίων ἄλλοι τε μνημονεύουσι καὶ ῎Εφορος ἔν τε τῇ ιη′ καὶ ἐν τῇ ιθ′ (= *F.Gr.Hist.* 70 F 73). If Hieronymus was in fact *strategos*, it is unlikely that he held the office in the summer of 395, as Athens and Sparta were not yet involved in the war which broke out between Boeotia and Phocis in this summer, and it is therefore improbable that an Athenian holding public office would be found actively engaged in the maritime war against the Spartans.

On Nicophemus, see *PA* 11,066 (II, p. 147). On the form of the name, P is supported by Xenophon (*Hell.* IV, 8. 8) and Lysias (XIX, 7ff.). Diodorus (XIV, 81. 4) calls him Nicodemus. In 393, Nicophemus was left as 'harmost' in Cythera by Conon and Pharnabazus (Xen. *loc. cit.*). In 389, along with his son Aristophanes, he was arrested and put to death without trial in Cyprus (Lysias, *loc. cit.*), where he had a wife and daughter in addition to his family in Athens (Lysias XIX, 36). Incidentally, Conon too had a second family in Cyprus; Lysias XIX, 36 mentions that he had a wife and a son there.

X, 2 (= Column xi, 12–28)

τῶν [δὲ] Ῥοδίων οἱ συνειδότες τὴν π̣[ρᾶξιν

The Rhodian conspirators are the sole executors of the *coup*. Conon, of course, was a party to the plot, and I have suggested (*CQ* n.s. xi (1961), 169) that, while refusing to help in the overthrow of the Diagoreans, he agreed to station some of his troops at the harbour and near the agora on the day of the *coup* in order to ensure the safe escape of the conspirators if their attempt should fail. Since the revolution was successful, there was no need for Conon's men to take any action at all.

Δωρίμαχος [μ]ẹṿ αὐτῶν

Dorimachus is unknown apart from this reference. He appears to have been the leader of the conspirators, but Kalinka's reading [ἦρχ?]εν seems grammatically unsuitable as well as too long for the space. Ed.pr. reads [μ]έν ⟨τις⟩ αὐτῶν.

'[Ἴ]ωμεν, ὦ ἄνδρες', ἔφη, 'πολῖται, ἐπὶ τοὺς τυράννους [τὴ]ν ταχίστην.'

This is the only direct speech in the extant portions of the *Hellenica Oxyrhynchia*. If, as we may assume, P was not given to the inclusion of direct speeches in his work, and as he appears to have made little use of rhetorical devices (the avoidance of hiatus, of which the unusual position of ἔφη here is an example, excepted), this short speech may owe its place in the text to the vivid account of some eyewitness informant of P.

βοήσαντος ἐκείνου τὴν [βο]ήθειαν

Cf. ed.pr. p. 223 n. 23–4: 'For such an accusative as τὴν βοήθειαν after βοήσαντος there is no near parallel, but [βο]ήθειαν seems inevitable, and the phrase is so easily intelligible that we prefer to regard the expression as one peculiar to our author rather than to treat it as corrupt.' That the phrase indicates any appeal for new support on the part of Dorimachus seems impossible, both from the carefully constructed sentence τῶν δὲ Ῥοδίων οἱ συνειδότες τὴν πρᾶξιν... Δωρίμαχος μὲν αὐτῶν... οἱ δὲ λοιποί..., which indicates that only those previously concerned in the plot responded to the call, and on grounds of general probability. There would not have been many persons in the agora to give support of much value; the general public could have had no prior information about the plot (or so, assuredly, would those against whom it was directed), and any such exhortation as that here recorded would have been a little perplexing to persons ignorant of the conspiracy. Jacoby, *F.Gr.Hist.* II C, 14, comments: 'nicht "das hilfskorps herbeirufen", sondern "den notruf erheben"'.

μετ' ἐγχειριδίων

Cf. [σύ]ν ἐγχειριδίοις a little above. Jacoby, *F.Gr.Hist.* IIC, 14, says 'charakteristisch für das...streben nach abwechselung'.

ἀποκτείνουσι τούς τε Διαγο[ρε]ίους καὶ τῶν ἄλλων πολιτῶν ἕνδεκα

The dangers of imposing the lesser penalty of banishment on deposed rulers are most apparent from the numerous examples of Greek exiles who sought the aid of foreign arms to reinstate them. What does seem remarkable about this revolution is that so few of the oligarchic leaders were executed. By comparison with similar revolutions elsewhere throughout the course of classical Greek history this one is rather notable for the moderation of the successful conspirators. In addition to the execution of the Diagoreans and eleven other citizens, a small number of others were sent into exile (X, 3), and it appears that these appealed to Sparta for assistance in 391. Cf. Xen. *Hell.* IV, 8. 20: ἐπεὶ δ' ἦλθον εἰς Λακεδαίμονα οἱ ἐκπεπτωκότες 'Ροδίων ὑπὸ τοῦ δήμου, ἐδίδασκον ὡς οὐκ ἄξιον εἴη περιιδεῖν 'Αθηναίους 'Ρόδον καταστρεψαμένους καὶ τοσαύτην δύναμιν συνθεμένους....οἱ Λακεδαιμόνιοι...ἐπλήρωσαν αὐτοῖς ναῦς ὀκτώ, ναύαρχον δὲ Ἔκδικον ἐπέστησαν.

πλῆθος

Cf. I, 2. On both occasions on which the word is used as a political term, it is applied to the whole citizen body summoned to an assembly (of Athens at I, 2; of Rhodes here). P also uses the term to indicate the 'main body' of soldiers in XV, 2.

X, 3 (=Column xi, 28–34)

κατέστησαν δημοκρατίαν

Again we may note the author's specification that it was the Rhodian conspirators (οἱ δὲ τὴν σφαγὴν ἐξεργασάμενοι) who took the initiative in setting up the democracy, and not Conon, despite his return from Caunus soon after the assembly had been convened. Cf. the precise reference to τῶν [δὲ] 'Ροδίων οἱ συνειδότες τὴν π̣[ρᾶξιν in X, 2 as being the sole executors of the *coup*.

τινας ὀλίγους

Cf. note at X, 2 on the murder of the Diagoreans and the subsequent moderation of the assassins. Although those who were exiled were probably, like those who were put to death, oligarchs, it seems preferable to regard ὀλίγους here as purely numerical, and not as a term with any political significance.

ἐπανάστασις

A technical term denoting a domestic political revolution as distinct from a revolt from an imperial power or a defection from an alliance. Cf. Thuc. II, 27. 2 (of Helots at Sparta) and VIII, 21 (of Samian democrats against the oligarchs).

XI, 1 (=Column xi, 34–8)

τούτου τοῦ θέρους

The summer of 395; cf. Diod. XIV, 81. 1; Xen. *Hell.* III, 5. 3; also Pausanias, III, 9. 9, who mentions in his account τόν τε σῖτον ἀκμάζοντα. The narrative of the outbreak of war between Boeotia and Phocis is resumed, after an excursus on the constitution of Boeotia and an examination of the causes of the war in the light of the political situation at Thebes, in XIII, 2ff.

τῶν ἐν ταῖς Θήβαις τινές.

These were Ismenias, Antitheus and Androcleidas; cf. XII, 1. Xen. *Hell.* III, 5. 1 substitutes Galaxidorus for Antitheus; Pausanias III, 9. 8 substitutes Amphithemis for Antitheus. Plutarch, *Lys.* XXVII, does not mention Ismenias, but refers to Androcleidas and Amphitheus. Antitheus, Amphithemis and Amphitheus are probably variant forms of the same name. On the responsibility of these men, see XIII, 2ff., which gives an account of the stratagem by means of which they are alleged to have provoked the outbreak of war.

οὐ γὰρ πολλοῖς [ἔ]τεσιν πρότερον

I.e. since 404 B.C. For a detailed examination of Theban politics in the few years before 395 B.C., see Cloché in *REG* XXXI (1918), 315–43.

XI, 2 (=Column xi, 38–column xii, 6)

εἶχεν δὲ τὰ πράγματα τότε κα[τὰ τὴ]ν Βοιωτίαν οὕτως·

For a general commentary on sections 2, 3 and 4 of this chapter, see Appendix 2. Among the many articles dealing with various aspects of the Boeotian Constitution as here described by P, some of the more important of which I cite elsewhere, mention may be made here of a number of excellent general surveys: Glotz, 'Le conseil fédéral des Béotiens', in

BCH XXXII (1908), 271–8; Cloché, *Thèbes de Béotie*, pp. 71–4; Larsen, *Representative Government in Greek and Roman History*, pp. 31 ff.; also 'The Boeotian Confederacy and Fifth Century Oligarchic Theory', in *TAPA* LXXXVI (1955), 40–50; Ehrenberg, *The Greek State*, pp. 123–4.

τότε

We know that the constitution described in this chapter was dissolved in 387/6 under the terms of the King's Peace (cf. Xen. *Hell.* v, 1. 33: Θηβαῖοι δ' εἰς τὰς σπονδὰς εἰσελθεῖν ἠναγκάσθησαν, αὐτονόμους ἀφέντες τὰς Βοιωτίας πόλεις), and thus 387/6 becomes the *terminus post quem* for the composition of P's work. It is almost certain that this constitution was in force for the whole of the period from 447, when Boeotia recovered independence from Athens, until the King's Peace. This view is supported by numismatic evidence. While most, if not all, of the sovereign cities of Boeotia issued their own coinage during the periods 456–447 and 386–374, Thebes appears to have been the only city to do so between 447 and 387; cf. Head, *Historia Numorum*[2], pp. 346 ff. (also in *Numismatic Chronicle* (1881), pp. 197 ff.); Hill, *Sources for Greek History* (new edition, Oxford, 1951), pp. 328–30 (C 1–3). We may further note that the author's use of the past tense throughout this section justifies the emphasis placed upon the word τότε in establishing the earlier terminus for the date of composition.

βουλαὶ [τό]τε τέττα[ρες παρ' ἑ]κάστῃ τῶν πόλεων κτλ.

The four councils in each of the cities appear to have been concerned solely with local affairs, contrary to the judgement of the first editors (ed.pr. p. 224). Cf. Larsen, *Representative Government*, p. 37: 'It may suffice to say that submission (by the confederacy) to all separate city councils could have worked only if the confederacy had been free from local antagonisms. In Boeotia, where measures favored by one city would have been opposed by other cities, it could never have worked.' Cf. further Appendix 2. Each of the councils in turn acted as a probouleutic body which made proposals to the other three. Resolutions adopted by all four became valid. The wording of the passage suggests that the three to which reference was made by the one presiding and probouleutic council voted separately, and that one negative vote was sufficient to prevent the adoption of any measure. This form of local government did not involve the abandonment of direct government, but restricted it to a property class. Not all citizens (πολῖται; i.e. citizens of each small city-state, for there seems to have been no federal citizenship as such; cf. Ehrenberg, *op. cit.* p. 123) were permitted to sit on the councils, but only those who had acquired a certain amount of property (πλῆθός τ[ι χρημά]-των). It may not be unreasonable to suggest that this property qualification may have amounted to a hoplite census.

At least ten cities had this form of local government in 395, for ten sovereign cities are mentioned in XI, 3: Thebes, Orchomenus, Thespiae, Tanagra, Haliartus, Lebadea, Coronea, Acraephium, Copae and Chaeronea. The system of four councils to administer strictly local affairs may even have extended to some of the places which, for federal purposes, were subject to these cities (e.g. Plataea to Thebes and Hysiae to Orchomenus). P does not refer to the places he names as being non-sovereign (Plataea, Hysiae, Eutresis, Thisbae) as either πόλεις or χωρία; the places formerly in the Plataean sympolity and at this time subject to Thebes (Scolus, Erythrae, Scaphae and some others) he calls χωρία. Such places would, I suggest, form one city-state with their larger neighbour and would therefore not have independent local councils. Larsen, *Representative Government*, p. 34, thinks that this was also the status of Eutresis and Thisbae, and is critical of Glotz's tendency (art. cit.) to look upon the smaller places as constituting separate cities: 'In all likelihood their status was not one of subjection but rather one of sympolity or union with the larger city—sympolity in this sense being used to indicate a union or merging of two or more cities into one state. Thus, to use an illustration, Eutresis and Thisbe undoubtedly continued to exist as towns, but their citizens were citizens of Thespiae just as the citizens of the towns and villages scattered throughout Attica were citizens of Athens.'

XI, 3 (= Column xii, 6–20)

τὸ δὲ τῶ[ν Βοι]ωτῶν τοῦτον ἦν τὸν τρόπον συντεταγμένον. κτλ.

P now passes from the government of the individual cities to the federal constitution. The division of Boeotia into eleven districts appears to have been in fairly close proportion to population. Thus Thebes, together with the places subject to her, made up four districts, while two other districts each comprised three small independent cities. Ehrenberg, *The Greek State*, p. 123, speaks of the federal constitution as combining 'in a strange and artificial way...the preponderance of Thebes with the claim to equal standing, raised by at least the most important of the other cities'. It would seem that this 'strange and artificial way' may have, in fact, amounted to little more than the principle of proportional representation.

ἕκαστον ἕνα παρείχετο βοιώταρχον

Each of the eleven districts supplied one Boeotarch. On the form of the word, P uses βοιώταρχος twice in the singular and βοιωτάρχης once in the plural in this chapter. Ed.pr. chose to read βοιωτάρχ⟨η⟩ν for βοιώταρχον, but Bartoletti retains the form found in P, citing Xen. *Hell.* III, 4. 4, οἱ Βοιώταρχοι. The supreme command of the Boeotian military forces was exercised by these officials. They supervised the composition and mobilization of the contingents which the several districts had to provide for the federal army (Diod. XV, 52; Paus. IX, 1. 6), and they formed a council of war entrusted with the conduct of military operations. It seems likely that the chief command was surrendered to one of the Theban Boeotarchs, just as the allies of Athens and Sparta submitted to the authority of these cities. Thucydides IV, 91 states that when Pagondas, one of the Theban Boeotarchs, gave battle at Delium in 424 contrary to the advice of the other Boeotarchs, he held the chief command, ἡγεμονίας οὔσης αὐτοῦ. Gomme, *A Historical Commentary on Thucydides*, III, 560 (note to IV, 91), comments: 'Presidency of the board of Boiotarchai changed regularly; but at what intervals and whether between all the boiotarchs, or only between the two Thebans, is not known. 93, 1: ἤδη γὰρ καὶ τῆς ἡμέρας ὀψὲ ἦν is certainly not evidence that it changed daily and that Pagondas must fight that day if the command was to be in his hands. It means that little time was left for battle that day and they must fight then if they were to catch the Athenians.' However, Pausanias IX, 13. 6 suggests that the decisions were generally taken by a majority vote of the Boeotarchs, and that, in consequence, the action taken by Pagondas was highly irregular. Cf. further Salmon, *L'Ant.Cl.* XXII (1953), 348–9.

δύο δὲ ὑπὲρ Πλαταιέων καὶ Σκώλου καὶ Ἐ̣ρ̣[υ]θρῶ[ν] καὶ Σκαφῶν καὶ τῶν ἄλλων χωρίων τῶν πρότερον μὲν ἐκείνοις συμπολιτευομένων

Fuhr, in a note on this section in *Berl.Phil.Woch.* (1912), col. 1,299, argues that Πλαταιέων is an error for Πλαταιῶν, the same error being found in Cod. Venetus F Dem. XIII, 24 and XVI, 4.

Thebes would have gained the right to appoint two further Boeotarchs with the capture of Plataea in 427 B.C. It would appear, therefore, that before 427 the number of Boeotarchs was nine, not eleven, and we have no evidence which would contradict this view, for the first mention of there being eleven Boeotarchs is in Thucydides' account of the battle of Delium in 424 (IV, 91). However, Thucydides here implies that there were two Theban Boeotarchs, not four, so perhaps two were actually sent from Plataea, although that city was dominated by Thebes. Scolus, Erythrae and Scaphae were situated east of Plataea, between the river Asopus and Mount Cithaeron. Strabo IX, 2. 24 associates these three places with Plataea: ἕτεροι δ' ἐν τῇ Πλαταιέων φασὶ τόν τε Σκῶλον καὶ τὸν Ἐτεωνὸν καὶ τὰς Ἐρύθρας. Eteonus, he states, was an earlier name for

Scaphae (which he calls Σκάρφη). Pausanias also mentions Erythrae (IX, 2. 1) and Scolus (IX, 4. 4) as belonging to Plataea. Cf. further ed.pr. p. 226 n. xii, 12–13.

τότε δὲ συντελούντων εἰς τὰς Θήβας.

For the term indicating the dependence of small Boeotian towns on the independent cities, cf. Thuc. IV, 76. 3 and Paus. IX, 3. 6. The date at which these towns became subject to Thebes is discussed at some length by the first editors (ed.pr. p. 226 n. xii, 12–13). They cite the mention in XII, 3 of the inhabitants of these three towns (along with those of Aulis, Schoenus and Potniae) migrating to Thebes through fear of an Athenian invasion. They argue that 431 (suggested to them by Walker) is the most likely date for this migration, since if the towns had been joined to Thebes before 431 it is difficult to see what period P could have meant by πρότερον, the period of their union with Plataea. We know from XII, 3 that the migration to Thebes took place in time of war, and that if this was previous to 431 it must have been before the formation of the Boeotian Confederacy as here described. The natural interpretation, however, is that the war mentioned in XII, 3 is the Peloponnesian War, and that the people of these towns moved to Thebes soon after its inception. It is also natural to suppose, in XI, 3, that these towns joined Thebes for purposes of federal administration at the same time as Plataea, i.e. 427, although the date of the migration, 431, is also quite possible. In any case, it is improbable that the addition of three towns so insignificant would have altered the Theban quota of Boeotarchs, if 431 is to be taken as the date of their union with Thebes, and it is fairly certain that Thebes gained the right to appoint two further Boeotarchs after the capture of Plataea in 427.

Ὀρχομένιοι καὶ Ὑσιαῖοι

Orchomenus, standing on a promontory on the north of the Copaïc plain, was the most serious rival to Thebes for predominance in Boeotia. It was among the first Boeotian cities to issue coinage (about 550 B.C.), and the absence of the league symbol on coins struck before 387 has given rise to the theory that Orchomenus was not a member of the league before 447, from which date until 387 only Thebes of the Boeotian cities issued coins (cf. Head, *Coins of Central Greece*, p. xxxvii, *Historia Numorum*², p. 346; and *Oxford Classical Dictionary*, *s.v.* Orchomenus). The evidence, however, is far from being conclusive; cf. ed.pr. p. 227 n. xii, 16.

It was noted by Wilamowitz (*ap.* ed.pr. p. 227) that the reference here is not to Hysiae near Plataea, but to Hyettus on Lake Copaïs, east of Orchomenus. The first editors comment that "Ὑσιαῖοι here probably indicates a real variation in the form of the name'. That this Hysiae was dependent on Orchomenus in 395, which seems very probable, was first suggested by Meyer. Cf. Paus. IX, 24. 3.

Θεσπιεῖς σὺν Εὐτρήσει καὶ Θίσβαις

Thespiae, near the eastern foot of Mount Helicon, was the chief city of south Boeotia. Its territory was extensive during the latter part of the fifth century (cf. Thuc. IV, 76. 3: αἱ δὲ Σῖφαί εἰσι τῆς Θεσπικῆς γῆς ἐν τῷ Κρισαίῳ κόλπῳ ἐπιθαλασσίδιοι), and it is thus not surprising to find that it provided two Boeotarchs. On its subject, Eutresis, cf. Strabo IX, 2. 28: Εὔτρησιν...κώμιον Θεσπιέων.

Ταναγραῖοι

Tanagra, the chief city of east Boeotia, was an early rival of Thebes, and it has been argued that it was the leader of the Boeotian League in the period immediately after the Persian Wars, because it was the only city to strike coins in the name of Boeotia between 480 and 456 (cf. Head, *Coins of Central Greece*, p. xxxviii, and *Historia Numorum*², p. 348). The first editors, however, regard this as a 'very doubtful inference'.

The fact that Tanagra controlled only one district at this period indicates that her territory was not as extensive as it had been and was again later in the fourth century. Cf. Meyer, p. 97. It appears from XII, 3 that in 431 Aulis, which later belonged to Tanagra (cf. Strabo IX, 2. 8; Paus. IX, 19. 8), was subject to Thebes (cf. note to XII, 3). For further discussion of the territory of Tanagra cf. ed.pr. p. 228 n. xii, 17. The editors conclude that Delium 'seems to have been the only place of much importance belonging to Tanagra in 395 B.C.' Cf. Thuc. IV, 76. 4; Strabo IX, 2. 7; Paus. IX, 20. 1.

Ἁλιάρτιοι καὶ Λεβαδεῖς καὶ Κορωνεῖς

Of these three cities which formed one district and provided a Boeotarch in rotation, Haliartus and Coronea are mentioned by Thucydides IV, 93 as being members of the league in 424. Lebadea, along with Acraephium (see below), would be among those mentioned by Thucydides as οἱ ἄλλοι οἱ περὶ τὴν λίμνην.

ἐξ Ἀκραιφνίου καὶ Κωπῶν καὶ Χαιρωνείας

Copae is mentioned by Thucydides IV, 93 as being a league member in 424. Chaeronea, however, did not gain her independence until after 424, at which time she was subject to Orchomenus; cf. Thuc. IV, 76. 3: Χαιρώνειαν ἣ ἐς Ὀρχομενὸν...ξυντελεῖ. The form of the name Ἀκραίφνιον used by P is otherwise found only in Paus. IX, 23. 5; 24. 1. Cf. Steph. Byz. *s.v.* (=*F.Gr.Hist.* 70 F 229 (Ephorus); 115 F 362 (Theopompus)): Ἀκραιφία· πόλις Βοιωτίας· οἱ δὲ Ἀκραίφιον· Παυσανίας δὲ ⟨Ἀκραίφνιον⟩ καὶ οὐδετέρως...τὸ ἐθνικὸν Ἀκραιφιαῖος καὶ Ἀκραίφιος...Ἔφορος δὲ καὶ Ἀκραιφνίους καὶ Ἀκραιφνεῶτας. Θεόπομπος δὲ τὰ Ἀκραίφνιά φησι καὶ τὸ ἐθνικὸν Ἀκραιφνιεύς. Cf. also ed.pr. p. 228 n. xii, 20.

XI, 4 (=Column xii, 21–31)

παρείχετο δὲ καὶ βουλευτὰς ἑξήκοντα κατὰ τὸν βοιώταρχον, καὶ τούτοις αὐτοὶ τὰ καθ' ἡμέραν ἀνήλισκον.

On the functions and organization of the federal council, see Appendix 2. The probability is that one-fourth of the council acted as a probouleutic body, in rotation, thus compelling the councillors to give up only a quarter of their time to full-time service. Glotz (*BCH* XXXII (1908), 272 and 275–7) and Cloché (*Thèbes de Béotie*, p. 73) interpret καὶ τούτοις αὐτοὶ τὰ καθ' ἡμέραν ἀνήλισκον as meaning that the councillors themselves were obliged to defray their day-to-day expenses. If this was so, the system of rotating one-fourth of the council as a probouleutic body would render such an obligation a less severe financial strain and would not restrict the office of councillor to too narrow an aristocracy of wealth. While I, personally, find this interpretation attractive, in that it suggests that Boeotia conformed to the common oligarchic principle that holders of public office received no assistance from public funds, it is linguistically difficult to accept τούτοις and αὐτοί as referring to the same persons. One would rather expect to read something like αὐτοὶ δὲ ἑαυτοῖς τὰ καθ' ἡμέραν ἀνήλισκον. I would not, however, go so far as Larsen, *Representative Government*, p. 205 n. 33 to chapter II, in saying that 'this view seems impossible'. The alternatives are that the local authorities paid the expenses of their own councillors (cf. ed.pr. p. 228 n. xii, 23; Bonner, *CP* V (1910), 414) or that they were paid by the federal government (cf. Swoboda and Busolt, *Gr. Staatskunde*, pp. 1,417f.). Larsen, *loc. cit.*, comments: 'Which of the two is correct makes little practical difference, for the districts contributed to the federal treasury in proportion to their representation. However, it seems best to take αὐτοί as referring to the citizens of the μέρος.'

For a theory on the choice of 660 as the full number of councillors, see Glotz, art. cit. His argument is that this was the lowest number which would ensure the representation of all the cities, independent or subject, but is based on an assumption about the number of subject towns not mentioned by name in P's narrative. Cf. p. 160.

περὶ χιλίους μὲν ὁπλίτας, ἱππέας δὲ ἑκατόν.

The number of hoplites supplied by each district to the federal army is approximate, but the full hoplite strength of the federal force would seem to have been about 11,000. As Thucydides IV, 93. 3 mentions 7,000 hoplites ἀπὸ πασῶν τῶν πόλεων at the battle of Delium, the interesting question has been raised whether the Boeotian League had adopted the practice of the Peloponnesian League, whereby two-thirds of the strength of each district was supplied for any particular campaign, except that in the event of one district being invaded that district should put its entire force in the field. See further Appendix 2.

τῶν κοινῶν ἀπέλαυον

That τὰ κοινά refers to a federal treasury was convincingly argued by Glotz, art. cit. Cf. the meaning of τῶν κοινῶν, the Athenian treasury, in II, 2. Grenfell and Hunt's translation, 'enjoyed the privileges of the league', is, perhaps, rather too vague. See further Appendix 2.

δικασ⟨τὰς⟩ ἔπεμπον

Boeotia clearly had a federal legal system, and it is possible that this was the system on which Athens modelled the legal organization of her second confederacy in 378. Cf. Tod, *GHI* II, 123.

XII, 1 (=Column xii, 31–column xiii, 5)

οἱ βέλτιστοι καὶ γνωριμώτατοι τῶν πολιτῶν

While it is reasonable to suppose that the leaders of the opposing factions would be γνωριμώτατοι in the sense of being the best-known men in Thebes, the term here indicates that they were of an upper social class, as in the case of the Athenian γνώριμοι mentioned in I, 2. The γνώριμοι to whom P refers as composing one of the Athenian parties appear not to have been the leading public figures, for the historian names none of them, whereas he makes special mention of Thrasybulus, Aesimus, Anytus, Epicrates and Cephalus. The term βέλτιστοι is in any case one applied to aristocratic or oligarchic factions by writers disposed to be hostile to democracy, as indeed P reveals some tendency to be. Xenophon, for instance, applies the term frequently to oligarchic parties. The interesting point here is that both the Theban factions are described by these terms; and not unnaturally, for both had to be of a specified census to qualify for political life and both appear to have been quite satisfied with the moderate oligarchic form of government of this period. It is true that Plutarch,

Pelop. v, 1, states that the party of Ismenias was φιλελεύθερον ἅμα καὶ δημοτικὴν εἶναι δοκοῦσαν, but he is referring to the period after the King's Peace. There is no evidence of an attempt to establish a democracy in Thebes until the revolution of 379, and this, I should think, largely reflects reaction after the breakdown of the existing constitution by the loss of Boeotia, the appeal to force by Leontiades, and, most of all, the Spartan occupation. The democratic movement may then have represented a temporary distrust of any form of representative government.

ὥσπερ καὶ πρότερον εἴρηκα I.e. in XI, 1.

Ἰσμηνίας κα[ὶ] Ἀντίθεος καὶ Ἀνδροκλ⟨είδα⟩ς

Ismenias appears to have been the leading figure of this group (cf. οἱ περὶ τὸν Ἰσμηνίαν in XII, 1), although Xenophon (*Hell.* III, 5. 4) once calls the party οἱ περὶ τὸν Ἀνδροκλείδαν, and P four times uses οἱ περί with the names of both men. Of Ismenias we know (apart from the references in P) that he received Persian money from Timocrates, the Rhodian (Xen. *Hell.* III, 5. 1; Paus. III, 9. 8), that he was polemarch of Thebes along with his opponent Leontiades in 383/2 (Xen. *Hell.* v, 2. 25) and that he was subsequently arrested, tried before three Spartan judges on charges of accepting Persian bribes and precipitating the war of 395–387, and condemned to death (Xen. *Hell.* v, 2. 30–6). Justin (v, 9. 8) mentions him as having given assistance to Thrasybulus, the Athenian, at the end of the Peloponnesian War: *itaque et Ismenias, Thebanorum princeps, etsi publicis non poterat, privatis tamen viribus adiuvabat.* The passage seems to imply that Ismenias had at that time little influence in Theban policy, and it is probable that the philo-Laconian party was still in the ascendancy. Plato mentions him twice, in *Repub.* I, 336A and *Meno* 90A.

Androcleidas is associated with Ismenias in the receipt of the money brought by Timocrates by P, Xenophon and Pausanias. Plutarch, *Lys.* XXVII, mentions Androcleidas, but not Ismenias, in this connection. Xenophon, *Hell.* III, 5. 4, states that οἱ περὶ τὸν Ἀνδροκλείδαν persuaded the Thebans to assist the Locrians in 395, and, v, 2. 35, couples Androcleidas with Ismenias as being most responsible for the Corinthian War. Cf. also Plut. *Pelop.* v on Spartan dislike of the party of Ismenias and Androcleidas. Androcleidas did not stand trial along with Ismenias, but was one of the 300 or so anti-Spartans who fled from Thebes to Athens when Ismenias was arrested; cf. Plut. *Pelop.* v–VI, *IG* II^2, 37, Xen. *Hell.* v, 2. 31. While in Athens he was assassinated by an agent of Leontiades. Cf. Plut. *Pelop.* VI, 2: οὐ μὴν ἀλλ' οἱ περὶ Λεοντίδαν πυνθανόμενοι τοὺς φυγάδας Ἀθήνησι διατρίβειν τῷ τε πλήθει προσφιλεῖς ὄντας καὶ τιμὴν ἔχοντας ὑπὸ τῶν καλῶν καὶ ἀγαθῶν, ἐπεβούλευον αὐτοῖς κρύφα. καὶ πέμψαντες ἀνθρώπους ἀγνῶτας Ἀνδροκλείδαν μὲν ἀποκτιννύουσι δόλῳ, τῶν δὲ ἄλλων διαμαρτάνουσιν.

Androcleidas, the correct Boeotian form of the name, is used uniformly by Xenophon (*Hell.* III, 5. 1; 5. 4; V, 2. 31; 2. 35). Ἀνδροκλῆς, which occurs at this point in P, appears to be a copyist's error; Ἀνδροκλείδας occurs in XIII, 1 and 3. The form Ἀνδροκλείδης, apparently an Attic variant, occurs in XII, 2. Jacoby, *F.Gr.Hist.* IIC, 15, comments: 'Der auffällige wechsel der namenformen Ἀνδροκλῆς (Theben *IG* VII, 2424), -είδας (aber Λεοντιάδης), -είδης geht trotz der vielen namenkorruptelen von P doch wohl auf den (böotischen) verfasser zurück.'

Antitheus is not mentioned elsewhere, but is probably identical with Amphithemis (Paus. III, 9. 8) and Amphitheus (Plut. *Lys.* XXVII). Xenophon (*Hell.* III, 5. 1) does not mention Antitheus, but names Galaxidorus (otherwise unknown) as one of the recipients of the money brought to Greece by Timocrates.

Λεοντιάδης καὶ Ἀσίας καὶ Κο⟨ιρα⟩τάδας, ἐφρόνουν δὲ—τὰ Λακεδαιμονίων

Leontiades, the leader of the philo-Laconian group, is well known from Xenophon and Plutarch. He may possibly be the son of Εὐρυμάχου τοῦ Λεοντιάδου, ἀνδρὸς Θηβαίων δυνατωτάτου (Thuc. II, 2. 3). Ἀσίας, called Ἀστίας in XII, 2, may be identical with Ἀρχίας, who is associated with Leontiades in the events of 379 B.C. by Xenophon (*Hell.* V, 4. 2; 4. 6), Plutarch (*Pelop.* V ff.) and Nepos (*Pelop.* III, 2). Jacoby, *F.Gr.Hist.* IIC, 15, accepts the identification of Asias with Archias, while Grenfell and Hunt, ed.pr. p. 229 n. xii, 34–5, thought it improbable. Gigante, p. 67, quotes, in support of Jacoby, Plutarch, *Pelop.* V, which contrasts the party of Ἀρχίας (*sic*) and Leontiades and Philip with that of Ismenias and Androcleidas to which Pelopidas adhered.

On the form of the name used by P, Bartoletti comments (*ad loc.*): 'quid vero Anonymus scripserit, incertum videtur'. Both Asias and Astias are attested by epigraphical evidence.

Grenfell and Hunt retained the reading of the papyrus Κορραντάδας, noting that this person may be identical with the Boeotian general Κοιρατάδας (cf. Xen. *Hell.* I, 3. 15 ff.; *Anab.* VII, 1. 33 ff.). Cf. also Meyer, p. 81 n. 5. Bartoletti restores Κο⟨ιρα⟩τάδας, this form being further attested by *Inscr.Gr.Septent.* I, 537.

The pro-Spartan activity of Leontiades' party is well known. Leontiades himself, as polemarch, arranged the seizure of the Cadmea in 382 with the Spartan Phoebidas (Xen. *Hell.* V, 2. 25 ff.) and was responsible for the arrest and subsequent trial of Ismenias. He died in 379 at the hands of Phyllidas and three others of the liberators of Thebes (Xen. *Hell.* v, 4. 7), or at the hands of Pelopidas and Damocleidas (Plut. *Pelop.* XI, 3–6). Before the accession to power of Ismenias' group, the pro-Spartan party had held the ascendancy for some considerable time (XII, 2), and had reaped the benefits of friendly relations with Sparta during the period of the occupation of Decelea.

αἰτίαν μὲ̣ν εἶχον ἀττικίζειν, ἐξ ὧν πρόθυμοι πρὸς τὸν δῆμον ἐγένοντο ὡς ἔφυγ⟨ε⟩ν κτλ.

The reference is to the exiled Athenian democrats at the end of the Peloponnesian War. On the help given to them by the supporters of Ismenias, cf. Diod. XIV, 32. 1: οἱ δ' ἐν ταῖς 'Αθήναις δυναστεύοντες τριάκοντα τύραννοι καθ' ἡμέραν οὐκ ἐπαύοντο τοὺς μὲν φυγαδεύοντες, τοὺς δὲ ἀναιροῦντες. τῶν δὲ Θηβαίων ἀγανακτούντων ἐπὶ τοῖς γινομένοις καὶ φιλοφρόνως τοὺς φυγάδας ὑποδεχομένων, Θρασύβουλος Στιριεὺς ὀνομαζόμενος, ὢν 'Αθηναῖος, ὑπὸ δὲ τῶν τριάκοντα πεφυγαδευμένος, συνεργούντων αὐτῷ λάθρᾳ τῶν Θηβαίων, κατελάβετο τῆς 'Αττικῆς χωρίον ὀνομαζόμενον Φυλήν... Cf. also Justin v, 9. 8: *itaque et Ismenias, Thebanorum princeps, etsi publicis non poterat, privatis tamen viribus adiuvabat* (sc. *Thrasybulum*). The friendship of this party to Athens is further illustrated by the alliance of 395 (Xen. *Hell.* III, 5. 16; Tod, *GHI* II, 101) and the flight of some of its members to Athens in 382, when Thebes was seized by the Spartans (Xen. *Hell.* v, 2. 31).

ἔφυγ⟨ε⟩ν

Restored by Wilamowitz. ἔφυγον p. Gigante retains ἔφυγον, citing x, 2–3: συνῆγον τὸ πλῆθος τὸ τῶν 'Ροδίων εἰς ἐκκλησίαν. ἄρτι δὲ σ υ ν ε ι λ ε γ μ έ ν ω ν α ὐ τ ῶ ν...

οὐ μὴν ἐφρόν[τιζον] τ̣ῶ̣[ν 'Α]θηναίων, ἀλλ' ε̣ἶ̣χ̣[ον κτλ.

The corruption of this sentence makes the meaning so obscure that variant readings of the last word include both ἀττικί]ζειν (Grenfell and Hunt) and λακωνί]ζειν (Kalinka). The first editors commented (p. 229 n. xiii, 1–5): 'The general sense of the passage appears to be that Ismenias and his party favoured Athens not for any regard for Athenian interests but from selfish motives, in order that they might use Athenian support in the contest with the pro-Spartan party at Thebes; cf. col. xiv, 6–16' (i.e. XIII, 1). From the passage cited by Grenfell and Hunt one would infer that the party wanted friendship with Athens in the interests of self-preservation. Athens might be an ally if the pro-Laconian group betrayed the city to Sparta. The event of 382 B.C. would thus seem to have been feared by some in Thebes as early as 403 B.C., but see note to XIII, 1.

XII, 2 (= Column xiii, 5–14)

πρ]οῆλθον πολλοὶ καὶ τῶν ἐν ταῖς [πόλεσι ταῖς κ]α[τὰ τὴ]ν Βοιωτίαν κα[ὶ] μετέ[σ]χον ἑκ[ατέρας τῶν ἑταιρει]ῶν ἐκείνοις.

It is interesting to note that the rivalry between the two parties extended throughout the Boeotian federation and was not simply a rivalry between Theban factions. P makes special mention of the fact that the party of Ismenias and Androcleidas became pre-eminent both in Theban politics and in the federal council: καὶ παρ' αὐτοῖς τοῖ[ς Θηβαίοις κ]αὶ [παρὰ] τῇ βο[υλ]ῇ τῶν Βοιωτῶν. This state of affairs might perhaps be best understood if my contention (see *Emerita* XXVIII (1960), 75 ff.) that the parties were primarily distinguished on grounds of foreign policy is correct. Any powerful movement towards either democracy or dissolution of the federation would seem to be most improbable, for, on the one hand, the Boeotian cities would hardly lend support to a pan-Boeotian democracy with a primary assembly meeting in Thebes, which would ensure in practice Theban predominance, and on the other hand it is difficult to imagine something in the region of half the citizens of Thebes wishing to concede independence to the Boeotian cities.

τ[ότε μὲν καὶ ἔτι μικ]ρῷ πρότερον

ἔτι added by Bartoletti 'propter spatium lacunae'.

The party of Ismenias gained the ascendancy very shortly after 404, or less than a decade before 395 (τότε). Cf. Cloché, in *REG* XXXI (1918), 315–43.

χρόνον δέ τι]να συχνόν

The ascendancy of the pro-Spartans at Thebes probably dates from 447, at the latest, and perhaps from before the period of Athenian domination of Boeotia.

διὰ κ̣[ράτους

Bartoletti's reading presents some difficulty in that it is improbable that Leontiades could have kept his position by force throughout a long period of war, and one must ask why he lost his position just at the time that his allies, the Spartans, were at their strongest. Further, the prosperity of Thebes during the alliance with Sparta may very well have made the policy of Leontiades popular in Boeotia, to a degree which would exclude the need to maintain his position by force. P, in fact, implies in his next sentence (XII, 3) that the wealth which accrued during the Decelean War was a cause of the ascendancy of Leontiades. διὰ π[ειθοῦς (Richards, *ap. OCT*) might be a more acceptable reading.

XII, 3 (=Column xiii, 15–28)

[ὅτ]ε γὰρ πολεμοῦντες οἱ Λακεδαιμ[όνιοι τοῖς] Ἀ[θην]αίοις ἐν Δεκελείᾳ διέτριβον κτλ.

The Spartans fortified Decelea in the spring of 413; cf. Thuc. VII, 19. 1. The reasons given here by P for the superiority of the philo-Laconians at Thebes are the proximity of the Spartans and the resulting material benefits to the Thebans.

ὁ πόλεμος

Clearly the Peloponnesian War.

ἀρξαμένων γὰρ ἀγ[ταίρ]ειν τῶν Ἀθηναίων τῇ Βοιωτίᾳ

Bartoletti adopts Kalinka's reading ἀν[ταίρ]ειν, which is perhaps more suitable to the context than ἀπ[ειλ]εῖν (ed.pr.). The only action ε]ὐθέως ὡς ὁ πόλεμος...[συνέστη... to which this passage could be a reference is the support given by Athens to Plataea. There were, of course, an expedition by Nicias against Tanagra in 426 (Thuc. III, 91) and the invasion of Boeotia in 424 at the time of the battle of Delium (Thuc. IV, 89. 1 ff.).

συνῳκίσθησαν [εἰ]ς αὐτὰς οἵ τ' ἐξ Ἐρυθρῶν καὶ Σκαφῶν καὶ Σκώλου κα[ὶ Αὐ]λίδος καὶ Σχοίνου καὶ Ποτνιῶν κτλ.

On Erythrae, Scaphae and Scolus see note to XI, 3. These towns had been subject to Plataea, probably until 431, and in 395, we are told, were subject to Thebes. Their proximity to Plataea may suggest that the siege of Plataea was the occasion of their migration to Thebes. This would not, however, explain the migration of the people of the other towns, and if P's reason is correct, they simply feared an invasion and, since they lived in unwalled towns, moved to Thebes almost as soon as the war began. Schoenus and Potniae were situated fifty and ten stades respectively to the north of Thebes. Cf. Paus. IX, 8. 1; Strabo IX, 2. 22; 24; 32. Even taking into consideration the πολλῶν ἑτέρων τοιούτων χωρίων, it is perhaps an exaggeration that the population of Thebes was doubled.

XII, 4 (= Column xiii, 28–36)

ἐπετείχισαν—μετὰ τῶν Λακεδ[αι]μ[ονί]ων

P specifies that the Thebans assisted in the fortification of Decelea; cf. Thuc. VII, 19. 1: οἱ Λακεδαιμόνιοι καὶ οἱ ξύμμαχοι. The idea appears to have come from Alcibiades; cf. Thuc. VI, 91. 6; VII, 18. 1.

τά τε γὰρ ἀνδράποδα καὶ τὰ λοιπὰ πάντ[α ⟨τὰ⟩ κατὰ τὸ]ν πόλεμον ἁλισκόμενα μικροῦ τιν[ος ἀργυρίο]υ παρελάμβανον

It appears that Athenian slaves who deserted to Decelea received no better fate than to be sold by the Spartans. Prisoners of war on occasion escaped to Decelea also; cf. Xen. *Hell.* I, 2. 14 (some Sicilians) and I, 3. 22 (Coeratadas, the Boeotian).

This section provides an interesting account of the way in which the Thebans took advantage of their alliance with Sparta during the Decelean War. Their proximity to the occupied area of Attica enabled them to carry all kinds of plunder back to their homes, and the systematic nature of their looting is illustrated by P's remark that they began with the timber and tiles of the Attic houses. It is interesting to note that at the beginning of the Archidamian War the inhabitants of Attica took away their household utensils and even the timber of the houses themselves (Thuc. II, 14. 1). One wonders why they did not do so later as well.

XII, 5 (= Column xiii, 36–column xiv, 6)

τότε δὲ τῶν Ἀθηναίων ἡ χώρα πολυτελέστατα τῆς Ἑλλάδος κατεσκεύαστο·

Cf. Thuc. II, 65. 2: οἱ δὲ δυνατοὶ (*sc.* τῶν Ἀθηναίων) καλὰ κτήματα κατὰ τὴν χώραν οἰκοδομίαις τε καὶ πολυτελέσι κατασκευαῖς ἀπολωλεκότες...

ἐπεπόνθει γὰρ μικρὰ κακῶς ἐν ταῖς ἐμβολαῖς ταῖς ἔμπροσθεν κτλ.

Cf., on this section, Hardy in *CP* XXI (1926). Grenfell and Hunt (ed.pr. p. 230) thought that μικρά was an undue minimization of the extent of the damage caused by the Spartan invasions in the Archidamian War. The devastation, they observed, was clearly shown by Thucydides to have been widespread. Hardy, however, argues plausibly that the devastation of Attica during the Decelean War was far greater than that inflicted during the Archidamian invasions in that much lasting and irreparable damage was done, whereas in the early invasions the damage was largely confined to annual crops. While the Archidamian War was in progress this damage seemed substantial to Thucydides, but he realized at the time of the Decelean devastations that the former had been comparatively mild. Hardy even suggests that Thucydides VII, 27 may have been one of P's sources. Nor is this suggestion unlikely, for the absence of P's customary citation of a former reference in his work when he mentions a subject he has dealt with previously may imply that this excursus is in the nature of a supplementary note, not to an earlier passage in P's own work, but to Thucydides' narrative. Cf. Bloch, *HSCP*, supp. vol. I (1940), p. 326.

Cf. Thuc. VII, 27. 3–5 on the devastation of Attica at this time: ἐπειδὴ γὰρ ἡ Δεκέλεια τὸ μὲν πρῶτον ὑπὸ πάσης τῆς στρατιᾶς ἐν τῷ θέρει τούτῳ τειχισθεῖσα, ὕστερον δὲ φρουραῖς ἀπὸ τῶν πόλεων κατὰ διαδοχὴν χρόνου ἐπιούσαις τῇ χώρᾳ ἐπῳκεῖτο, πολλὰ ἔβλαπτε τοὺς Ἀθηναίους, καὶ ἐν τοῖς πρῶτον χρημάτων τ' ὀλέθρῳ καὶ ἀνθρώπων φθορᾷ ἐκάκωσε τὰ πράγματα. 4 πρότερον μὲν γὰρ βραχεῖαι γιγνόμεναι αἱ ἐσβολαὶ τὸν ἄλλον χρόνον τῆς γῆς ἀπολαύειν οὐκ ἐκώλυον· τότε δὲ ξυνεχῶς ἐπικαθημένων, καὶ ὁτὲ μὲν καὶ πλεόνων ἐπιόντων, ὁτὲ δ' ἐξ ἀνάγκης τῆς ἴσης φρουρᾶς καταθεούσης τε τὴν χώραν καὶ λῃστείας ποιουμένης, βασιλέως τε παρόντος τοῦ τῶν Λακεδαιμονίων Ἄγιδος, ὃς οὐκ ἐκ παρέργου τὸν πόλεμον ἐποιεῖτο, μεγάλα οἱ Ἀθηναῖοι ἐβλάπτοντο. 5 τῆς τε γὰρ χώρας ἁπάσης ἐστέρηντο, καὶ ἀνδραπόδων πλέον ἢ δύο μυριάδες ηὐτομολήκεσαν, καὶ τούτων τὸ πολὺ μέρος χειροτέχναι, πρόβατά τε πάντα ἀπωλώλει καὶ ὑποζύγια.

XIII, 1 (= Column xiv, 6–16)

οἱ δὲ περὶ τὸν Ἀ[ν]δροκλείδαν κα[ὶ τὸν Ἰσμηνίαν ἐ]σπούδαζον ἐκπολεμῶσαι τὸ ἔθνος [πρὸς τοὺς Λακεδα]ιμονίους

P may be a little unfair in charging the party of Ismenias and Androcleidas with primary responsibility for the outbreak of the war, although in doing so he is in agreement with Xenophon, *Hell.* III, 5. 3–5, and Pausanias III, 9. 9. For further discussion see Accame, *Ricerche intorno alla guerra corinzia*, ch. II, and my article in *Emerita* XXVIII (1960), 75–86, entitled 'Internal Politics and the Outbreak of the Corinthian War'.

βουλόμενοι μὲν καταλῦσαι τ[ὴν ἀρχὴν αὐτῶ]ν ἵνα μὴ διαφθαρῶσιν ὑπ' ἐκείνων διὰ [τοὺς λακων]ίζοντας

A slight pro-Spartan bias which is detectable in P seems to blind him to an important (if not the greatest) cause of hostility to Sparta in Greece, and that is dissatisfaction on the part of the Peloponnesian and other allies with their treatment at the end of the Peloponnesian War, and on the part of everyone, especially subjects, with the overbearing nature of Spartan imperialism. Cf. II, 2, where P ignores this factor in accounting for the opposition to Sparta in Athens, Argos, Corinth and Boeotia. As for the motive given here for desiring a war, (*a*) the fear would not really seem to have been justified, for no such attempt to gain material support from the Spartans had been made by the philo-Laconians and no such attempt was made until some five years after the Corinthian War ended. It looks as if this motive may have been supplied later in the light of the event of 382 B.C. (*b*) The desire for open war seems very rash, since the philo-Laconians might side with the enemy, and despite the confidence of the anti-Spartans it could hardly be certain that Athens would become an active ally. We should note too that the Thebans were already at war before the alliance of Corinth and Argos was secured.

ῥᾳδίως

Surely an exaggeration. Not even the most enthusiastic anti-Laconian would think this. Cf. XIII, 2: οὐδέποτε γὰρ οὔτε Θηβαίους οὔτε τοὺς ἄλλους Βοιωτοὺς πεισθήσεσθαι πολεμεῖν Λακεδαιμονίοις ἄρχουσι τῆς Ἑλλάδος.

ὑπολα]μβάνοντες βασιλ[έ]α χρήματα π[α]ρέξε[ιν ὅπερ ὁ π]αρὰ τοῦ βαρβάρου π[ε]μφθεὶς ἐπηγγέλλετο

The envoy in question is Timocrates, the Rhodian. Cf. note to II, 2. It becomes evident from the present passage that Timocrates, in addition to distributing grants of money to anti-Spartan factions in Greece, had authority from the King to promise further financial assistance for the future. Cf. Accame, *Ricerche intorno alla guerra corinzia*, p. 29, and Barbieri, *Conone*, pp. 92ff. The view of Lenschau (*Phil. Woch.* LIII (1933), 1,325–8) that the messenger mentioned in this passage is someone other than Timocrates does not seem to me to be a very probable hypothesis.

⟨τοὺς δὲ⟩ [Κορινθίου]ς

This restoration of Grenfell and Hunt is obviously correct. For some reason Kalinka rejected [Κορινθίου]ς in favour of [ἔτι δ' ἴσω]ς; Kalinka's reading is strongly criticized by Lipsius in *Berl.Phil.Woch.* (1917), col. 1,574.

τούτους γὰρ ἐχθροὺς τοῖς Λακεδαιμ[ονίοις ὄ]ντας

It is worth noting that in the case of the Corinthians this hostility to Sparta, apparently widespread, could hardly have been based on grounds of domestic politics, for Corinth remained an oligarchy until 392. Opposition to Sparta in Corinth evidently cut across party distinctions, and the change of outlook in foreign affairs of this city surely provides the most obvious example of growing distaste for the behaviour of the Spartans since their victory in the Peloponnesian War.

τοὺς πολίτας (πολειτασ p). The emendation of Richards, *ap. OCT*, τοὺς ὁπλίτας, seems unnecessary.

XIII, 2 (= Column xiv, 16–24)

ἀπὸ μὲν τοῦ φανεροῦ χαλεπῶς ἔχειν ἐπιτίθεσθαι τούτοις· κτλ.

The logic of this argument appears faulty, for Ismenias and Androcleidas were supported by the majority of Thebans and of Boeotians (XII, 2) and, in my view, chiefly on grounds of foreign policy. The charge thus seems to be directed against these men in an individual capacity, whereas it is difficult to see what individual gain they could hope for from war, being already the most influential persons in both city and federation.

Λακεδαιμονίοις ἄρχουσι τῆς Ἑλλάδος·

Cf. Xen. *Hell.* III, 1. 5: πᾶσαι γὰρ τότε αἱ πόλεις ἐπείθοντο ὅ τι Λακεδαιμόνιος ἀνὴρ ἐπιτάττοι. See further Parke, 'The Development of the Second Spartan Empire', in *JHS* L (1930), 37–79.

διὰ ταύτης τῆς ἀπάτης

I have suggested in *Emerita* XXVIII (1960), 75–86, that this stratagem may have been a fiction of Ismenias' political opponents.

ἀνέπεισαν ἄνδρας τινὰς Φωκέων ἐμβαλεῖν εἰς τὴν Λοκρῶν τῶν Ἑσπερίων καλουμένων

The version of Xenophon (*Hell.* III, 5. 3) is that the Theban leaders persuaded the Opuntian Locrians χρήματα τελέσαι from the disputed territory near Parnassus, whereupon the Phocians invaded Locris. The point of contact between Xenophon and P is that both represent the Phocians as being the first to invade the territory undisputedly belonging to their neighbours. Pausanias (III, 9. 9) indicates that the Locrians, at the instigation of the party of Ismenias, cut down the ripe corn in the disputed area and drove away the livestock. The Phocians retaliated by invading Locris. Diodorus (XIV, 81. 1) simply states: Φωκεῖς πρὸς Βοιωτοὺς ἔκ τινων ἐγκλημάτων εἰς πόλεμον καταστάντες ἔπεισαν τοὺς Λακεδαιμονίους συμμαχεῖν κατὰ τῶν Βοιωτῶν. It is doubtful whether the Locrians in question were the western (Ozolian) Locrians, as stated by P, or the

Opuntian (eastern) Locrians, as stated by Xenophon. Pausanias, in naming οἱ ἐξ Ἀμφίσσης Λοκροί, agrees with P. Both were later allied to the anti-Spartan confederates. In the battle of Corinth (394 B.C.) the Opuntians supplied fifty head of cavalry and the Ozolians a contingent of light-armed troops (Xen. *Hell.* IV, 2. 17). Both fought at the battle of Coronea in 394 (Λοκροὶ ἀμφότεροι, Xen. *Hell.* IV, 3. 15; cf. Xen. *Ages.* II, 6; Plut. *Ages.* XLVII). On the alliance between Locris and Athens in 395, see Tod, *GHI* II, 102.

XIII, 3 (=Column xiv, 25–37)

ἔστι τοῖς ἔθνεσιν τούτοις ἀμφισβητήσιμος χώρα περὶ τὸν Παρνασσόν

Cf. Xen. *Hell.* III, 5. 3: τῆς ἀμφισβητησίμου χώρας Φωκεῦσί τε καὶ ἑαυτοῖς (*sc.* Λοκροῖς); and Paus. III, 9. 9: γῆ...ἐτύγχανεν οὖσα ἀμφισβητήσιμος.

The use of the present tense, ἔστι, here, and in ἐπινέμουσι (below) and διάκεινται (XIII, 4), indicates that the work was composed before the end of the Sacred War, 346 B.C. thus being the *terminus ad quem* for the composition.

περ[ὶ] ἧς καὶ πρότερόν ποτε πεπολεμήκασιν, κτλ.

On this section see McKay, 'The Oxyrhynchus Historian and the Outbreak of the Corinthian War', in *CR* n.s. III (1953), 6–7. In the past the normal course of these disputes had been: (1) One side grazed sheep on the disputed land. (2) The other side gathered in force and made a raid on the flocks. (3) Both sides sought legal proceedings or arbitration. McKay points out that on this occasion the first abnormal step was the retaliation of the Locrians (ἀνθαρπασάντων ἀνθ' ὧν ἀπέβαλον προβάτων) at the point at which a peaceful solution was usually sought. Thus he argues that the Theban leaders would have approached the Locrians and not the Phocians (as indeed happens in Xenophon's account). He concludes that P and Xenophon both seem to have heard an incomplete or inaccurate account, and to have enlarged upon it as each thought necessary. It might well be argued to the contrary, however, that the wealth of detail and background in P's version suggests he had heard a most complete account of the stratagem and reproduced it with characteristic diligence. This apparent inconsistency might then lend support to the possibility of the stratagem being a fabrication of the political opponents of Ismenias (cf. *Emerita* XXVIII (1960), 75–86).

XIII, 4 (= Column xiv, 37–column xv, 15)

οἱ δὲ Λοκροὶ—πέμψαντες πρέσβεις εἰς Βοιωτοὺς κτλ.

Pausanias III, 9. 10 records the Locrian appeal to Thebes, and it may be inferred from Xenophon's account (*Hell.* III, 5. 4), in which Ismenias and Androcleidas persuade the Thebans to assist the Locrians. We may note the greater accuracy of P in speaking of 'the Boeotians', for a decision of this nature would certainly be taken by the federal council, before which the Locrian ambassadors would appear. The apparent ease with which the Boeotians were persuaded to help the Locrians, while they would never have been persuaded to oppose the Spartans (XIII, 2), might suggest that the intervention of Sparta was not at this stage regarded as a probability.

Φω[κεῖς δέ,—πρέσβεις δ[ὲ] π̣α̣[ραχρῆμα πέμψαν]τες πρὸς Λακεδαιμονίους κτλ.

According to the more succinct accounts of Xenophon and Pausanias the Phocians appealed to Sparta after the Boeotians (Xenophon and Pausanias say Thebans) had invaded Phocis. Neither mentions the fruitless attempt by the Spartans to make the Boeotians submit to arbitration. The tone of the Spartan demand would appear from P to be in keeping with the high-handed character of Spartan behaviour since 404 B.C. The Spartans do not appear at this juncture to have been particularly interested in making war on Boeotia, and the success of the Phocian appeal, with the intervention of Sparta, must have been recorded by P after the end of the London papyrus, that is after the narrative of Agesilaus' campaign in Phrygia Minor in XVII. The further remark of Pausanias (III, 9. 11), evidently obtained from some Athenian or philo-Athenian source, that the Athenians sent an embassy to Sparta requesting that there should be no recourse to arms against Thebes, but that the matter should be submitted to arbitration, is dismissed by Grenfell and Hunt as 'an improbable story which looks like a perversion of the proposals of the Spartans' (ed.pr. p. 233). However, it is quite possible that this mission is factual and was recorded by P also, for, since the Spartans at the time of the Athenian request had evidently decided upon war, it would occur in P's account later than chapter XVII. The remainder of chapter XIII, narrating the Boeotian invasion of Phocis, makes no further mention of the Spartans and does not indicate that they had yet resolved to march on Boeotia.

XIII, 5 (=Column xv, 15–32)

P is our only informant of the course of the Boeotian invasion of Phocis, which he describes in considerable detail. P's statement in XI, 1 that these hostilities began in the summer of 395 would accord with Pausanias' remark (III, 9. 9) that the Locrians had cut down τὸν σῖτον ἀκμάζοντα. Grenfell and Hunt suggest May or June as the date of the dispute between Locris and Phocis, July or August for the Boeotian invasion of Phocis, and September or October for the battle of Haliartus (Xen. *Hell.* III, 5. 17ff.). Between the invasion of Phocis and the battle of Haliartus Lysander won over Orchomenus (Xen. *Hell.* III, 5. 6), and the Boeotians concluded a defensive alliance with the Athenians (Tod, *GHI* II, 101; Xen. *Hell.* III, 5. 7ff.). I would assign these events to August or September of 395.

ἐμβα]λόντες δὲ διὰ ταχέων εἰς τὴν Φωκίδα

The words διὰ ταχέων may indicate that the invasion was made with a hastily gathered force, not amounting to anything like the full complement of federal troops. The purpose of the invasion was evidently punitive, as may be inferred from the devastation of the land over a fairly extensive area of Phocis and the half-hearted and rather unsuccessful attacks on towns. The capture of the προάστιον of the Phanoteis was the only successful assault (and hardly an impressive one), while attempts on the towns of the Parapotamii and Daulii failed, as did the later attack on Hyampolis. In the case of Hyampolis there appears to have been no plan to attack the town, the idea first presenting itself as the troops happened to be passing that way on their return to Boeotia. If P's narrative adheres strictly to the chronological sequence of events, the invasion and withdrawal could not have lasted more than two months at the most.

[πορθ]ήσαντες τήν τε τῶν Παραποταμίων χώραν καὶ Δαυλίων καὶ Φανοτέων

Although the location of the ἀμφισβητήσιμος χώρα is uncertain beyond P's description of it as being περὶ Παρνασσόν, it is quite possible that these were the peoples concerned in the initial Phocian attack on the Locrians, especially if the Locrians in question were in fact the Western Locrians, or, as Pausanias describes them, οἱ ἐξ Ἀμφίσσης.

περὶ τὴν Ἐλάτειαν καὶ τοὺς Πεδιέας

If we accept the view of P and Pausanias that the Western Locrians were those initially involved in the dispute, the subsequent Boeotian invasion of the district of Elatea may have given rise to the other view (of Xenophon) that the Locrians concerned were the Opuntians. Elatea was a town of strategic importance commanding the route from Phocis to Boeotia by the Cephissus valley, and also that to Opus in Locris. (Cf. the consequences of the fortification of Elatea by Philip of Macedon in 339 B.C.) However, the nature of Boeotian activity in the area—ravaging of land, but no attempt on the town—suggests no strategic motive for marching to that region.

Πεδιέας would seem to refer to the people rather than the town, although Herodotus, VIII, 33, uses this form of the town.

{πρὸς} παρ' Ὑ⟨άμ⟩πολιν: προσπαρυηνπολιν p

'The corruption of παρ Υαμπολιν into προς Παρυην πολιν was detected by both Blass and Wilamowitz' (ed.pr. p. 233 n. xv, 26). Gigante reads Ὕαν πόλιν, citing Strabo IX, 2. 3 (=Jacoby, *F.Gr.Hist.* 70 (Ephorus) F 119): Ὕαντες δὲ τῆς Φωκίδος Ὕαν πόλιν ᾤκισαν. Cf. also Strabo IX, 3. 15: Ὑάμπολις (Ὕα μετὰ ταῦτα ἐκλήθη ὑπό τινων), εἰς ἣν ἐκ Βοιωτίας ἐκπεσεῖν ἔφαμεν τοὺς Ὕαντας· ἔστι δ' ἐν τῇ μεσογαίᾳ μάλιστα καὶ αὕτη, πλησίον τῶν Παραποταμίων, ἑτέρα οὖσα τῆς ἐν τῷ Παρνασσῷ Ὑαμπείας.

ἀποπειρᾶσθαι τῆς πόλεως·

For the expression cf. Thuc. II, 93. 1; IV, 121. 2, etc., although Thucydides tends to use the active for an attempt on a city.

ἀποβαλόντες δὲ τῶν στρατιωτῶν ὡς ὀγδοήκοντα

One cannot make any guess about the numbers of the Boeotian army from this solitary figure relating to losses sustained at Hyampolis. The attempt on the place would seem to have been an ill-conceived venture with inadequate forces. That the real purpose and only effect of the invasion was to devastate some Phocian land is also indicated by Xenophon (*Hell.* III, 5. 3), οἱ Θηβαῖοι ἀντεμβαλόντες εἰς τὴν Φωκίδα ἐδῄουν τὴν χώραν, and Pausanias (III, 9. 10), τὴν Φωκίδα ἐπόρθησαν.

XIV, 1 (=Column XV, 32–9)

Chapters XIV and XV constitute an important source for the activity of Conon during the late summer and autumn of 395, for not only does the Oxyrhynchus historian record the circumstances of the Persian fleet with his customary detail, but Xenophon remains completely silent on the subject of the naval operations at this period and minor sources provide only the barest outline, which may, in any case, be of doubtful reliability.

The mutiny of Conon's troops, to which the whole of chapter XV is devoted, is mentioned by only one other source available to us, Justin VI, 2. 11, and that in a bare statement of its occurrence.

παρειληφότος ἤδη Χειρικράτους τὰς ναῦς τὰς τῶν Λακεδαιμονίων καὶ τῶν συμμάχων, ὃς ἀφίκετο ναύαρχος διάδοχος τῷ Πόλλιδι

Cheiricrates (*P.Lak.* 758) is not known from any source other than P. Pollis' assumption of office is mentioned in IV, 2; there is a further reference to Cheiricrates in XVII, 4. While the arrival of Cheiricrates is placed by P earlier than the events of the present narrative, it cannot have been much earlier (whatever date we assign to the arrival of Pollis (IV, 2)) and I therefore conclude that it must have occurred shortly after midsummer or towards the end of the summer of the year 395. Cf. ed.pr. p. 210 n. iii, 21. We know of no positive action being taken by Cheiricrates against Conon.

In the light of the statement in the present passage of Cheiricrates appointment as nauarch, a difficulty is presented by Xenophon's record of the nauarchia of Peisander, who held the office at the time of the battle of Cnidus, in which he was killed. Xenophon (*Hell.* III, 4. 29) dates the appointment of Peisander to the time when Agesilaus was on his way to invade Phrygia, i.e. the late summer of 395. The appointment of Peisander is also mentioned by Plutarch (*Ages.* X) and Pausanias (III, 9. 6). Cheiricrates' appointment seems to have been a regular one and he appears from XVII, 4 still to have been the Spartan nauarch later in the autumn of 395, in fact *after* the invasion of Phrygia by Agesilaus. The solution suggested by Pareti in *Memorie Accad. Torino* LIX (1909), 135–7, is that Peisander was given an extraordinary command by Agesilaus, while Cheiricrates remained officially the nauarch. Cf. Barbieri, *Conone*, p. 140. The alternative, and, I suggest, preferable view is that taken by Grenfell and Hunt (ed.pr. p. 234 n. XV, 33), who consider the reference to Cheiricrates as nauarch in XVII, 4 to be an indication not of any extraordinary nature of Peisander's office, but of Xenophon's erroneous chronology. They assume that Xenophon has simply given too early a date for the succession of Peisander to the nauarchia (no doubt after a rather brief tenure of the office by Cheiricrates), and that the appointment of Peisander by Agesilaus would thus have been made during the winter of 395/4. Cf. also Jacoby, *F.Gr.Hist.* II C, 18.

βουλόμενος δὲ συμμεῖξαι τῷ Φαρναβάζῳ κα[ὶ] τῷ Τιθραύστῃ καὶ χρήματα λαβεῖν ἀνέβαινεν ἐκ τῆς Καύνου πρὸς αὐτούς.

The departure of Conon to consult Pharnabazus and Tithraustes regarding the arrears of pay owing to his men, immediately after the arrival of Cheiricrates as successor to Pollis, must be assigned to the late summer of 395. Diodorus (XIV, 81. 4–6) states that Conon went to Babylon and conversed with the Great King himself on the subject of pay for his troops. This visit to Artaxerxes is synchronized with the Boeotian War by Diodorus, and in the opinion of Grenfell and Hunt (ed.pr. p. 234 n. XV, 37ff.) the present passage amply vindicates the correctness of Diodorus' date as against the implications of Nepos (*Conon* III) and Pausanias (III, 9. 2) that Conon went to Persia in the winter of 396/5. The first editors noted further that such a visit to the King by Conon, occurring after the events recorded by P, would not be surprising since the 220 talents obtained from Tithraustes (XIV, 3) cannot have been sufficient to meet the demands of the troops; see my note to XIV, 3. The mutiny described in XV is a further indication of the grave situation in which Conon found himself so long as the arrears of pay for his sailors and land-forces were withheld. On the other hand Barbieri (*Conone*, pp. 135–6) considers it unlikely that Conon met Artaxerxes in person, commenting: 'Il racconto di Diodoro, anche se in sostanza esatto, sembra voler mettere eccessivamente in risalto la figura di Conone ed il prestigio di cui egli godeva presso il ré persiano.' This view is supported by the evidence of Nepos (*Conon* III, 2–4) and Justin (VI, 2. 12–13). The latter states: *itaque Conon diu rege per epistulas frustra fatigato ad postremum ipse ad eum pergit, a cuius aspectu et conloquio prohibitus est quod eum more Persarum adorare noluit.*

These authors indicate that Conon communicated with the King by letter through the agency of Tithraustes. We know from P XIV, 3 that by the time of the visit of Conon to Artaxerxes, whether or not a personal meeting took place, Tithraustes had already returned to the court, leaving Pasiphernes and Ariaeus in charge of affairs in Sardis. Since Conon had previously held talks with Tithraustes (as noticed in the present passage), the Persian could be expected to be well acquainted with the circumstances of Conon's forces and might therefore be a highly suitable intermediary between Conon and Artaxerxes. Cf. Meyer, p. 79 n. 4.

Barbieri, *loc. cit.*, while accepting the word of Nepos and Justin that Conon did not meet the King in person, rejects the reasons they give for the failure of such a meeting to take place: 'L'episodio è trattato diffusamente da Nepote e Giustino per mettere in luce il carattere fiero e dignitoso di Conone, alieno dall'abbassarsi a compiere un atto barbarico in contrasto col prestigio di un ateniese.' Yet it is difficult to see what other reason there may have been. Conon obviously did not refuse to see the King, for he went to Persia with that express intention. The only alternative is that Artaxerxes refused to see Conon, but since a satisfactory solution of the problems regarding the troops in his service would undoubtedly have been to his advantage he would only have refused Conon a hearing under some such circumstances as those outlined by Justin and Nepos.

Barbieri is surely right, however, in rejecting Diodorus' claim that the appointment of Pharnabazus to military command was made at Conon's suggestion at this meeting, which Diodorus accepts, with Artaxerxes. For it appears that Pharnabazus had already been appointed to the supreme command by the King. Cf. Diod. XIV, 39. 2: (Φαρνάβαζος) ἐπέστησεν αὐτὸν (Κόνωνα) ἐπὶ τὴν θάλατταν ἡγεμόνα; and Ctesias, *Pers. ap.* Phot. 44b38 (=*F.Gr.Hist.* 688 F 30): ὑπὸ Φαρναβάζου ναύαρχος Κόνων ἐγένετο. Tissaphernes had previously been the commander-in-chief of all naval and military operations (Xen. *Hell.* III, 2. 13), and the authority of Pharnabazus had probably been increased on the death of Tissaphernes. Conon, far from being given a choice of his Persian colleague, is more likely to have given his formal agreement to the King's appointment of Pharnabazus. Nor was Pharnabazus an equal colleague of Conon (as implied by Diodorus XIV, 81. 6 and Nepos, *Conon* IV, 2) but was his superior in both naval and land operations (Xen. *Hell.* IV, 8. 3 and 6) and was officially the nauarch at the battle of Cnidus (Xen. *Hell.* IV, 3. 11).

XIV, 2 (=Column XV, 39–column XVI, 15)

προσοφειλόμενος μισθὸς πολλῶν μηνῶν

The period appears to have been fifteen months; cf. Isoc. *Paneg.* 142: πεντεκαίδεκα δὲ μηνῶν τοὺς στρατιώτας τὸν μισθὸν ἀπεστέρησεν (*sc.* βασιλεύς).

ἐμισθοδοτ[οῦ]ντο γὰρ ὑπὸ τῶν στρατηγῶν κακῶς, ὃ ποιεῖν ἔθ[ος] ἐστὶν ἀεὶ τοῖς πολεμοῦσι⟨ν⟩ ὑπὲρ βασιλέως κτλ.

P now gives some interesting observations on the difficulties experienced by mercenary troops in the service of the Great King in obtaining their wages. The use of the present tense, ἔθ[ος] ἐστίν, here, and αἴτιός ἐστι⟨ν⟩, ὀλιγωρεῖ, εἴωθε, below, is a further indication that the work was composed before the fall of the Persian Empire. On the experience of the Spartans during the Decelean War, cf. Thuc. VIII, 45. 2; 83. 2–3; 99. It is noteworthy that P, despite his obvious acquaintance with Thucydides' work (cf. Flor.pap. II), places all the blame on the King, whereas Thucydides suggests that the pay was sometimes withheld as a result of the particular policy of an individual satrap, or, as in the Decelean War, as a consequence of the intrigues of Alcibiades.

Λακεδαιμόνιοι⟨ς⟩ λακεδαιμονιοι p, corrected by Wilamowitz in order to avoid hiatus. Gigante, p. 71, makes the further point that this reading provides 'la maggiore scorrevolezza del periodo già di per sé scabroso per il triplice mutamento di soggetto (στρατιῶται, στρατηγοί, τριήρεις)'.

κατ[ε]λύθησαν

Cf. Isoc. *Paneg.* 142: τὸ μὲν ἐπ' ἐκείνῳ (*sc.* βασιλεῖ) πολλάκις ἂν διελύθησαν (*sc.* στρατιῶται).

διὰ τὴν Κύρου προθυμίαν

For the expression, see XVI, 6: διὰ τὴν 'Ραθάνου προθυμίαν. Cf. also XV, 6. On Cyrus, see Xen. *Hell.* I, 4. 3; 5. 2; 6. 18; II, I. 11–15. One might add, however, that the προθυμία of Cyrus was not the only factor in the preservation of the Peloponnesian fleet, for it would appear that with the sending of Cyrus it became no longer simply the policy of individual satraps to assist the Spartans, but the set purpose of the Persian King.

XIV, 3 (=Column xvi, 15–29)

Τιθραύστης δέ,—ἀποστέλλει τινὰς τῶν μεθ' αὐτοῦ βαρβάρων ἵνα μισθὸν δῶσι τοῖς στρατιώταις, ἔχοντας ἀργυρίου τάλαντα διακόσια καὶ εἴκοσι⟨ν⟩

The sum of 220 talents can have been little more than a token payment when compared with that owing to Conon's troops for a fifteen-month period (cf. Isoc. *Paneg.* 142 above) of service during which pay had been withheld. I recall the calculation by Meyer of the approximate sum required to provide pay for one year for a fleet of 100 ships, assuming 200 men to each ship. If the daily rate of pay were 4 obols (i.e. $\frac{2}{3}$ drachma; cf. Xen. *Hell.* I, 5. 7) the annual sum would be:

$$\frac{2}{3} \times 200 \times 100 \times 360 = 4{,}800{,}000 \text{ drachmae}$$
$$= 800 \text{ talents}$$

Cf. Meyer, pp. 75–6, Barbieri, *Conone*, p. 110 n. 2. This payment, although not satisfying the demands of the troops, may probably be regarded as terminating the fifteenth-month period mentioned by Isocrates; alternatively the return of Conon from Persia early in 394 could be taken as the end of the period during which the troops were unpaid (cf. further De Sanctis, *Atti Accad. Torino* LXVI (1931), 164).

τῆς οὐσίας τῆς Τισσαφέρνους

On the death of Tissaphernes, see ch. VIII and notes.

Τιθραύστης—ἀνέβαινεν ὡς βασιλέα

Tithraustes had been sent to Lydia for the express purpose of doing away with Tissaphernes (cf. Diod. XIV, 80. 7; Xen. *Hell.* III, 4. 25; Polyaen. VII, 16. 1; Plut. *Ages.* X, 5). Although it appears from these sources that Tithraustes was given full powers in the province of Tissaphernes at the time of his mission, it is not clear whether he was intended to replace Tissaphernes as satrap. If not, he would now have no legitimate reason for remaining in Lydia after the execution of Tissaphernes. We do know that Tiribazus became satrap of the former province of Tissaphernes, but we hear no mention of him in connection with any events before the winter of 393/2. Cf. Xen. *Hell.* IV, 8. 12.

'Αριαῖον καὶ Πασιφέρνη

For Ariaeus cf. VIII, 1 (*bis*) and VIII, 2. On his part in the assassination of Tissaphernes see notes to chapter VIII. It appears that he was still in charge of Sardis during the winter of 395/4. Cf. Xen. *Hell.* IV, 1. 27: ἀπιόντες εἰς Σάρδεις πρὸς 'Αριαῖον.

Pasiphernes, not known from any other source, may possibly have been mentioned in IV, 3; cf. note *ad loc.*

XV, 1 (= Column xvi, 29–column xvii, 6)

The whole chapter is devoted to a detailed account of the mutiny of the Cypriot mercenaries serving under Conon, which appears to have arisen from the rumour that, after the long period in which the troops had received no pay (cf. XIV, 2), the money which had recently become available to Conon was to be distributed only to the sailors and marines and not to the other men, among whom were the Cypriots. The only other known record of the mutiny is that of Justin, VI, 2. 11: *sed Cononem seditio militum invadit, quos praefecti regis fraudare stipendio soliti erant: eo instantius debita poscentibus quo graviorem sub magno duce militiam praesumebant.* It seems probable that Justin's statement derives from P, not only since the mutiny is overlooked by Xenophon and Diodorus, but because the notice of the customary treatment of the soldiers in respect of their pay is reminiscent of P XIV, 2, ἐμισθοδοτ[οῦ]ντο γὰρ ὑπὸ τῶν στρατηγῶν κακῶς κτλ. The date of the mutiny I take to have been the beginning of autumn 395. Cf. also ed.pr. p. 220 (late summer or autumn), Meyer, pp. 64, 79 (autumn), p. 75 (late summer), Zunkel, *Diss. Jenensis* 1911, p. 42 (autumn), Pareti, *St.It.Fil.Class.* XIX (1912), 443 (second half of the θέρος), De Sanctis, *Atti Accad. Torino* LXVI (1931), 184 (the end of 395), Barbieri, *Conone*, p. 134 (beginning of autumn).

τῶν δὲ Κυπρίων οἱ μετὰ τοῦ Κόνωνος

To judge by the contrast drawn between these Cypriot troops and the ὑπηρεσίαι and ἐπιβάται (below), they were probably a land force put at Conon's disposal by Evagoras (cf. Barbieri, *Conone*, pp. 132–3). It is unlikely, as far as appears from P, that they were very numerous, perhaps a few hundred at the most; cf. Meyer, p. 76.

εἰς τὴν Καῦνον

Cf. XIV, 1. Conon had sailed from Rhodes to Caunus in order to proceed from there to have talks with Tithraustes and Pharnabazus regarding the arrears of pay owing to his troops.

οὕτω ουτω p.

Wilamowitz (*ap.* ed.pr.) preferred to emend the text to ὑπό, to obviate what Grenfell and Hunt called 'an extremely awkward construction' (p. 236) resulting from the retention of οὕτω. Bartoletti follows Kalinka and Gigante in preserving the reading of the papyrus. For this reading, see Kalinka, *Gött.gel.Anzeigen* (1917), p. 416 and Gigante, p. 71, note to XV, 1.

ἄνδρα Καρπασέα τὸ γέ[ν]ος

The failure of P to name this man could well be intentional as a means of implying contempt (cf. Meyer, p. 76; ed.pr. p. 236; Barbieri, *op. cit.* p. 133). It is, of course, possible that he was unable to ascertain the man's name. On Carpasia, cf. Stephanus Byz. *s.v.*, = Jacoby, *F.Gr.Hist.* 115 (Theopompus) F 19: Καρπασία· πόλις Κύπρου...ὁ πολίτης Καρπασεώτης ὡς Μαρεώτης. καὶ τὸ κτητικὸν Καρπασεωτικός...Θεόπομπος ἐν δεκάτῳ Καρπασεῖς αὐτούς φησιν, ἴσως ἀπὸ τοῦ Κάρπασος, ὡς Ἀντίοχος Ἀντιοχεύς, ἀφ' οὗ Καρπάσεια. The agreement of P with Theopompus on the form of the adjective does not, of course, provide any argument for the identification of P with Theopompus, as claimed by the first editors. Cf. Jacoby, *F.Gr.Hist.* II C, 18.

ἀφ' ἑκάστης [τάξεως

For the reading τάξεως see Meyer, p. 76 n. 2. Grenfell and Hunt read νεώς, although recognizing that the Cypriots concerned were a land force.

XV, 2 (= Column xvii, 6–13)

After the return of Conon to Caunus (κατελ̣[θόντος τοῦ Κό]νωνος), noticed in XV, 1, it appears, despite the lacunae, that the Carpasian discussed the question of pay with him and that Conon gave an assurance that there would be no discrimination such as had been rumoured.

τὸ πλῆθος τὸ τῶν στρατιω[τῶν

Apparently the Cypriot soldiers, whose camp was outside the city.

XV, 3 (= Column xvii, 13–33)

τῶν Μεσσηνίω[ν] τινὲς τῶν τῷ Κόνωνι παρακολουθεῖν εἰωθότων

The Messenians were quite probably from Naupactus. Conon had been on friendly terms with the Messenians of Naupactus as early as 414/13 (Thuc. VII, 31. 4–5), and on their expulsion from Naupactus in 401 some may well have fled to Cyprus; cf. Meyer, p. 76 n. 3 and Barbieri, *op. cit.* p. 133 n. 1.

[οὐ] μετὰ τῆς ἐκείνου γν[ώ]μης

On the expression cf. I, 1. Barbieri, *op. cit.* p. 133 n. 2, comments: 'volendo far apparire Conone alieno da atti crudeli e inumani, mette in risalto che i Messeni agivano di loro iniziativa'. Such reasoning would presumably regard the crucifixion of the Carpasian (XV, 5) as wholly justified.

τὸ τῶν ἔξ[ω Κυπρ]ίων [πλῆθος

I.e. the Cypriots outside the city. The excellent restoration ἔξ[ω Κυπρ]ίων is due to Lipsius.

ὁ [δ]ẹ̀ Κόνων [.....] κτλ.

For the sense, cf. Meyer, p. 77: 'Konon springt schleunigst durch das Tor in die Stadt zurück.'

[ε]ἰς τὴν πόλιν I.e. Caunus.

ὥς γέ τινες ἔλεγον

As noticed by the first editors (ed.pr. p. 236), it is the professed purpose of the Cypriots themselves which is here indicated, and not any reservation on P's part, in which case ὥς τινες λέγουσι would be expected.

XV, 4 (= Column xvii, 33–column xviii, 3)

[μ]έλλον[τες τοὺς ἐκ] τῆς 'Ρόδου παρ[α]λαβόν[τε]ς εἰς Κύπρον πλε[ῖν,......]εύσαντες δὲ τῆς α.αγ[..]γιοιου καὶ παρακ[αλέσαν]τες τοὺς βουλομέ[νους τῶν Κ]υπρίων, βαδι[......] πρὸς τὴν ἀκρόπο[λιν, ἵνα τὴ]ν ἀρχὴν τ[.........] καταλύσωσι⟨ν⟩ ὡς [αἰτίου μό]νου πάν[των αὐτοῖς τῶ]ν κακῶν, κτλ.

The text of xv, 4 is the subject of my article 'The Mutiny of Conon's Cypriot Mercenaries' in *Proceedings of the Cambridge Philological Society*, n.s. VIII (1962), 13–16. I have there tried to demonstrate that previous restorations of the crucial lacunae in this section do not yield adequate sense, and suggested the following alternatives: Bartoletti's insertion of a comma after εἰς Κύπρον πλε[ῖν at the end of xv, 3, where all earlier editors placed a full stop, and proposal (in his apparatus) of βαδι[εῖσθαι] for the previously accepted reading βαδί[ζουσιν] make all the section under review refer to the intentions of the Cypriot soldiers, and not to what they actually did. This opens the way for acceptance of Kalinka's reading ἐπιπλ]εύσαντες δὲ τῇ Σαλα[μῖ]νι ὅ[π]ου, the only real objection to which had been that the mutineers obviously did not sail to Cyprus. Salamis is the only name we know which fits this lacuna (the scribe would have used the spelling Σαλαμεῖνι), and a place-name is clearly what is required. If this reading is right, however, Wilamowitz's restoration of τ[οῦ Κόνωνος], which appealed to earlier editors, Kalinka included, yields no sense, for no attack on the authority of Conon could have been intended by an assault on Salamis. The man in question is one against whom the mutineers hoped to rally support in Cyprus; he is also the man they blamed for their grievances. He could have been not Conon, but the man who placed the troops at Conon's disposal, presumably Evagoras. His power *could* be assailed by an attack on Salamis, and τ[οῦ Εὐαγόρου], which I proposed, exactly fills the lacuna after ἀρχήν.

ἀ]ποπλεύσαντες ἀπὸ τῆς .[..................]

It is at this point, I suggested (art. cit.), that P would have returned to the narrative of what the Cypriots actually did, and so I restored ἀπὸ τῆς Κ[αύνου... For the general sense of this passage, cf. Bartoletti's note: 'Cyprios milites, opinor, e Cauno navibus egressos, ob aliquam difficultatem, vel potius propter navigandi inscitiam, quominus iter pergerent impeditos esse, eodemque, unde abierant, propere redisse.'

XV, 5 (= Column xviii, 3–22)

Κόνων δὲ κατηγμέ[νων αὐτῶν προσ]ελθὼν κτλ.

The reference is clearly to the return of the mutineers to Caunus after their brief and apparently unsuccessful voyage.

Λεώνυμον τὸν τ[ῶν πεζῶν ὕπαρχον

The position held by Leonymus is not certain. He was in command of οἱ φρουροὶ οἱ Ἕλληνες οἳ τὴν Καῦνον φρουροῦσι and a number of Carian troops. If τ[ῶν πεȝῶν is right, the absence of any indication to the contrary would suggest that he was an officer in charge of a garrison of Persian infantry; Meyer, p. 75, comments: 'eine persische Besatzung unter dem Kommandanten Leonymos liegt', and Barbieri, *Conone*, p. 133, describes Leonymus as 'il comandante persiano di Cauno'. It is evident that he was not a subordinate of Conon. Bartoletti, in his *index verborum*, describes him as 'Cauniorum dux'. Meyer read τ[ῆς Καύνου for τ[ῶν πεȝῶν.

ἐκ τῆς πόλεως

The camp of the Cypriots was outside the city; cf. XV, 2–3.

XV, 6 (= Column xviii, 23–33)

ο]ἱ καταλειφθέντες ἐν τῇ Ῥόδῳ

I take this to mean those of the Cypriots who had been left in Rhodes at the time of Conon's departure for Caunus on his way to visit Tithraustes (XIV, 1), assuming that the mutineers had not been able to sail to Rhodes and pick up their compatriots, as had been their intention (XV, 3).

χαλεπ]ῶς ἐνεγκόντες

An excellent restoration by Bartoletti, who cites Flor.pap. I, 2 and Lond. pap. XIII, 2; XV, 1.

τοὺς μὲν ἄρχοντας τοὺς [ὑπὸ τοῦ Κόνω]νος καταστάντας

These ἄρχοντες had probably been given a special command by Conon on his departure from Rhodes. On Conon's practice, cf. the appointment of Nicophemus and Hieronymus to a general supervisory authority while he was on a previous visit to Caunus (X, 1). Diodorus XIV, 81.4 mentions Hieronymus and Nicophemus (whom he calls Nicodemus) as being left in command when Conon visited the Great King at the time of the

Boeotian War. The failure of P to name these two on the present occasion would seem to me to be an indication that Diodorus' record of a visit to Artaxerxes and P's account of a visit to Tithraustes do not refer to the same event, but that Conon visited the Persian King (or set out to do so) later than the time of the present narrative, i.e. after the end of the extant fragments of P. Cf. further my note to XIV, 1.

τὸ μὲν οὖν βασιλικὸν στρατό[πεδον οὕτ]ως εἰς μέγαν κίνδυνον προελθὸν διὰ Κόνων[α καὶ] τὴν ἐκείνου προθυμίαν ἐπαύσατο τῆς ταραχῆ[ς.

Cf. De Sanctis, *Atti Accad. Torino* LXVI (1931), 184: these events 'vengono riferite con tutti i particolari, per celebrare la sagacia con cui Conone ha superato le difficoltà'.

προθυμίαν

Cf. XIV, 2 and XVI, 6.

XVI, 1 (= Column xviii, 33–column xix, 9)

Chapters XVI and XVII record the details of the campaign of Agesilaus in Phrygia in the autumn of 395. This campaign has been admirably discussed by Dugas, *BCH* XXXIV (1910), especially pp. 76–90. The discrepancies between P and Xenophon on the particulars of this part of the war in Asia are not so marked as those in their respective accounts of the spring campaign in Lydia (P VI–VII), but the two historians differ greatly in their selection of material. P provides more information than Xenophon about the itinerary and the actual military operations of the Spartan king.

'Α]γησίλαος δὲ παρα[π]ορευόμ[εν]ος εἰς τὸν Ἑλλήσπ[ο]ντον ἅμα τῷ στρατ[ε]ύματ[ι τῶν Λ]ακεδαιμονίων κ[α]ὶ τῶν συμμάχων

It appears from the itinerary of Agesilaus after the battle of Sardis, as recorded by P, VII, that the Spartans and their allies returned along the Maeander to Ephesus, and that Ephesus was therefore the starting point for the present march to Phrygia, which, in all probability, was made by the main coast road to the north. P mentions no place on the route before the plain of Thebe, which is just to the south of Mt Ida by Adramyttium. Xenophon gives no details at all as to the activity of Agesilaus after the battle of Sardis (*Hell.* III, 4. 21 ff.) apart from recording his negotiations with Tithraustes (on which see note below). The first geographical location specified by Xenophon is the plain above Cyme (*Hell.* III, 4. 27), and without the more complete information furnished by P one might assume that Agesilaus had taken a fairly direct route from Sardis to Cyme by way of the valley of the Hermus. (The 'plain above Cyme' must refer to that at the mouth of the Caicus. The distance from Cyme to Adramyttium—about fifty miles—is too great for Xenophon's expression to mean the plain of Thebe.) Cyme, although not mentioned by P, would certainly have been on Agesilaus' route from Ephesus to the plain of Thebe. While in the plain above Cyme, Agesilaus received an additional command over the Peloponnesian fleet with the authority to appoint as admiral anyone he should choose; cf. Xen. *Hell.* III, 4. 27: ὄντι δ' αὐτῷ ἐν τῷ πεδίῳ τῷ ὑπὲρ Κύμης ἔρχεται ἀπὸ τῶν οἴκοι τελῶν ἄρχειν καὶ τοῦ ναυτικοῦ ὅπως γιγνώσκοι καὶ καταστήσασθαι ναύαρχον ὅντινα αὐτὸς βούλοιτο. Cf. also Plut. *Ages.* X, 5. The further statement of Xenophon (*Hell.* III, 4. 29) that Agesilaus appointed Peisander to the nauarchia at this point would seem, however, to be erroneous chronologically; cf. my note to XIV, 1.

ὅσον μὲν χ[ρόνο]ν ἐβάδιζε διὰ τῆ[ς] Λυδίας [ο]ὐδὲν κακὸν ἐποί[ει τοὺς] ἐνοικοῦντας, β[ουλ]όμενος ἐμμ[έν]ειν ταῖς σπον[δ]αῖ[ς τ]αῖς πρὸς Τιθραύ[στ]ην γενομ[έναις·]

The truce negotiated by Agesilaus and Tithraustes after the death of Tissaphernes may well have been recorded in a lost section of P either immediately after the account of Tissaphernes' execution in chapter VIII or, if Bartoletti's view (that chapter IX concerns Cyrus the Younger and is occasioned by the account of Tissaphernes' death) is correct, after chapter IX; Diodorus' brief reference to Cyrus (XIV, 80. 6) precedes his mention of the truce made by Agesilaus and Tithraustes (XIV, 80. 8): αὐτὸς δὲ (*sc.* Τιθραύστης) τὸν 'Αγησίλαον πείσας εἰς λόγους ἐλθεῖν ἑξαμηνιαίους ἀνοχὰς ἐποιήσατο. The implication of Diodorus' wording may be, as Dugas remarks (*loc. cit.*), that the two contracting parties met personally. The more detailed account of Xenophon (*Hell.* III, 4. 25–6), however, indicates that Tithraustes negotiated with Agesilaus through the agency of envoys. The Spartan king, given an assurance that the Asiatic Greeks would remain autonomous while paying their traditional tribute to Persia, was first asked to sail home on the grounds that his adversary, Tissaphernes, had been put to death. This, he said, he could not do without instructions from Sparta. Tithraustes then suggested that Agesilaus should march into the territory of Pharnabazus while awaiting further orders from home, and he agreed to do so after obtaining thirty talents for provisions for his troops during their march through Tithraustes' territory. Xenophon does not specify the duration of the truce. Isocrates, *Paneg.* 153, makes the duration eight months, instead of six as in Diodorus' version: τὴν μέν γε μετ' Ἀγησιλάου στρατιὰν ὀκτὼ μῆνας ταῖς αὑτῶν δαπάναις διέθρεψαν. It appears from the present passage of P that one clause of the treaty was that Agesilaus should not molest the Lydians or pillage their land while marching through it. The payment of thirty talents by Tithraustes would thus seem to have been in the nature of compensation for the supplies which the Greeks might have extracted from the inhabitants and land of Lydia.

ἐπειδὴ δὲ κα[τ]ῆ̣ρ̣εν εἰς τὴν χ̣[ώραν] τὴν Φαρν[αβά]ζου κτλ.

Grenfell and Hunt commented (ed.pr. p. 239 n. xviii, 38) that καταίρειν 'is often used by Thucydides for arriving by sea, but is rare in the sense of coming by land'. The use of the word in this latter sense by Theopompus (*F.Gr.Hist.* 115 F 265: Antiattic. καταραι· ἀντὶ τοῦ ἐλθεῖν. Θεόπομπος) led the first editors to hint, erroneously, that the passage of Theopompus and the present passage of P might be identical. Liddell and Scott (9th ed., Jones and McKenzie) list the present use of the word by P under 'of ships', but that this instance does not, in fact, belong to that category becomes apparent from a closer acquaintance with the context. It is, rather, probable that the use of the word to indicate arrival by land is characteristic of P, who appears to use it also at VIII, 2: κα]τῆρεν εἰς [---.

From the point of the arrival of Agesilaus in the territory of Pharnabazus P becomes superior to the accounts of Xenophon and Plutarch in respect of detail concerning his itinerary. Xenophon gives only a brief statement (*Hell.* IV, 1. 1): ὁ δὲ Ἀγησίλαος ἐπεὶ ἀφίκετο ἅμα μετοπώρῳ εἰς τὴν τοῦ Φαρναβάζου Φρυγίαν, τὴν μὲν χώραν ἔκαε καὶ ἐπόρθει, πόλεις δὲ τὰς μὲν βίᾳ, τὰς δ' ἑκουσίας προσελάμβανε. It has been aptly noted by Grenfell and Hunt (ed.pr. p. 239 n. xviii, 39) that P and Xenophon were writing from very different points of view. Hence, in order to illustrate the personality of Agesilaus, Xenophon writes at considerable length on the more dramatic episodes of the campaign, notably the negotiations with the king of Paphlagonia (*Hell.* IV, 1. 2–15), while the military operations do not command much of his attention, no doubt because, as appears from P, there were no notable victories to report. The failure of Agesilaus' attacks on Leonton Cephalae, Gordium and Miletou Teichos is passed over in silence. P, on the other hand, gives an informative account of the itinerary and military ventures, but is not over-concerned with incidentals (such as the marriage of the daughter of Spithridates) which make interesting anecdotes but are scarcely serious matter to the military historian. Plutarch, who generally follows Xenophon, is also very brief (*Ages.* XI, 1): αὐτὸς δὲ (*sc.* Ἀγησίλαος) τὸν στρατὸν καταστήσας εἰς τὴν ὑπὸ Φαρναβάζῳ τεταγμένην χώραν οὐ μόνον ἐν ἀφθόνοις διῆγε πᾶσιν, ἀλλὰ καὶ χρήματα συνῆγε πολλά.

The boundary between the provinces of Tithraustes and Pharnabazus must have been very close to the valley of the Caicus if it did not in fact coincide with the river. Cf. Xen. *Hell.* III, 1. 10; Dugas, art. cit. p. 78; Beloch, *Gr.Gesch.* II, 294 n. 2.

παραλλάξα[ς τ]ό τε Θήβης πεδίον καὶ τ[ὸ 'Απίας] καλούμενον ε[ἰσ]έβαλεν εἰς τὴν Μυσία[ν

The plain of Thebe, crossed by Agesilaus, is that country to the south of Mt Ida in which stands Adramyttium. Agesilaus returned to the plain of Thebe after his departure from Dascylium in the spring of 394 (Xen. *Hell.* IV, 1. 41: ἀφικόμενος δ' εἰς Θήβης πεδίον κατεστρατοπεδεύσατο περὶ τὸ τῆς 'Αστυρηνῆς 'Αρτέμιδος ἱερόν). The restoration τ[ὸ 'Απίας] καλούμενον is due to Wilamowitz (*ap.* ed.pr.). The plain of Apia is not far to the east of Thebe (that is, in the direction of Mysia and Mt Olympus) along the west bank of the Macestus, north of Mt Temnus. Cf. Strabo XIII, 1. 70: Τῆμνον δ' ἐστὶν ὄρος, ὃ διορίζει τοῦτό τε καὶ τὸ καλούμενον 'Απίας πεδίον, ὃ ὑπέρκειται ἐν τῇ μεσογαίᾳ τοῦ Θήβης πεδίου· ῥεῖ δ' ἐκ τοῦ Τήμνου ποταμὸς Μύσιος, ἐμβάλλων εἰς τὸν Κάϊκον ὑπὸ ταῖς πηγαῖς αὐτοῦ. Cf. Polybius V, 77. 9.

Agesilaus pressed forward into Mysia wishing to obtain recruits from among the Mysians, and some, it appears, joined him (ὅσοι μὲν οὖν [τῶν Μυ]σῶν μετέχειν ἠροῦντο τῆς στρατείας). As for those who did not, he ravaged their land. On Mysia and its boundaries, cf. Beloch, *Gr.Gesch.* II, 294 n. 2; Ramsay, *Historical Geography of Asia Minor*, p. 145; Reinach, *Revue Archéologique* (1908), p. 373. Dugas, art. cit. pp. 78–9, suggests that the Mysians were a backward nation of marauders, and recalls the proverbial Μυσῶν λείαν.

εἰσὶ γὰρ οἱ πọλ̣[λ]ọὶ [τ]ῶν Μυσῶν αὐ[τόνομοι καὶ] βασιλέως οὐχ ὑπακούον[τ]ες.

That the Mysians were independent at this time was already known from Xenophon, *Hell.* III, 1. 13, *Anab.* I, 6. 7; 9. 14; II, 5. 13; III, 2. 23, etc.

XVI, 2 (= Column xix, 9–39)

ἐπειδὴ δὲ προϊὼν ἐγένετο κατὰ μέσο[ν μάλι]στα τ[ὸ]ν "Ολυμπον τὸν Μύσιον καλούμεν[ον κτλ.

It is not easy to see why Agesilaus should have entered this difficult and mountainous country when he could, if, as it appears, he wished to avoid

Dascylium, have passed to the south of the Mt Olympus region and reached the valley of the Tembris from that of the Rhyndacus. Dugas (art. cit.) suggests that Agesilaus went astray, or was misled, and did not appreciate the peril until it was too late. The extent of the dangers surrounding the Greeks in the region of Mt Olympus may be inferred from the sudden change of attitude towards the Mysians on the part of Agesilaus. Having delivered a virtual ultimatum to these people to join him or suffer the consequences of refusal, he had ravaged the land of those who rejected his demand. Now, finding himself in difficult country and wishing to make a safe crossing of the Mt Olympus region, he sends representatives to the Mysians and concludes a treaty with them.

παρέντ[ε]ς δὲ π̣.[.......τῶν Π]ε[λ]οποννησίων καὶ τῶν συμ[μ]ά-χ[ων, ἐπιθέμενοι τ]οῖς τελευταίοις αὐτῶν καταβά̣λ̣λ[ουσι...

π̣ο̣[λλούς Grenfell and Hunt; ⟨τοὺς⟩ π̣ο̣[λλούς Wilamowitz; τὸ̣ [πλῆθος Lipsius; 'Fortasse π̣λ̣[είστους et lacunae et vestigiis magis aptum', Bartoletti.

The Mysians, however, did not adhere to the treaty, but, falling upon the Greek rearguard in the narrow defiles of Mt Olympus, killed some fifty of them. Agesilaus, in order to punish the Mysians for the injury they had inflicted, had recourse to an ambush similar in some respects to that with which he had surprised Tissaphernes earlier (VI, 5). In this case, however, the troops employed for the ambush were left behind when the army moved forward, whereas in the previous case they had been sent ahead of the main body of troops. There would not seem to me to be any grounds for regarding the two ambuscades as 'suspiciously conventional', as did the first editors (ed.pr. p. 130). Some 130 Mysians perished in the encounter (XVI, 3), the rest fleeing in terror to their villages. The Greek troops stationed in the ambush were πολλοὺς τῶν μ[ισθοφ]όρων τῶν Δερκυλιδείων καλουμένων. This band of mercenaries, obviously, from its name, formed by Dercylidas and now employed by Agesilaus, is not known from any other source. As Grenfell and Hunt commented (ed.pr. p. 240 n. xix, 23), 'they were no doubt veterans who had served under Cyrus'. Cf. Meyer, p. 36 and Jacoby, *F.Gr.Hist.* IIC, 19.

[κ]α̣τεστρατοπέδευσ⟨ε⟩ν

This restoration, and an alternative -πεδεύσαν⟨το⟩, were suggested by Fuhr, *Berl.Phil.Woch.* (1910), coll. VII, 4 and XVII, 1 and 4. -πεδευσαν p.

XVI, 3 (= Column xix, 39–column xx, 10)

τῶν μὲν Μυσῶν, ὧν ἦσαν [οἱ ἀποθανόντες, ἕκαστοι κή]ρυκας πέμψαντες α̣[................ἀνείλον]το τοὺς νεκροὺς ὑ[ποσπόνδους·

The restoration of Castiglioni, *Gnomon* IV (1928), ἀ[νοχὰς ἐποιοῦντο καὶ ἀνείλον]το, may well be on the right lines, although Bartoletti expresses doubt about the initial α. For phrases similar to ἀνείλοντο τοὺς νεκροὺς ὑποσπόνδους, see VII, 1 and Flor.pap. 1, 1.

'Αγησίλαος δὲ λαβὼν ἐκ τῶν] κωμῶν τινας καθ[ηγεμόνας

As Dugas (art. cit.) aptly commented, it is inconceivable that Agesilaus would have entered unknown mountainous territory without already having guides. He may have felt the need for these to be replaced if he had in fact been misled into the perilous region of Mt Olympus (cf. note above, XVI, 2), but it is perhaps more probable that the guides taken from the Mysians at this time were intended to serve as hostages to guarantee that there should be no new assault on the Greek army.

ἀναπαύσας....] ἡμέρας τοὺς στρ[ατιώτας

Kalinka reads τρεῖς, which is a fair guess (cf. VII, 1), but no more.

ἦγεν εἰς] τὸ πρόσθεν τ[ὸ] στράτευμα, καὶ κα[τα]βιβάσας [εἰς τὴ]ν χώραν τῶν Φ[ρ]υγῶν, οὐκ εἰς [ἥ]ν τοῦ προτέρου [θέρ]ους ἐνέβαλεν, ἀλ[λ' ε]ἰς ἑ[τέ]ραν ⟨οὖσαν⟩ [ἀ]πόρ[θ]ητον, κα[κῶ]ς αὐτὴν ἐποίει

The region entered would presumably be the valley of the Sangarius, or more particularly, perhaps, the valley of its tributary, the Tembris, since it was probably up this valley that Agesilaus reached the town of Leonton Cephalae (XVI, 5). This area of Phrygia Magna had not been ravaged previously and provided an opportunity for the acquisition of sufficient plunder for the needs of the army. P points out that this was not the region invaded by Agesilaus in the previous summer (396), when he reached Dascylium in Hellespontine Phrygia, that is the Phrygia παραθαλαττίδιος of XVII, 3. Cf. Diod. XIV, 79. 3; Xen. *Hell.* III, 4. 11ff.

Σπι[θρ]α̣δάτη[ν

This form of the name is found in the papyrus here and at XVI, 4; also in Ctesias, *Pers. ap.* Phot. 42b37, = *F.Gr.Hist.* 688 F 15. The form Σπιθριδάτης, which appears in XVI, 4 and 6 and XVII, 1, is attested by Xenophon, *Hell.* III, 4. 10; IV, 1. 2ff.; 20ff.; *Anab.* VI, 5. 7; *Ages.* III, 3; V, 5; and by Plutarch, *Ages.* XI; *Lys.* XXIV; also Arrian, *Anab.* I, 12. 8. Yet

Grenfell and Hunt (ed.pr. p. 240 n. xx, 9ff.) state that the form Σπιθραδάτης is more correct (cf. the variant forms of Ῥαθάνης, XVI, 6). Considering it necessary to decide upon one form throughout, the first editors and Meyer read only Σπιθραδάτης, Lipsius and Gigante only Σπιθριδάτης. Bartoletti, like Kalinka and Jacoby, retains both forms in his text, adding rightly 'quid Anonymus scripserit, incertum est'. On Spithridates and his son see further below.

XVI, 4 (= Column xx, 10–21)

ὁ δὲ Σπιθραδά[τ]ης τὸ μὲν γένος ἦν Πέρ[σης, δι]ατρίβω[ν] δ̣ὲ̣ π̣ρ̣ὸ̣ς̣ τῷ Φαρναβάζῳ καὶ θεραπεύων [ἐκεῖ]ν̣ο̣ν̣, ε̣ἶ̣[τα δὲ εἰς] ἔχθραν καταστὰς πρὸς αὐτόν, φοβηθεὶς μ̣[ὴ κατα]λ̣η̣φ̣θ̣ῇ̣ καὶ κακόν τι πάθῃ, παραυτίκα μὲ[ν] ἀπέ[φυγεν] εἰς Κύζικον, ὕστερον δ[ὲ] ὡς Ἀγη[σ]ί[λαο]ν [ἧκεν ἄγω]ν [Με]γαβάτην υ⟨ἱ⟩ὸν νέον ὄντα καὶ καλόν.

Cf. Xen. *Hell.* III, 4. 10: ὁ Λύσανδρος αἰσθόμενος Σπιθριδάτην τὸν Πέρσην ἐλαττούμενόν τι ὑπὸ Φαρναβάζου, διαλέγεται αὐτῷ καὶ πείθει ἀποστῆναι ἔχοντα τούς τε παῖδας καὶ τὰ περὶ αὐτὸν χρήματα καὶ ἱππέας ὡς διακοσίους. καὶ τὰ μὲν ἄλλα κατέλιπεν ἐν Κυζίκῳ, αὐτὸν δὲ καὶ τὸν υἱὸν ἀναβιβασάμενος ἧκεν ἄγων πρὸς Ἀγησίλαον. ἰδὼν δὲ ὁ Ἀγησίλαος ἥσθη τε τῇ πράξει καὶ εὐθὺς ἀνεπυνθάνετο περὶ τῆς Φαρναβάζου χώρας τε καὶ ἀρχῆς. Cf. also Xen. *Ages.* III, 3; Plut. *Ages.* XI, 2; *Lys.* XXIV, 1. Spithridates is mentioned by Xenophon, *Anab.* VI, 5. 7, as being a lieutenant of Pharnabazus. In the *Hellenica*, *loc. cit.*, Xenophon gives rather more detail than does P about his subsequent defection to Agesilaus, indicating that he was persuaded to do so by Lysander. Xenophon dates his meeting with Agesilaus to 396, before the campaign of that year. P gives no indication of the date, and although one might infer, *ex silentio*, that Spithridates joined Agesilaus during the present campaign of autumn 395 there is nothing in P's narrative which contradicts or gives reason to doubt Xenophon's dating of the event. As Dugas (art. cit.) suggests, Agesilaus had probably met Spithridates the previous year and at this point in the campaign of 395 was rejoined by him. I would add, further, that the present section looks like one of the digressions to which P is prone, and that, in consequence, not only the reference to Spithridates' former association with Pharnabazus, but also that to his joining Agesilaus, may belong in time to a period earlier than the present campaign, indeed to the date specified by Xenophon.

Xenophon, *Ages.* III, 3, is the only source to indicate a specific reason for Spithridates' enmity towards Pharnabazus, an enmity which in turn led to his flight to Agesilaus through fear of arrest. The satrap, it appears, was prepared to marry the daughter of the Great King, but wished to take

Spithridates' daughter without offering her marriage. Spithridates interpreted this as a personal insult. The daughter, who is not mentioned by P, is an important figure in Xenophon's account of the negotiations between Agesilaus and the Paphlagonian king (*Hell.* IV, 1. 2–15) in that he was persuaded by Agesilaus to marry her. She does not appear to have accompanied her father when he joined Agesilaus, however (*Hell.* IV, 1. 14–15), and may have been left at Cyzicus (cf. *Hell.* III, 4. 10). On the detail that Spithridates first fled to Cyzicus and subsequently came to Agesilaus, P and Xenophon (*Hell.* III, 4. 10) are in agreement.

As for Spithridates' son, Megabates, described here as young and handsome, P mentions briefly Agesilaus' attachment to him and suggests further that the boy was his main reason for accepting the friendship of Spithridates (μάλιστα μὲν ἕνεκα τοῦ μειρακίου). The relationship between Agesilaus and Megabates is mentioned at greater length by Xenophon, *Ages.* V, 4–5, and Plutarch, *Ages.* XI, but only indirectly implied in Xen. *Hell.* IV, 1. 6 and 28.

P gives as the second reason (ἔπειτα δέ) for Agesilaus' favourable reception of Spithridates the hope that the Persian would be of service as a guide and 'in other respects'. Dugas suggests that after his experience in the region of Mt Olympus (XVI, 2) Agesilaus would not wish to advance into unknown territory without a reliable guide. This would, of course, be true, but it is probable that the initial meeting of Agesilaus and Spithridates took place the previous year and if, as I have suggested, the present section is in the nature of a digression, the hope expressed here that Spithridates would act as a guide would not refer in particular to the march into Phrygia Magna beyond Mt Olympus, but would represent a general wish felt by Agesilaus the previous year. Xenophon implies (*Hell.* III, 4. 10) that one reason for the initial welcome extended to Spithridates was the opportunity he presented for obtaining information about the territory and government of Pharnabazus, and this would seem very reasonable. The knowledge of Pharnabazus' affairs which Spithridates may have had is the most obvious of the 'other respects' mentioned by P.

⟨ἡγούμενος⟩ ἡγεμόνα κτλ. is due to Crönert, coll. XVII, 2, in *Literarisches Zentralblatt* LIX (1908), 22–4. Grenfell and Hunt read ἡγεμόνα τε τῆς στρατιᾶς ⟨ἡγούμενος⟩ αὐτοῖς ἔσεσθαι.

XVI, 5 (= Column XX, 21–9)

ἀφικνεῖται πρὸς χωρίον, ὃ καλεῖται Λεόντων Κεφαλαί.

Accompanied by Spithridates and his son, Agesilaus led the army forward, ravaging the territory of Pharnabazus, and reached the town of Leonton

Cephalae. The exact location of the place is a matter of some uncertainty. Agesilaus must have reached it by way of the valley of the Tembris or the Sangarius, and it presumably lay in the region of one of these rivers, in view of the fact that he marched thence to Gordium. Dugas (art. cit. p. 81) retains the view of Hirschfeld (*Berl.Phil.Woch.* (1891), cols. 1,386f.) that the town was on the site of the modern Afyonkarahisar, but Meyer, p. 25 n. 1, considers this to be untenable. It is probably true that if Agesilaus had already intended to make for Gordium, or if he had already been advised by Spithridates to advance towards Paphlagonia (XVI, 6 would suggest, however, that this advice was given after the failure to capture Gordium), the site of Afyonkarahisar would be too far out of his way to the south. It is also possible, of course, that Leonton Cephalae was an objective itself, in which case a location well to the south of the general direction of the march from Mysia to Paphlagonia would not necessarily be impossible. Ramsay, *Cities and Bishoprics of Phrygia*, pp. 229 and 423, places Leonton Cephalae near Ayaz-Inn. It is known from Plutarch (*Themist.* XXX) that the town was on the main highway from Sardis to Susa, and Meyer, *loc. cit.*, objects to Ramsay's view: 'aber durch dieses Gebiet hat die Heerstrasse schwerlich geführt'. Meyer's statement seems to be based on grounds of probability rather than certainty. Plutarch (*loc. cit.*) uses the form of the name Λεοντοκέφαλον; Appian, *Mithr.* 19 has Λεόντων Κεφαλή, and adds ὃ τῆς Φρυγίας ἐστὶν ὀχυρώτατον χωρίον. Note further Meyer, p. 25: 'Der etwas weiter südlich gelegene Ort Λέοντος Κώμη mit heissen Salzquellen (Athen. II, 43B) hat mit Λεόντων Κεφαλαί nichts zu tun. Benannt sind diese Orte offenbar nach den in diesem ganzen Gebiet sehr zahlreichen mit Löwen dekorierten Denkmälern.'

καὶ ποιησάμενος πρὸς αὐτὸ προσβολάς, ὡς οὐδὲν ἐπέραινεν, ἀναστήσας τὸ στράτευμ[α] προῆγεν εἰς τὸ πρόσθε⟨ν⟩ πορθῶν καὶ λεηλατῶν τῆ[ς] χώρας τὴν ἀκέραιον.

The failure of this assault, and of those on Gordium (XVI, 6) and Miletou Teichos (XVII, 3), is overlooked by Xenophon, who states too simply (*Hell.* IV, 1. 1): πόλεις δὲ τὰς μὲν βίᾳ, τὰς δὲ ἑκουσίας προσελάμβανε. P, it may be noted, does not indicate that a single city was taken by force. As Dugas rightly asserts, it is difficult indeed to doubt (as does Busolt, *Hermes* XLIII (1908), 270) the precise account of P in respect of these places and to accept the more general statement of Xenophon. It would appear rather that Xenophon, hearing of the rich plunder gathered from the Phrygian countryside, assumed that Agesilaus had carried all before him, fortified towns included. In fact his inability to take any strongly fortified place probably made Agesilaus aware of the inadequacy of his force for a trial of strength with Pharnabazus, and the suggestion by Spithridates of an alliance with the king of Paphlagonia (XVI, 6) may have been intended to provide a means of increasing the numerical strength of the Greek army; cf. XVII, 2 and Xen. *Hell.* IV, 1. 3, where Agesilaus is reported to have been given 1,000 head of cavalry and 2,000 foot-soldiers by the Paphlagonian king. Despite the acquisition of these troops the assault on Miletou Teichos (XVII, 3) was also a failure.

πορθῶν καὶ λεηλατῶν

On the vocabulary, cf. XVI, 1: λεηλατῶν καὶ πορθῶν. Cf. Xen. *Hell.* IV, 1. 1 (of the present campaign): τὴν μὲν χώραν ἔκαε καὶ ἐπόρθει.

XVI, 6 (=Column xx, 29–38)

ἀφικόμενος δὲ πάλιν πρὸς Γόρδιον, χωρίον ἐπὶ χώματος ᾠκοδομημένον καὶ κατεσκευασμένον κα⟨λ⟩ῶς

πάλιν, *weiter*: Jacoby, *F.Gr.Hist.* IIC, 19. Agesilaus had not previously been to Gordium. On this use of πάλιν see note to VII, 1. κα⟨λ⟩ῶς: κακωσ p.

Gordium was situated on the Sangarius, a little to the south of the confluence of the Tembris and that river. We now know that it was on or near the highway from Sardis to Susa, by which Agesilaus may have marched from Leonton Cephalae, since remains of the road have been found near the site of Gordium now being excavated. In view of the situation of Gordium upon a mound and the inability of Agesilaus to capture it, despite assaults made for a period of six days, it is surely correct to assume with the first editors that κακῶς in the papyrus is an error. The arguments of Gigante (p. 76), who supports Kalinka's retention of the papyrus reading, that κακωσ is a *lectio difficilior* to be preserved seem to me to have little foundation. The assertion of P that Gordium was not taken owing to the energy of Rhathanes (see below) is not incompatible with the supposition—and the apparent probability—that the town was well fortified, although Gigante's view is that a well fortified site could withstand assault without the need for resolute defence on the part of those within. He is right, however, in claiming that the citation by Grenfell and Hunt of the phrase κατεσκευασμένον καλῶς (*F.Gr.Hist.* 115 (Theopompus) F 31) is irrelevant, for Theopompus is no longer seriously considered a possible author of *Hell.Oxy.* On the other hand, the passage of Thucydides (VIII, 31. 3: προσβολὴν ποιησάμενος τῇ πόλει οὔσῃ ἀτειχίστῳ καὶ οὐ δυνάμενος ἑλεῖν, ἀπέπλευσεν κτλ.) quoted by Gigante 'a conferma della mia opinione' may be thought equally irrelevant. It is also pertinent to ask why, if the place was fortified, it should not have been fairly well fortified. On recent excavations at Gordium see *Archaeological Reports*, 1959–60, pp. 35ff., 1964–5, pp. 41ff. and the reports of discoveries made there since 1950 by R. Young and G. R. Edwards, being published annually in *AJA*.

διὰ τὴν 'Ραθάνου προθυμίαν

For the expression see XIV, 2: διὰ τὴν Κύρου προθυμίαν. Cf. also XV, 6. Rhathanes is mentioned by Xenophon (*Anab.* VI, 5. 7; *Cyrop.* VIII, 3. 32) as one of Pharnabazus' lieutenants at the time of the march of the ten thousand, and (*Hell.* III, 4. 13) as commanding, along with Bagaeus, the bastard brother of Pharnabazus, a detachment of cavalry which engaged Agesilaus' troops near Dascylium in the campaign of 396. Rhathanes is here in command of Gordium. Xenophon uses the form 'Ραθίνης (cf. the variant forms of the name Spithridates; see note to XVI, 3). The papyrus reading πήγησωντογενοσ must clearly be corrected to Π⟨έρσ⟩ης ὢν τὸ γένος, despite the attention drawn to the word πήγης by the scribe, who marked the paroxytone accent (cf. ed.pr. p. 240 n. XX, 35). The only other accent to appear in the London papyrus is in the unplaced fragment 45, where]ήε[is found.

κελεύοντος τοῦ Σπιθριδάτου εἰς Παφλαγονίαν πορεύεσθαι

Cf. Xen. *Hell.* IV, 1. 2: λέγοντος δὲ τοῦ Σπιθριδάτου ὡς εἰ ἔλθοι πρὸς τὴν Παφλαγονίαν σὺν αὐτῷ, τὸν τῶν Παφλαγόνων βασιλέα καὶ εἰς λόγους ἄξοι καὶ σύμμαχον ποιήσοι, προθύμως ἐπορεύετο, πάλαι τούτου ἐπιθυμῶν, τοῦ ἀφιστάναι τι ἔθνος ἀπὸ βασιλέως.

XVII, 1 (= Column XX, 38–column XXI, 4)

π[ρὸς τὰ ὅρια τῆς τε Φρυ]γίας καὶ τῆς Παφλαγον[ί]ας

τε was added by Kalinka; cf. VII, 3: τῆ]ς τ[ε Λυδίας] καὶ τῆς Φρυγίας.

It is probable that Agesilaus followed the main Sardis to Susa route from Gordium as far as the Halys (cf. Anderson in *JHS* XIX (1899), 95) and then turned north following the river downstream as far as the borders of Paphlagonia, where he pitched camp. The words εἰς Παφλαγονίαν πορεύεσθαι (XVI, 6) must therefore be rendered 'towards Paphlagonia' rather than 'into Paphlagonia'. The words of Xenophon, *Hell.* IV, 1. 3, ἐπεὶ δὲ ἀφίκετο εἰς τὴν Παφλαγονίαν, need not imply penetration beyond the frontiers of the country; cf. Plutarch, *Ages.* XI, 1: καὶ προελθὼν ἄχρι Παφλαγονίας. It does not necessarily follow from the fact that

Agesilaus ordered a trireme to be equipped to bring the daughter of Spithridates to Paphlagonia (Xen. *Hell.* IV, 1. 15), that he had crossed the country and had reached the sea. Indeed the expression of P (XVII, 2), ἀπήγα[γε] διὰ ταχ[έων τὴν στρατιὰν ἐπὶ θ]άλατταν (i.e. the Propontis), would seem a little strange if Agesilaus were already on the sea coast, albeit of the Euxine. It is further improbable that Agesilaus would have led his army, accustomed to ravaging the country through which it passed without restraint, into the territory of a king whose alliance he sought. Cf. Dugas, *BCH* XXXIV (1910), 83.

The Paphlagonians, like the Mysians, were in practice independent of the Persian Empire at this time (cf. Xen. *Anab.* V, 6. 6), but in contrast to the Mysians were organized under the authority of a king.

τὸν δὲ Σπ[ι]θριδάτη[ν πρὸς Γύην ἔπεμψε]ν· ὁ δὲ πορευθεὶς καὶ πείσας ἐκεῖ[νον ἐπανῆκεν αὐτὸν] ἄγων.

πρὸς Γύην ἔπεμψε]ν Rühl, *Rhein.Mus.* LXVIII (1913), 197. A variety of forms of the name of the Paphlagonian king is found: Γύης p (at XVII, 2); Ὄτυς Xen. *Hell.* IV, 1. 3–14 (11 times); Κότυς Xen. *Ages.* III, 4 and Plut. *Ages.* III; XI. The Paphlagonian king Θῦς (Theopompus *ap.* Athen. IV, 144F and X, 415D = *F.Gr.Hist.* 115F 179) or Thuys (Nepos, *Datam.* II–III) may well be the same man. Meyer comments (p. 26 n. 3): 'Die Namensform Kotys ist offenbar Assimilation an den bekannten thrakisch-bithynischen Namen und eine sehr alte, schon von Plutarch benutzte, Korrektur in Xenophon's Agesilaos. Γύης im Papyrus wird Schreibfehler sein.' Grenfell and Hunt had noted that the form Γύης is not in itself objectionable (cf. Γύγης), but 'in view of the errors in the papyrus does not carry much weight' (ed.pr. p. 241). Wilamowitz (*ap.* ed.pr.), regarding Θῦς as the correct form, proposed its restoration in P XVII, 2, where γυησ could be corrupt for τυησ = Θῦς. Kalinka and Gigante read Τύης. Bartoletti comments 'nulla est via qua ad ipsius Anonymi manum perveniamus'. There can, further, be no real certainty which attempt to transliterate into Greek the barbarian name comes closest to the original and there can, therefore, be no firm ground for emending the reading of p, or, for that matter, the readings of any of the other texts.

αὐτὸν] ἄγων is due to Rühl (*loc. cit.*); ed.pr. has πρέσβεις] ἄγων. The very reasonable restoration of Rühl would bring P and Xenophon (*Hell.* IV, 1. 3: ἦλθεν Ὄτυς καὶ συμμαχίαν ἐποιήσατο) into agreement that there was a personal meeting between Gyes (or Otys) and Agesilaus, and that the Paphlagonian king came to Agesilaus, who was, in P's version, encamped on the borders of the country.

XVII, 2 (=Column xxi, 4–13)

᾿Αγησίλαος δὲ ποιησάμεν[ο]ς̣ [σπονδάς

Xenophon (*Hell.* IV, 1. 2–15) gives a lengthy account in dramatic form of the conversation between Agesilaus and the Paphlagonian king, yet the only details he provides of the terms of the treaty are that 1,000 horsemen and 2,000 peltasts were placed at Agesilaus' disposal (P probably agrees on these figures; see next note but two) and that a marriage was arranged between the king and the daughter of Spithridates. P makes no mention of the marriage, and it is perhaps unlikely that it was as significant an event in relation to the agreement between Agesilaus and Otys as Xenophon suggests, for Spithridates does not seem to have been a man of great rank or influence, and, whatever the beauty of the girl, Otys would have been marrying someone of inferior family.

ἐποιεῖτο δὲ τὴν πορε[ί]αν οὐκέτ[ι τὴν αὐτὴν ὁδόν, ἥν]περ ἦλθε⟨ν⟩, ἀλλ' ἑτέραν, ἡγ[ού]μενος διὰ [τοῦ Σαγγαρίου] δ̣ιεξιο̣[ῦσιν ἀκο]π̣ω̣τέρως [ἔ]σεσθαι τοῖς σ[τρατιώταις.

τοῦ Σαγγαρίου is due to Dugas, *BCH* XXXIV (1910), 86. Ed.pr. reads τῆς Βιθυνίδος. The restoration of Dugas seems preferable, for the territory of the Bithynians at the beginning of the fourth century was limited and probably did not extend as far south as that part of the Sangarius along which Agesilaus would naturally march on his way to Cius in Mysia. Cf. Meyer, *Gesch. von Troas*, p. 101; Reinach, *Trois Royaumes de l'Asie Mineure*, p. 93. Dugas further notices that a detour north of the Sangarius into what might more precisely be called Bithynia would have been both futile and dangerous, for the country is mountainous and its people, although often at war with Pharnabazus (Xen. *Hell.* III, 2. 2), might well remember the devastations of their land by Dercylidas in 399.

Γύης

On the form of the name see note above, XVII, 1.

ἱππέας μ[ὲν περὶ χιλί]ους, πεζοὺς δὲ πλείου[ς δισχι]λ̣[ί]ων

The numbers restored here bring P into agreement with Xenophon (*Hell.* IV, 1. 3) and Plutarch (*Ages.* XI, 3). It appears, however, that in P's account the Paphlagonian king sent these troops after Agesilaus had set out on his march towards the sea, whereas Xenophon suggests that they were left by the king at the time of his interview with Agesilaus. This is in any case a minor discrepancy (and only a discrepancy if our inferences are right), and Dugas is mistaken in his view that Xenophon's version is only a consequence of a supposed personal meeting between the two men. For Dugas, reading πρέσβεις] (with the first editors) for αὐτὸν] in XVII, 1 (see note *ad loc.*), and preferring P's account as it appeared from this reading, discounted a personal meeting between Agesilaus and the Paphlagonian king. It is perhaps more probable, however, that the troops would be sent at a later date, for, if the meeting took place on the borders of the country, Otys (or Gyes), going for peaceful talks, might not have brought sufficient troops with him to be able to dispense with 3,000 of them on the spot. On the other hand, if he had been accompanied by a large army, that would be an indication of suspicion on his part (and quite understandable) and would answer Dugas's argument that the king would not have trusted Agesilaus sufficiently to visit him in person.

XVII, 3 (= Column xxi, 13–24)

καταγ[αγὼν δὲ τὸ στρ]άτευμα κατὰ Κίον τῆς Μυσίας, [πρῶ]τον μ[ὲν περιμείν]ας ἡμέρας αὐτοῦ δέκα κακῶς ἐποίε[ι] τοὺς Μυσο[ὺς πάλ]ịṿ ἀνθ' ὧν ἐπεβούλευσαν αὐτῷ περὶ τὸν Ὄλυμπον

At Cius in Mysia, near to the coast due west of Lake Ascania, Agesilaus made a halt of ten days, during which he made punitive raids on the Mysians for their treacherous attack on the Greek army in the region of Mt Olympus (cf. XVI, 2–3). P is the only authority for these contacts with the Mysians.

[ὕσ]τερον δὲ προῆγε τοὺς Ἕλληνας διὰ τῆ[ς] Φρυγίας τῆς παρ[αθα]-λαττιδίου

Leaving Cius, Agesilaus entered the Hellespontine region of Phrygia, here called παραθαλαττίδιος. This form of the adjective is also found in Thuc. VI, 62. 3 and Dio Cass. LIV, 9.

καὶ προσβαλὼν πρὸς χ[ω]ρίον τὸ καλούμ[εν]ον Μιλήτου Τεῖχος, ὡς οὐκ ἠδύνατο λαβεῖν, ἀπῆγε [το]ὺς στρατιώτας.

Miletou Teichos is to be identified with the city later known as Μιλητούπολις or Μιλητόπολις; cf. Ramsay, *Historical Geography of Asia Minor*, p. 159. Cf. Strabo XII, 8. 10: ὑπέρκεινται δὲ τῆς Δασκυλίτιδος ἄλλαι δύο λίμναι μεγάλαι, ἥ τε Ἀπολλωνιᾶτις ἥ τε Μιλητοπολῖτις. πρὸς μὲν οὖν τῇ Δασκυλίτιδι Δασκύλιον πόλις, πρὸς δὲ τῇ Μιλητοπολίτιδι Μιλητούπολις, πρὸς δὲ τῇ τρίτῃ Ἀπολλωνία ἡ ἐπὶ Ῥυνδάκῳ λεγομένη. See also Strabo XIV, 5. 29. Lake Miletopolitis is identical with Manyas Gölü, the lake here called Apolloniatis being Apolyont Gölü. The exact location of Miletopolis is not certain, but must have been on the Rhyndacus or the Macestus, either somewhat north-east of Lake Manyas (i.e. about ten miles from the coast) or to the south-east of the lake (about twenty miles from the coast). See Calder and Bean, *A Classical Map of Asia Minor*, supplement to *Anatolian Studies* VII (1957), which marks both possible sites. Agesilaus' attempt to storm the place was unsuccessful, as were those on Leonton Cephalae (XVI, 5) and Gordium (XVI, 6). Xenophon makes no mention of Agesilaus' incursion inland from Cius, stating briefly that after his conference with the king of Paphlagonia αὐτὸς ἐπὶ Δασκυλείου ἀπεπορεύετο (*Hell.* IV, I. 15).

ποιούμενος δὲ τὴν πορείαν παρὰ τὸν Ῥύνδακον ποταμὸν ἀφ[ι]κνεῖται π[ρ]ὸς τὴν Δασκυλῖτιν λίμνην, ὑφ' ᾗ κεῖται τ[ὸ] Δα⟨σ⟩κύλιο[ν], χωρίον ὀχυρὸν σφόδρα καὶ κατεσκευασμ[έ]νον ὑπὸ βασιλέως, οὗ καὶ τὸν Φαρνάβαζον ἔλεγον ἀ[ρ]γύριον ὅ[σον] ἦν αὐτῷ καὶ χρυσίον ἀποτίθεσθαι.

Following the course of the Rhyndacus, Agesilaus reached the Δασκυλῖτις λίμνη, which, despite the statement of Strabo XII, 8. 10 (see p. 145) that there were three separate lakes in this region, may be identical with Lake Manyas. Dascylium has generally been supposed to have been situated on the sea coast to the east of Cyzicus (cf., e.g., Calder and Bean, *A Classical Map of Asia Minor*), although such a site does not help to identify the lake called in antiquity Dascylitis. However, there are now grounds for placing Dascylium at the south-east corner of Lake Manyas, where Ekrem Akurgal's discoveries suggest the relics of the palace of Pharnabazus; cf. J. M. Cook, *Archaeological Reports*, 1959–60, pp. 34–5. Strabo XII, 8. 10 mentions both lake and city: πρὸς τῇ Δασκυλίτιδι (*sc.* λίμνῃ) Δασκύλιον πόλις. While P stresses the strong fortifications of Dascylium, Xenophon (*Hell.* IV, I. 15–16) emphasizes its pleasant surroundings and the location there of Pharnabazus' palace: ἐπὶ Δασκυλείου ἀπεπορεύετο, ἔνθα καὶ τὰ βασίλεια ἦν Φαρναβάζῳ, καὶ κῶμαι περὶ αὐτὰ πολλαὶ καὶ μεγάλαι καὶ ἄφθονα ἔχουσαι τὰ ἐπιτήδεια, καὶ θῆραι αἱ μὲν καὶ ἐν περιειργμένοις παραδείσοις, αἱ δὲ καὶ ⟨ἐν⟩ ἀναπεπταμένοις τόποις, πάγκαλαι. παρέρρει δὲ καὶ ποταμὸς παντοδαπῶν ἰχθύων πλήρης. ἦν δὲ καὶ τὰ πτηνὰ ἄφθονα τοῖς ὀρνιθεῦσαι δυναμένοις. ἐνταῦθα μὲν δὴ διεχείμαζε, καὶ αὐτόθεν καὶ σὺν προνομαῖς τὰ ἐπιτήδεια τῇ στρατιᾷ λαμβάνων. The κῶμαι mentioned by Xenophon could have been situated between the lake and the city, if Dascylium *was* on the coast, and the river abounding in all kinds of fish could be the Odryses.

After his failure to take Miletou Teichos, Agesilaus seems to have made no attempt on Dascylium, but made his encampment on the shores of the lake.

XVII, 4 (= Column xxi, 24–39)

μετεπέμπετο Πά[γ]καλον, ὃς ἐπιβάτης τῷ ναυάρχῳ Χειρικράτει πεπλευκὼ[ς] ἐπεμελεῖτο τοῦ Ἑλλησπόντου πέντε τριήρεις ἔχων.

Pancalus is not otherwise known (cf. *P.Lak.* 584). ἐπιβάτης was thought by Grenfell and Hunt (ed.pr. p. 241 n. xxi, 25–6) to be 'somewhat curious and possibly an error for ἐπιστολεύς'. Bauer, however (*Wiener Studien* XXXII (1910), 315), distinguished ἐπιβάτης as the commander of a small detachment of ships, while ἐπιστολεύς would be a deputy for the nauarch; but Jacoby (*F.Gr.Hist.* IIC, 20) comments: 'ein eigentlicher "titel" ist es wohl nicht'. For ἐπιβάτης, see Thuc. VIII, 61. 2, Xen. *Hell.* I, 3. 17. On Cheiricrates, the Spartan nauarch, see XIV, 1 and note *ad loc.* Xenophon (*Hell.* III, 4. 29) indicates that Peisander was nauarch at this time, being appointed by Agesilaus while the king was in the plain above Cyme at the beginning of the autumn campaign of 395. P, however, here implies that Cheiricrates was still in office at the end of that campaign.

εἰσπλεύσαντος εἰς τὴν λίμνην

As Agesilaus had made no attempt on Dascylium but had encamped on the shores of the Lake Dascylitis, it was into the lake that Pancalus brought his triremes rather than into the port of Dascylium—if, indeed, Dascylium was a port; see note above, XVII, 3. On the navigability of the lake see Plut. *Lucullus* IX, 8: τῆς δὲ Δασκυλίτιδος λίμνης πλεομένης ἀκατίοις ἐπιεικῶς εὐμεγέθεσι, τὸ μέγιστον αὐτῶν ὁ Λεύκολλος ἀνελκύσας καὶ διαγαγὼν ἁμάξῃ πρὸς τὴν θάλατταν ὅσους ἐχώρει στρατιώτας ἐνεβίβασεν.

ἐκεῖ[νον μὲν] ἐκέλευσεν ὁ Ἀγησίλαος ἐνθέμενον ὅσα τῶν [διηρπασμ]-ένων ἦ⟨ν⟩ πλείονος ἄξια διαγαγεῖν εἰς τ[.]ọ.[.....περ]ị Κύζικον, ὅπως {αν} ἀπ' αὐτῶν μισθὸς τῷ [σ]ṭ[ρατεύματι] γένοιτο·

In drawing attention to this incident, P, as Dugas observes, illustrates the practical side of Agesilaus' character. The transportation of the more valuable parts of the booty gained from the ravages of the Phrygian countryside to the safety of Cyzicus or its vicinity would ensure a source of payment for the troops. The position of the Greeks near Dascylium was somewhat perilous, not least, as appears from Xen. *Hell.* IV, 1. 17, on account of the over-confident spirit of the soldiers, whose lack of caution subsequently invited a surprise attack from Pharnabazus' cavalry.

εἰς τ[.]ọ.[.....περ]ị Κύζικον: εἰς τ[όπ]ον [ὀχυρόν, proposed by Crönert (*Literarisches Zentralblatt* LIX (1908)), is a possibility despite Bartoletti's view that 'litterae οπ spatio repugnant' and Gigante's observation that the word τόπος does not recur in the papyrus. Cf. *OCT*, 'τ[όπ]ον fort. caperet prior lacuna'. The traces of a letter after τ[.]ọ would accord well with ṿ and were restored as such in ed.pr. The alternative view is that a place-name was specified here (cf. Bartoletti, 'nomen loci latere videtur'), and while the suggestion is in itself reasonable one cannot even guess which place might be in question. Artace, which would be suitable geographically, does not accord with p, for τ[.]ọṿ would have to become τὴν or τὴν 'A.

τοὺς δὲ στρατιώτας τοὺς ἀπὸ τῆς Μ[υ]σία[ς ἀπέλυσε πρ]οστάξας αὐτοῖς ἥκειν εἰς τὸ ἔαρ

Cf. XVI, 1: ὅσοι μὲν οὖν [τῶν Μυ]σῶν μετέχειν ἠροῦντο τῆς στρατείας... As it appears from P's geographical details that these Mysians joined Agesilaus after his crossing of the plain of Apia but before his arrival in the region of Mt Olympus, their homes were obviously not far from Dascylium.

παρα[σκ]ευα[ζόμενος τ]ὸν ἐπιόντα χειμῶνα βαδίζειν εἰς Καππα[δοκίαν

Grenfell and Hunt (ed.pr. p. 241 n. xxi, 35–9) commented: 'τ]ὸν ἐπιόντα χειμῶνα is to be connected closely with παρα[σκ]ευα[ζόμενος, not with βαδίζειν, a winter campaign being, of course, out of the question'. They translate (ed.pr. p. 238): 'The soldiers from Mysia he dismissed with orders to return in the spring, as he was preparing during the coming winter to invade Cappadocia, having heard', etc. The sentence construction does not seem to me to admit such an interpretation, however, for παρασκευαζόμενος, subordinate to ἀπέλυσε and probably offering some explanation for the dismissal of the Mysians until spring, should refer to the time of the dismissal. A more acceptable explanation of the difficulty inherent in the text is the tentative restoration of Bartoletti, ⟨μετὰ⟩ τὸν ἐπιόντα χειμῶνα. Jacoby's assumption (*F.Gr.Hist.* IIA, 35) of a grave corruption which he emended to τὸ ἐπιὸν θέρος is thus rendered unnecessary.

Xenophon (*Hell.* IV, 1. 41) does not mention Cappadocia specifically, but indicates that Agesilaus had ambitious plans for the future. Before he could attempt to execute these plans he was recalled to Greece (Xen. *Hell.* IV, 2. 2ff.) Grenfell and Hunt noted (ed.pr. p. 242) that in any case 'the plan itself was based on a complete misunderstanding of the geography'. See further below.

ἀκού]ων ταύτην τὴν χώραν διατείνειν ὥσ[περ ταινία]ṿ στενὴν ἀρξα[μ]ένην ἀπὸ τῆς Ποντικῆς [θαλάττης μ]έχρι Κιλικίας κ[αὶ] Φοινίκης, καὶ τ[ὸ] μῆκος [αὐτῆς εἶν]αι τοσοῦτο[ν ὥσ]τε τοὺς ἐκ Σινώπ[η]ς βαδί[ζοντας---

Agesilaus' erroneous conception of the geography is in keeping with the misguided view of the Greeks that Asia Minor was 'a kind of triangle, of which the apex was formed by a comparatively narrow isthmus joining Sinope to the Gulf of Issus' (ed.pr. p. 242; *q.v.* further).

ταινία]ṿ στενήν

Herodotus I, 72 describes Cappadocia as αὐχήν.

τοὺς ἐκ Σινώπ[η]ς βαδί[ζοντας

Cf. Hdt. II, 34: ἡ δὲ Αἴγυπτος τῆς ὀρεινῆς Κιλικίης μάλιστά κῃ ἀντίη κεῖται. ἐνθεῦτεν δὲ ἐς Σινώπην τὴν ἐν τῷ Εὐξείνῳ πόντῳ πέντε ἡμερέων ἰθέα ὁδὸς εὐζώνῳ ἀνδρί. ἡ δὲ Σινώπη τῷ Ἴστρῳ ἐκδιδόντι ἐς θάλασσαν ἀντίον κεῖται. Cf. also Hdt. I, 72: μῆκος ὁδοῦ εὐζώνῳ ἀνδρὶ πέντε ἡμέραι ἀναισιμοῦνται. Consequently Grenfell and Hunt suggested that the sentence in P might continue with something like ἐντὸς πέντε ἡμερῶν εἰς Σόλους πορεύεσθαι.

As Herodotus reckons a day's journey at 200 stades (IV, 101. 3) or 150 stades (V, 53), and the actual distance from Sinope to Soli or the Gulf of Issus is over 300 miles (say 2,500 stades), his estimate of the distance is far too low, even if the εὔζωνος ἀνήρ could travel faster than the average traveller. Hesychius, *s.v.*, defined εὔζωνος as μὴ ἔχων φορτίον. Scylax 102 also gives five days as the time taken on the journey from Sinope to Soli; Ps.-Scymnus 917ff. gives seven days. Even Pliny, *NH* VI, 7, thought the distance only 200 Roman miles: *oppida Gamge, Carusa, Amisum liberum a Sinope* CXXX M *passuum, eiusdem nominis sinus tanti recessus, ut Asiam paene insulam faciat,* CC M *passuum haut amplius per continentem ad Issicum Ciliciae sinum.* The time quoted by Herodotus has been explained as that taken by relays of Persian postal runners; cf. Wiedemann, *Herodots zweites Buch*, p. 145.

APPENDIX 1

THE BATTLE OF SARDIS

The battle of Sardis, fought between the armies of Agesilaus and Tissaphernes either in the valley of the Hermus or on the banks of the Pactolus, took place in the spring of 395 B.C. The nature and course of the battle admit of no immediate certainty, not on account of lack of information, of which we have on the contrary a good deal, but because the two main sources, P and Xenophon, differ so greatly in their versions of what actually happened. Let us, therefore, review the two versions.

Hellenica Oxyrhynchia VI, 4–6

Approaching Sardis by way of the Hermus valley and harassed by the forces of Tissaphernes in close attendance, Agesilaus decided to deliver a surprise attack. A number of hoplites (perhaps 900) and light-armed troops (perhaps 500) were therefore placed under the command of Xenocles, a Spartiate, and sent by night in advance of the army with instructions to lie in ambush and prepare for battle when the main body of the army marched past them. The Persians, whom we know from Diodorus' account (based upon P) to have made attacks on the Greek rearguard, were presumably following quite closely. Next day the Greeks advanced, with the Persians in pursuit as usual. When Xenocles considered the time opportune for the surprise attack, his men charged at the double. The Persians, in no formation to give battle, fled at once, whereupon Agesilaus despatched his cavalry and light-armed soldiers in pursuit. About 600 of the Persians were killed, but the pursuit was then abandoned, as there was little chance of overtaking the majority of the barbarians, who were either on horseback or unarmed. Returning from the chase, the Greeks attacked the Persian camp, which was poorly guarded, and captured supplies, prisoners, and miscellaneous booty including the property of Tissaphernes himself. The Persians retired with Tissaphernes to Sardis, in fear of the Greeks, while Agesilaus, setting up a trophy and returning the enemy dead under a truce, spent three days in plundering the countryside and then led his army away towards Phrygia Magna.

The account of Diodorus (XIV, 80. 2–4), which is clearly derived from P's version, nevertheless differs from it in three particulars: (1) Agesilaus is represented as attacking before Xenocles, who only acts on a given signal. (2) Diodorus speaks of a καρτερὰ μάχη, whereas the Persians, according to P, offered no resistance. (3) The number of Persians killed is given as 6,000 instead of 600. These differences are adequately explained by Dugas,[1] the first two resulting from the fact that Diodorus did not use P's work directly as a source, but the work of Ephorus, which in turn was based directly on P, the third being assumed an error of transmission in the MSS. καρτερὰ μάχη, as noticed by Jacoby,[2] is an Ephorean phrase, but the tendency of Ephorus to exaggerate the importance of battles makes it unnecessary to suppose that here Xenophon's *Hellenica* was his source. As we shall see, the battle in Xenophon's version was a far more serious affair than in that of P.

Xenophon, *Hellenica* III, 4. 21–5

ὁ δ' Ἀγησίλαος οὐκ ἐψεύσατο, ἀλλ' ὥσπερ προεῖπεν εὐθὺς εἰς τὸν Σαρδιανὸν τόπον ἐνέβαλε. καὶ τρεῖς μὲν ἡμέρας δι' ἐρημίας πολεμίων πορευόμενος πολλὰ τὰ ἐπιτήδεια τῇ στρατιᾷ εἶχε, τῇ δὲ τετάρτῃ ἧκον οἱ τῶν πολεμίων ἱππεῖς. καὶ τῷ μὲν ἄρχοντι τῶν σκευοφόρων εἶπε⟨ν ὁ ἡγεμὼν⟩ διαβάντι τὸν Πακτωλὸν ποταμὸν στρατοπεδεύεσθαι, αὐτοὶ δὲ κατιδόντες τοὺς τῶν Ἑλλήνων ἀκολούθους ἐσπαρμένους εἰς ἁρπαγὴν πολλοὺς αὐτῶν ἀπέκτειναν. αἰσθόμενος δὲ Ἀγησίλαος, βοηθεῖν ἐκέλευσε τοὺς ἱππέας. οἱ δ' αὖ Πέρσαι ὡς εἶδον τὴν βοήθειαν, ἠθροίσθησαν καὶ ἀντιπαρετάξαντο παμπληθέσι τῶν ἱππέων τάξεσιν. ἔνθα δὴ ὁ Ἀγησίλαος γιγνώσκων ὅτι τοῖς μὲν πολεμίοις οὔπω παρείη τὸ πεζόν, αὐτῷ δὲ οὐδὲν ἀπείη τῶν παρεσκευασμένων, καιρὸν ἡγήσατο μάχην συνάψαι, εἰ δύναιτο. σφαγιασάμενος οὖν τὴν μὲν φάλαγγα εὐθὺς ἦγεν ἐπὶ τοὺς παρατεταγμένους ἱππέας, ἐκ δὲ τῶν ὁπλιτῶν ἐκέλευσε τὰ δέκα ἀφ' ἥβης θεῖν ὁμόσε αὐτοῖς, τοῖς δὲ πελτασταῖς εἶπε δρόμῳ ὑφηγεῖσθαι. παρήγγειλε δὲ καὶ τοῖς ἱππεῦσιν ἐμβάλλειν, ὡς αὐτοῦ τε καὶ παντὸς τοῦ στρατεύματος ἑπομένου. τοὺς μὲν δὴ ἱππέας ἐδέξαντο οἱ Πέρσαι· ἐπεὶ δ' ἅμα πάντα τὰ δεινὰ παρῆν, ἐνέκλιναν, καὶ οἱ μὲν αὐτῶν εὐθὺς ἐν τῷ ποταμῷ ἔπεσον, οἱ δ' ἄλλοι ἔφευγον. οἱ δ' Ἕλληνες ἐπακολουθοῦντες αἱροῦσι καὶ τὸ στρατόπεδον αὐτῶν. καὶ οἱ μὲν πελτασταί, ὥσπερ εἰκός, εἰς ἁρπαγὴν ἐτράποντο. ὁ δ' Ἀγησίλαος κύκλῳ πάντα καὶ φίλια καὶ πολέμια περιεστρατοπεδεύσατο. καὶ ἄλλα τε πολλὰ χρήματα ἐλήφθη, ἃ ηὗρε πλέον ἢ ἑβδομήκοντα τάλαντα, καὶ αἱ κάμηλοι δὲ τότε ἐλήφθησαν, ἃς Ἀγησίλαος εἰς τὴν Ἑλλάδα ἀπήγαγεν. ὅτε δὲ αὕτη ἡ μάχη ἐγένετο, Τισσαφέρνης ἐν Σάρδεσιν ἔτυχεν ὤν.

The same account, with a few insignificant variations, appears in Xenophon's *Agesilaus*, I, 29–32. Of the briefer accounts of other authors, we may note that Plutarch, *Agesilaus* X, 1–4, follows Xenophon except in that he represents Tissaphernes as having taken part in the battle, and appears to waver between the versions of P and Xenophon in deciding in

[1] *BCH* XXXIV (1910), 68.

[2] *F.Gr.Hist.* IIC, 12.

what order the Greek troops engaged in the battle. Plutarch mentions the cavalry and peltasts as attacking first, the hoplites later. Nepos, *Agesilaus* III, 4–5, is apparently based on Xenophon's account, and Pausanias III, 9. 6 on that of Diodorus, placing the battle against Tissaphernes in the valley of the Hermus.

The discrepancies between P and Xenophon, then, are considerable. In the first place P has previously indicated that the Greeks were approaching Sardis along the Hermus valley from the region of Sipylus, while Xenophon implies that their approach was from Tmolus along the Pactolus. Then, in P's account Tissaphernes and his army followed the Greeks, perhaps from Sipylus, and caused them some trouble by attacks on the rearguard. In Xenophon's version the Persian cavalry seem to make their first appearance immediately before the battle commenced. Tissaphernes appears to take part in the battle in P, but Xenophon states that he was in Sardis at the time. Xenophon gives no hint of the ambush which P describes in detail, and makes no mention of Xenocles in connection with the battle. The first to attack, according to P, were the hoplites and light-armed forces under Xenocles, the Greek cavalry and the rest of the light-armed troops joining in later. According to Xenophon, the Greek cavalry attack first, followed by selected hoplites and peltasts. In the one version the Persians offer no resistance, taking to flight at the first Greek charge; in the other a pitched battle takes place. In P's version the Greeks return from their pursuit of the Persians in order to reach the Persian camp, yet Xenophon indicates that it was while pursuing the Persians that the Greeks reached their camp.

Hatzfeld comments most aptly that 'seule la circonstance du pillage du camp de Tissapherne... permet de croire qu'il s'agit du même événement'.[1] One might add, however, that both historians locate the scene of the battle near the Persian camp, and, if one concedes that the initial Persian raids in P's version cannot be regarded as part of the battle proper, both represent the Greeks as being the first to attack. Yet one may with justification consider these to be minor points of agreement by contrast with the points on which the two versions differ, and it may not, therefore, be unprofitable to re-examine the possibility that the two historians are not, in fact, referring to the same battle.

Such a hypothesis presents an immediate difficulty, recognized by Grenfell and Hunt,[2] in that if Agesilaus had won two important victories, it is not likely that Xenophon would have omitted one of them. Yet there is a distinct possibility that Xenophon's account of this particular part of the campaign of 395 is in a state of considerable confusion, and that clearly caused by a lack of information about the movements of the Greek

[1] Xénophon, *Helléniques* I–III, ed. Budé, p. 142 n. 1. [2] Ed.pr. p. 217.

army. Xenophon's primary source of information concerning the campaigns of Agesilaus in Asia may well have been his own eyewitness. His informative account of the preparations at Ephesus before the march to Sardis (*Hell.* III, 4. 16–19), while of little relevance to the military operations, reads like that of an eyewitness, for the events would clearly have impressed those who were in Ephesus at the time and saw the gymnasia and hippodrome filled with Greek soldiers exercising themselves in athletics and riding, or the market-place inundated with unaccustomed merchandise, horses and weapons of war. This narrative provides sharp contrast with the section which follows, recording the march of Agesilaus to Sardis. Xenophon, when compared with P or Diodorus, appears to know no details whatever of the route taken by the Greeks, nor of any incidents occurring during the march. The reason for this contrast, I suggest, is that Xenophon remained in Ephesus when Agesilaus left. Let us recall *Hellenica* III, 4. 20: Ἐν δὲ τούτῳ τῷ χρόνῳ (i.e. while the army was at Ephesus) καὶ ὁ ἐνιαυτὸς ἤδη ἀφ' οὗ ἐξέπλευσεν ὁ Ἀγησίλαος διεληλύθει, ὥστε οἱ μὲν περὶ Λύσανδρον τριάκοντα οἴκαδε ἀπέπλεον, διάδοχοι δ' αὐτοῖς οἱ περὶ Ἡριππίδαν παρῆσαν. τούτων Ξενοκλέα μὲν καὶ ἄλλον ἔταξεν ἐπὶ τοὺς ἱππέας, Σκύθην δὲ ἐπὶ τοὺς νεοδαμώδεις ὁπλίτας, Ἡριππίδαν δ' ἐπὶ τοὺς Κυρείους... The appointment of Herippidas was no doubt in succession to Xenophon himself,[1] of whom we hear no more until his departure from Ephesus in the following spring to return to Greece with Agesilaus.[2]

Now if this hypothesis is accepted, it becomes probable that the apparent deficiencies of Xenophon's account of the spring campaign of 395 by comparison with that of P[3] are due to his lack of first-hand knowledge and the uncertain memory of his informants. The result could be either that Xenophon's account of the battle of Sardis is so incomplete or inaccurate as to render it barely recognizable as the same battle as that described by P, or that Xenophon was, in fact, recording another battle, the skirmish (for it is little more) narrated by P being overlooked along with the other details of the march from Ephesus to Sardis. Let us examine the possibilities of this second alternative.

In the first place, the two supposed battles would have taken place at about the same time and in about the same region in view of their positions in the narratives of P and Xenophon. It ought, therefore, to be possible, with the considerable information at our disposal, to attempt a reconstruction of events to include both supposed engagements. Can we, then, find any possible 'points of contact' between the two historians other than the rather slight agreements in their accounts of the actual battle

[1] Cf. Xen. *Hell.* III, 2. 7, and Hatzfeld, ed. Budé, note to p. 122 on p. 164.
[2] Xen. *Anab.* V, 3. 6. [3] Cf. Dugas, *BCH* XXXIV (1910), 58–76.

which have already been noticed? The following might be suggested: (1) Xenophon speaks of three days spent advancing through a country devoid of enemy troops and acquiring abundant provisions after Agesilaus entered the region around Sardis. This was *before* the battle. P speaks of three days spent ravaging the region around Sardis *after* the battle. Could these be the same three days? (2) Xenophon indicates that the Greeks were scattered in search of plunder *before* the battle. P mentions the abandoning of the πλινθίον and the search for plunder *after* the battle.

A reconstruction based on these observations would then be something in the nature of the following: the Persians caught up with the Greeks around Sipylus, whereupon Agesilaus formed the πλινθίον, and the ambush of Xenocles, not by any means a full-scale battle, took place in the valley of the Hermus (all as in P's version). Xenophon, giving no details of the march to Sardis, makes no mention of this brief encounter. From this point one would have to equate the two versions as follows:

Hell.Oxy.	Xenophon
(1) The barbarians retire to Sardis. The Greeks stay in the region for three days and ravage the whole country.	The Greeks enter the immediate vicinity of Sardis and march for three days through a country devoid of foes, plundering as they go.
(2) Then (on the fourth day presumably) they march forward towards Phrygia Magna. The soldiers, no longer in a column, are allowed to forage as they wish. Tissaphernes and his troops follow at some distance.	On the fourth day the Persian cavalry appear and attack some Greeks who are foraging. The Persian infantry is well behind and, like Tissaphernes, does not engage in the battle. The Greeks rout the Persian cavalry.
(3) Tissaphernes had been in Sardis.	Tissaphernes was still in Sardis.

Such a reconstruction, however, must be rejected for two reasons: (1) It is not so much the omission by Xenophon, as the first editors argued, of what would be the first of the two battles, as the omission of the second by P which would be inexplicable, and highly improbable. (2) In the *Agesilaus* (I, 33–4), although not in the *Hellenica*, Xenophon does accord with P in mentioning the devastation of the plain of Sardis after the battle.

One is compelled to conclude, therefore, that the two highly discordant accounts refer in fact to one and the same battle. How, then, does one explain the remarkable lack of agreement between the sources?

The greater detail in P's account, not only concerning the battle, but also in the record of the events which preceded and followed it, might reasonably lead one to the assumption that this version is derived from a reliable authority. The description of the ambush and the mention by name of Xenocles as leading the detachment entrusted with its execution are not the sort of details which would be readily invented or conjectured by an historian such as P, unless our general impressions regarding his character and approach to history are wildly mistaken. Meyer[1] suggested that P's source here was probably some kind of camp journal; it seems likely, at any rate, that P was able to consult some documentary evidence, and that probably compiled during the actual course of the campaign. If P's account is indeed based upon such a source, it is more likely to be reliable than that of Xenophon, which, to my mind, appears to have been based on the verbal report of a participant made at some later date. The implication of this argument is that one should seek the causes of the discrepancies between the two versions in that of Xenophon, and consider the possibility of Xenophon's account, rather than that of P, being erroneous in respect of certain details of the battle.

Two studies along these lines, by Cornelius[2] and Dugas,[3] particularly merit our attention. Cornelius, while accepting Xenophon's description of the battle as reliable, finds the answer to the problem of his disagreement with P in the supposition that Xenophon has recorded only a partial view of the battle, that is, a view obtained by a participant who was unable to see the broader aspects of the engagement beyond that part in which his own duties fell. While this view is not in itself improbable, the further suggestion by Cornelius, albeit made in a most tentative manner, that the participant in question was Xenophon himself, possibly being the ἄρχων τῶν σκευοφόρων mentioned in *Hell.* III, 4. 22, would seem to me to be most unlikely. In the first place, as I have suggested before, there are grounds, if not strong ones, for believing that Xenophon may have stayed in Ephesus when the army marched to Sardis. In the second place, I regard the case for the emendation of *Hell.* III, 4. 22 from καὶ τῷ μὲν ἄρχοντι τῶν σκευοφόρων εἶπε διαβάντι τὸν Πακτωλὸν ποταμὸν στρατοπεδεύεσθαι to καὶ τῷ μὲν ἄρχοντι τῶν σκευοφόρων εἶπε⟨ν ὁ ἡγεμὼν⟩ κτλ. (coll. Xen. *Ages.* I, 30) as very strong. Such an emendation makes it clear that the ἄρχων τῶν σκευοφόρων was not a Greek at all, but a Persian.

The alternative explanation of Xenophon's version of the battle is that the historian was not present at the time and was rather remiss in his inquiries into the details (just as he appears to have made no attempt to

1 *Theopomps Hellenika*, p. 146.

2 'Die Schlacht bei Sardes', *Klio* XXVI (1933), 29–31.

3 'La campagne d'Agésilas en Asie Mineure', *BCH* XXXIV (1910), 66–73.

discover the details of the route taken from Ephesus to Sardis), while his informant seems to have had no very precise knowledge or memory of the actual encounter. On some such assumption as this, Dugas has provided most attractive reasons for some of the discrepancies between Xenophon and P:

(1) Xenophon represents the Greek cavalry as attacking first because he knew that Xenocles led the first attack and that Xenocles was normally in command of the cavalry. He did not know, however, that on this occasion Xenocles had a special mandate and was given a special body of troops with which to execute his task.

(2) From this false assumption Xenophon is obliged to introduce the Greek hoplites at a later stage in the battle, knowing that some hoplites participated, but never imagining that they might have been under the command of Xenocles.

(3) The place at which the battle took place, Xenophon knew, was on the route by which the Greeks reached Sardis from Ephesus, and some little distance before their arrival at Sardis. His lack of information about the route leads him to suppose that the river near the scene of the battle was the Pactolus and not the Hermus.

(4) It is natural that Xenophon should assume that the Persians fled across the Pactolus towards their camp, for he knew nothing of the ambush, in consequence of which, following P, the Persians had been cut off from their camp.

(5) Xenophon's incomplete account leaves a mystery surrounding the whereabouts of the Persian infantry. Only the Persian cavalry took part in the battle, but if the σκευοφόροι had already arrived on the scene of the battle the infantry could not be far behind, and would have arrived in time to intervene if the battle was, in fact, as Xenophon indicates, a full-scale engagement of considerable duration.

The account of Xenophon, therefore, would appear to be a reconstruction of events based on a few established facts: that the cavalry, almost alone of the Persians, took part; that Xenocles led the first attack; that other Greek troops later joined battle. I am led to the same conclusion as Dugas. The version of P gives the clearer and more satisfactory picture of the battle of Sardis. The Persian cavalry and infantry had spent the night before the battle in camp. In the morning, the cavalry, as was customary, advanced first, while the infantry raised camp without particular haste. The battle must have been of short duration, giving the Greeks time to pursue the Persian cavalry some way across the plain, return, and still reach the Persian camp before the infantry set out. Taken unawares, the Persian infantry fled without offering resistance, leaving the camp in the hands of Agesilaus.

APPENDIX 2

THE CONSTITUTION OF BOEOTIA

Hellenica Oxyrhynchia, chapter XI, has contributed greatly to our knowledge in that we are here presented with an account in some detail of the political organization both of the individual cities of Boeotia and of the Boeotian Confederacy. The importance of the chapter, despite its being in the nature of a digression from the main narrative, is beyond question, and the first editors considered it 'the most valuable portion of the whole papyrus'.[1] Their view has found ample support among scholars, for of the many published works treating of the historical content of the papyrus, as distinct from questions such as that of the authorship, more have been concerned with the Boeotian Constitution than with any other subject.[2] It may not be out of place, however, to suggest, when one considers the mass of highly interesting new material provided by the papyrus on the campaigns of Agesilaus or on the activity of Conon, that the relative value of the section on the Boeotian Constitution may have been a little exaggerated because of a greater interest among historians in general in political history than in military history.

The constitution described in this chapter is that which was in force before the dissolution of the Boeotian League under the terms of the King's Peace.[3] In the absence of any evidence to the contrary it is highly probable that this had been the form of the constitution since the recovery of independence from Athens in 447, and this view is supported by the evidence of Boeotian coins, which during the period 447–386, in sharp contrast with the period 457–447, do not bear as legends the names of the individual cities of Boeotia, Thebes alone excepted.[4]

The various cities of Boeotia all had the same form of local government. In each city there were four councils; each of these in rotation acted as a probouleutic body which brought proposals before the other three.

[1] Grenfell and Hunt, ed.pr. p. 119, and again p. 224.

[2] Particular mention should be made of: Glotz, *BCH* XXXII (1908), 271–8; Goligher, *CR* XXII (1908), 80–2; Swoboda, *Klio* X (1910), 315–34; Bonner, *CP* V (1910), 405–17; Cloché, *Thèbes de Béotie*, pp. 71–4; Larsen, *Representative Government*, pp. 31 ff., and *TAPA* LXXXVI (1955), 40–50; Ehrenberg, *The Greek State*, pp. 123–4.

[3] Cf. Xen. *Hell.* V, 1. 33: Θηβαῖοι δ' εἰς τὰς σπονδὰς εἰσελθεῖν ἠναγκάσθησαν, αὐτονόμους ἀφέντες τὰς Βοιωτίας πόλεις.

[4] Cf. Head, *Historia Numorum*², p. 346.

Resolutions adopted by all four became valid. The historian's wording suggests that the four voted separately and that one negative vote was sufficient to reject any motion. Not all citizens were eligible to become councillors, but only those able to satisfy a certain property qualification. In this respect the constitution conformed to Greek oligarchic theory, and was considered in antiquity to be oligarchic.[1] We know that at Thebes a law excluded from office those who had been artisans within a period of ten years.[2] At Thespiae it was something of a disgrace to learn a mechanical job or to work the land with one's hands,[3] while at Orchomenus the census seems to have been based on a measure of forty-five medimni.[4] In general, in view of the prominence of Boeotian hoplites, it may not be unreasonable to suggest that the property qualification was the equivalent of a hoplite census. It is very likely that there was also an age qualification for magistracy.

For purposes of federal administration Boeotia was divided into eleven districts or wards, not geographical, but in proportion to population. Thus Thebes controlled four wards, two for the city, and two for Plataea, Scolus, Erythrae, Scaphae and some other small towns which were at this time subject to Thebes although they had previously formed one state with Plataea. Orchomenus together with Hysiae made up two wards, and Thespiae along with Eutresis and Thisbae a further two. Tanagra formed one ward, and the six smaller sovereign cities made up two, Haliartus, Lebadea and Coronea being grouped together to form one, and Acraephium, Copae and Chaeronea the other. Each ward supplied one Boeotarch. In the two wards comprising three sovereign cities, one of the three provided the Boeotarch in rotation. Similarly each ward supplied sixty bouleutae for the federal council, which sat in the Cadmea at Thebes. The first editors, citing Thucydides v, 38. 2 (ταῖς τέσσαρσι βουλαῖς τῶν Βοιωτῶν...αἵπερ ἅπαν τὸ κῦρος ἔχουσι), misinterpreted the organization and functions of the federal council. They commented:[5] 'The present passage, however, brings out a new fact of

[1] Thuc. v, 31. 6: αὐτοῖς (*sc.* Βοιωτοῖς) ὀλιγαρχουμένοις. Cf. Thuc. iv, 76. 2.

[2] Arist. *Pol.* 1278a25: ἐν Θήβαις δὲ νόμος ἦν τὸν δέκα ἐτῶν μὴ ἀπεσχημένον τῆς ἀγορᾶς μὴ μετέχειν ἀρχῆς; 1321a26: τὴν δὲ μετάδοσιν γίνεσθαι τῷ πλήθει τοῦ πολιτεύματος ἤτοι καθάπερ εἴρηται πρότερον, τοῖς τὸ τίμημα κτωμένοις, ἢ καθάπερ Θηβαίοις, ἀποσχομένοις χρόνον τινὰ τῶν βαναύσων ἔργων...

[3] Heracleid. *fr.* 43: παρὰ Θεσπιεῦσιν αἰσχρὸν ἦν τέχνην μαθεῖν καὶ περὶ γεωργίας διατρίβειν. καὶ διὰ τοῦτο πένητες οἱ πλείους ἦσαν καὶ Θηβαίοις οὖσι φειδωλοῖς πολλὰ ὤφειλον.

[4] Arist. *ap.* Pollux x, 165: ἐν δὲ Ἀριστοτέλους Ὀρχομενίων πολιτείᾳ μέτρον ἔστιν Ὀρχομενίων τετταράκοντα πέντε μεδίμνους χωροῦν Ἀττικούς.

[5] Ed.pr., p. 224 note xi, 38ff.

considerable value, that the four βουλαί were not councils of the Boeotian League as a whole, but existed in each of the separate states which formed the federation. Thucydides' expression ταῖς τέσσαρσι βουλαῖς τῶν Βοιωτῶν is therefore somewhat misleading, since the natural supposition is that he meant βουλαί of the league. There was indeed, in addition to the four βουλαί in the individual states, one federal βουλή for Boeotia,...but it is clear that Thucydides is not referring to this.' The immediate objections to their view that the supreme authority rested with the state councils and not the federal council were voiced by Glotz (*BCH* XXXII (1908), 271–8) and Goligher (*CR* XXII (1908), 80–2). The objections are the following:

(1) The historian indicates that he has been describing purely local affairs by the words καὶ τὰ μὲν ἴδια διετέλουν οὕτω διοικούμενοι, and then passes to federal affairs: τὸ δὲ τῶν Βοιωτῶν τοῦτον ἦν τὸν τρόπον συντεταγμένον. His description of the four councils in each of the cities falls within the section relating to local affairs.

(2) Thucydides, in the passage quoted, is dealing with a point of foreign policy. If the local councils had full power in deciding foreign affairs an incredible degree of inefficiency must have resulted. No decision could ever be reached without considerable delay if all the local councils had to be consulted, and foreign ambassadors would presumably have had to tour all the cities of Boeotia to announce their mission. Further, the impression gained from Thucydides is that the Boeotarchs put their proposition on one occasion only, and, it follows, to one council.

(3) If the federal council did not decide matters of foreign policy, what ever could its function have been?

(4) If the view of the first editors is to be accepted, the words of Thucydides are not 'somewhat misleading', but (in the words of Goligher) totally wrong and display complete ignorance of the Boeotian Constitution of his own day.

(5) Thucydides uses *boule*, *boulai*, and *Boiotoi* of the same body. The singular is inexplicable if he meant the councils in each of the cities.

(6) If the local councils had the supreme authority, one cannot explain the position in the league always attributed to Thebes, nor the claim by Xenophon (*Hell.* V, I. 36) that the cities had long been desirous of autonomy by the time of the King's Peace, for they would already have been autonomous.

Both Glotz and Goligher offered the interpretation which is now widely accepted,[1] and is certainly correct. The federal council was in fact organized

[1] Cf. also, e.g., Bonner, *CP* V (1910), 405 ff., Cloché, *Thèbes de Béotie*, pp. 72f., Larsen, *Representative Government*, p. 37, and Ehrenberg, *The Greek State*, p. 123.

on the same principle as the local councils. It was divided into four, with one quarter acting as a probouleutic body. The term προδιαγνόντες used by Thucydides (v, 38. 3) at least hints at this procedure. The federal council was supreme in all affairs concerning the federation, and, in particular, in matters of foreign relations.

The influence of Thebes in the federal council may well have been great, for 240 of the 660 councillors were supplied by that city, and their presence at the Cadmea would always be assured.

In accordance with the practice of Greek oligarchies the councillors had to defray their own expenses.[1] The Boeotian oligarchy was, however, moderate, in the sense that the property requirement was not above the means of a good proportion of the population. This would be ensured, partly, by the system of dividing the councils, local and federal, into four parts, for the councillors could to all appearances devote about three-quarters of their time to their own private affairs. The fact that the whole council was consulted by the presiding quarter may illustrate a general Greek hesitance to give full powers to a representative body, for (in the case of the federal council) 660 is rather a large number of councillors if efficient conduct of business had been the primary objective. Glotz argued that 660 is the lowest number which would ensure the representation of all the cities, however small, but his thesis rests on the assumption that there were two cities, not mentioned by name, in addition to those specified by P, in the Plataean sympolity. There may, of course, have been more. The Boeotian form of moderate oligarchy[2] may well have been the prototype for the constitution εἰς τὸν μέλλοντα χρόνον for Athens, outlined in Arist. *Ath. Pol.* xxx. If so, we may infer that there was an age qualification of thirty years for Boeotian councillors, and it might appear that each section of the council presided for a year, making a four-year term of office for the full council. It is argued, however, with reason, that in view of usual Greek practice the councillors in Boeotia were elected for a term of one year, each division acting as a committee for one quarter of the year.

The statement that each of the eleven wards supplied one Boeotarch has put an end to discussion about the number of Boeotarchs. Thucydides[3] mentions eleven in 424 B.C., but there was some doubt whether this

[1] In this view I follow Glotz, *BCH* xxxii (1908), 272 and 275–7, and Cloché, *Thèbes de Béotie*, p. 73. Against this interpretation see Larsen, *Representative Government*, p. 205 n. 33.

[2] Thuc. iii, 62. 3 calls it ὀλιγαρχία ἰσόνομος.

[3] iv, 91: τῶν ἄλλων Βοιωταρχῶν οἵ εἰσιν ἕνδεκα οὐ ξυνεπαινούντων μάχεσθαι...Παγώνδας ὁ Αἰολάδου Βοιωταρχῶν ἐκ Θηβῶν μετ' Ἀριανθίδου τοῦ Λυσιμαχίδου...

number was inclusive of the Theban Boeotarchs. It is, however, possible that before 427 there were only nine Boeotarchs, if the two sent from Plataea (or from Thebes on Plataea's behalf) after that date brought the number up to eleven. Although the federal council had full power in dictating the policy of the confederacy, the Boeotarchs exercised considerable authority as commanders-in-chief of the military forces and having charge, to an extensive degree, of diplomatic negotiation. Thucydides (v, 38. 3) seems to hint that it was normal for the federal council to be guided by the advice of the Boeotarchs.

There were ten sovereign cities in the federation as here described. Seven of them—Thebes, Haliartus, Coronea, Copae, Thespiae, Tanagra and Orchomenus—were known from Thucydides (IV, 93) to have been members of the confederacy in 424. P adds to these Lebadea, Acraephium and Chaeronea. It is clear, however, that some changes must have taken place during the period 447–395 B.C. in the number or identity of the independent cities in the federation, for we know that in 424 Chaeronea was subject to Orchomenus.[1] It is not specified whether the non-independent cities (Hysiae, Eutresis, Thisbae, Plataea, Scolus, Erythrae, Scaphae, etc.) also had local councils. This would seem to depend on whether P considered them to be πόλεις, for the local councils were established παρ' ἑκάστῃ τῶν πόλεων (XI, 2). If these places had local councils with any effective powers, they could scarcely be considered subject to the greater cities, such as Thebes and Orchomenus, in any practical sense. On the other hand, if Thucydides' mention (IV, 91) of Pagondas and Arianthidas as being Boeotarchs ἐκ Θηβῶν indicates a distinction between the two representing Thebes and the two representing Plataea and the other places subject to Thebes, it is not improbable that the Boeotarchs of the latter two wards controlled by Thebes were often Plataeans or natives of the smaller places. These places were in 395 συντελούντων εἰς τὰς Θήβας (*Hell.Oxy.* XI, 3); the term appears to be a technical one, cf. Thuc. IV, 76. 3: Χαιρώνειαν ἣ ἐς 'Ορχομενὸν... ξυντελεῖ; cf. also Paus. IX, 3. 6, indicating probably that the lesser places (those described by Pausanias as ἐλάσσονος λόγου) formed one πόλις or city-state with one of the independent cities, and were only subject to this extent, while having equal rights within the city-state.[2] The smaller places would not, therefore, be πόλεις, indeed the papyrus refers to some at least of those subject to Thebes as χωρία (XI, 3), and would not have their own local councils.

Each of the eleven wards was obliged to furnish a corps of approxi-

[1] Thuc. IV, 76. 3.

[2] For further discussion of the status of these places see Larsen, *Representative Government*, p. 34.

mately 1,000 hoplites and 100 horsemen.[1] These figures make interesting comparison with our other records of Boeotian military contingents, and it has been plausibly suggested[2] that the Boeotian Confederacy had adopted the system of the Peloponnesian League by which two-thirds of the forces of each member state were obliged to serve on league campaigns, except when war was carried into the territory of one member state, in which event that particular state fought with its full military force. Thus at the battle of Delium in 424 the district of Tanagra, being invaded by the enemy, would put its full number of 1,000 hoplites into the field, while two-thirds of the hoplites from the other ten districts, about 6,666 in all, would participate. The number which results is fairly close to that given by Thucydides (IV, 93. 3), 7,000 hoplites plus 500 peltasts (possibly sent in lieu of hoplites by some district). This force was, in Thucydides' words, ἀπὸ πασῶν τῶν πόλεων. If the number of hoplites specified by Thucydides (V, 57) as serving in the Peloponnese in 419, 5,000 plus 500 hamippoi, falls a little short of the number we should expect, it is to be noted that on this occasion the Boeotian cavalry, which numbered 1,000 at Delium, was only 500 strong, and, further, Thucydides (V, 60. 3) indicates that the Boeotians had here only picked troops, λογάδες. Other figures worthy of attention are 5,000 hoplites and 800 cavalry at Nemea in 394 (Xen. *Hell.* IV, 2. 17), when the district of Orchomenus was not represented, and 12,000 hoplites and 2,000 cavalry at the capture of the Cadmea in 379 (Diod. XV, 26. 4). These latter figures may be exaggerated, for Plataea, Thespiae and Orchomenus were at the time allied to Sparta, yet in the circumstances it is quite possible that the normal strength of the army could have been exceeded considerably.

The hoplites were apparently divided into λόχοι (Thuc. IV, 91) when on active service, and were commanded by λοχαγοί (Xen. *Hell.* V, 2. 30). The Boeotians also had a force of light-armed infantry; 10,000 such soldiers fought at Delium (Thuc. IV, 93. 3; Diod. XII, 69. 3). They may well have been free men of less than hoplite census, and, as a result, probably, deprived of political franchise.

The total force of Boeotian cavalry, following P, was 1,100 strong. The

[1] For an exhaustive survey of Boeotian military organization see P. Salmon, *L'Ant.Cl.* XXII (1953), 347–60.

[2] Cf. Seymour, *CR* XXXVI (1922), 70, and *CR* XXXVII (1923), 63. The view had been expressed before the discovery of P's work by Kromayer in *Klio* III (1903) and by Busolt in *Hermes* XL (1905). However, Gomme, *Historical Commentary on Thucydides*, III, 563 (note on IV, 93. 3), suggests with good reason that it is unlikely that there would be so little difference in the numbers of the Boeotian army when on a foreign campaign and when fighting in defence of an invaded region of Boeotia.

proportion of horsemen to infantrymen would thus be one to ten, compared with the proportion of one to at least thirteen at Athens in 431 (Thuc. II, 13). This figure for Boeotia does not, however, take into account light-armed infantrymen, of whom, on two occasions at least, the battle of Delium and the campaign in the Peloponnese in 419, there were as many as there were hoplites (Thuc. IV, 93. 3 and V, 57). It does appear, none the less, that the Boeotian army included an unusually high proportion of cavalry, and that in the early fourth century that proportion increased still further, perhaps to one cavalryman for every six hoplites; cf. Diod. XV, 26. 4 and Xen. *Hell.* IV, 2. 17. The cavalry was probably recruited from the rich citizens, as at Athens and elsewhere, for only the wealthy could afford the expense of maintaining a horse. It may well have been drawn from a superior property class of land-owning aristocrats. The chief command of the cavalry was in the hands of a hipparch (Hdt. IX, 69; Thuc. IV, 72. 4), although he must have been subject to the direction of the Boeotarchs. Peculiar to the Boeotian army were the ἅμιπποι πεζοί, auxiliaries carried by the cavalry who fought on foot beside their respective cavalrymen (Thuc. V, 57. 2; Xen. *Hell.* VII, 5. 24). Later in the fourth century Athens appears to have adopted this form of combat; cf. Arist. *Ath. Pol.* XLIX, 1.

It was suggested by Glotz that the meaning of τῶν κοινῶν ἀπέλαυον is not 'they enjoyed the privileges of the league' as translated by the first editors, but that τὰ κοινά here refers to a federal treasury. This appears to me to be highly probable, for the historian immediately follows this statement with the words καὶ τὰς εἰσφορὰς ἐποιοῦντο, 'they made their contributions', and if τὰ κοινά were to mean vaguely 'privileges of the league', the later remark that the Boeotians shared equally all things good and bad would be a needless and even more vague repetition. The historian is merely stating that in all matters, financial, legal and others, the members shared in proportion to their provision of federal officers and military contingents. If we agree that τὰ κοινά means the treasury (as indeed τὰ κοινά of the Athenians seems to do in chapter II, 2), the interpretation of the closing sentence of chapter XI will be that the treasury, as well as the federal council, was situated in the Cadmea at Thebes.

The special mention of federal judges being sent by the proportionally represented wards has given rise to the reasonable suggestion that it was from Boeotia that the Athenians derived the idea of a federal legal system which is reflected in the organization of the Athenian Confederacy of 378.[1]

In conclusion it is interesting to note that from 447 to 427 the Thebans, controlling only two wards, would have had no greater administrative

[1] Cf. Tod, *GHI* II, 123.

power (as distinct from influence) than Orchomenus or Thespiae. Even when with the addition of the two wards represented by Plataea and the small towns in that locality Thebes controlled four, with the advantage of being assured of the attendance in the federal council of all the Theban councillors, who had no travel problems, it would appear that the cities of the confederacy were not really subject to Thebes in any oppressive sense. The organization of the federation on strictly proportional representation seems to have been scrupulously fair to all members. The dissatisfaction which spread through the Boeotian cities would seem to have been dissatisfaction with a federal system denying full autonomy in all matters to the individual city, and not dissatisfaction with this particular federation or with Thebes, beyond the envy or even resentment which is only too often felt by members of an alliance in respect of its most influential, and usually most valuable, member. The desire for autonomy with the city-state as the political unit was a constant feature of Greek political life, but the successful operation of federal representative government, demonstrated by the Boeotians for a not inconsiderable period, is an indication of what the Greeks might have achieved in the field of government had not their city-state particularism prevented them.

BIBLIOGRAPHY[1]

I. EDITIONS OF 'HELLENICA OXYRHYNCHIA'

Grenfell, B. P. and Hunt, A. S. 'Theopompus (or Cratippus), Hellenica', in *Oxyrhynchus Papyri* v (London, 1908), 110–242.
Grenfell, B. P. and Hunt, A. S. *Hellenica Oxyrhynchia cum Theopompi et Cratippi fragmentis*. Oxford, 1909.
Meyer, E. *Theopomps Hellenika*. Halle, 1909.
Lipsius, J. H. *Cratippi Hellenicorum fragmenta Oxyrhynchia*. Bonn, 1916.
Jacoby, F. *Die Fragmente der griechischen Historiker*. II, Berlin, 1926, A, pp. 17–35, C, pp. 6–20.
Kalinka, E. *Hellenica Oxyrhynchia*. Leipzig, Teubner, 1927.
Bartoletti, V. 'Nuovi frammenti delle "Elleniche di Ossirinco"', in *Papiri greci e latini* XIII, 1 (Florence, 1949), pp. 61–81.
Gigante, M. *Le Elleniche di Ossirinco*. Rome, 1949.
Maas, P. *Nova Hellenicorum Oxyrhynchiorum Fragmenta*, published for the Oxford Philological Society, Oxford, 1949; also in *CQ* XLIV (1950), 8–11.
Bartoletti, V. *Hellenica Oxyrhynchia*. Leipzig, Teubner, 1959.

II. OTHER PUBLICATIONS

(in alphabetical order of authors)

Accame, S. 'Le fonti di Diodoro per la guerra deceleica', in *Rend. Accad. Lincei* XIV (1938), 347–451.
—— 'Trasibulo e i nuovi frammenti delle Elleniche di Ossirinco', in *Riv.Fil.* XXVIII (1950), 30–49.
—— *Ricerche intorno alla guerra corinzia*. Naples, 1951.
Anderson, J. G. C. 'Exploration in Galatia cis Halym', in *JHS* XIX (1899), 52–134 and 280–318.
Barber, G. L. *The Historian Ephorus*. Cambridge, 1935.
Barbieri, G. *Conone*. Rome, 1955.
Bartoletti, V. Review of Gigante, *Gnomon* XXII (1950), 380–4.
Bauer, W. 'Die spartanischen Nauarchen der Jahre 397–395', in *Wiener Studien* XXXII (1910), 296–314.
Beloch, K. J. *Griechische Geschichte*. 2nd ed., Strassburg, and Berlin and Leipzig, 1912–27.

[1] A few works cited in my commentary which are not listed in this Bibliography were not available to me. For a near exhaustive bibliography of relevant publications up to 1959 see Bartoletti's Teubner edition.

Bloch, H. 'Studies in Historical Literature of the Fourth Century B.C.: I. The Hellenica of Oxyrhynchus and its Authorship', in *Athenian Studies Presented to W. S. Ferguson*, *HSCP*, supp. vol. I (1940), pp. 303–41.
Boissevain, U. Ph. 'Zu dem neuen griechischen Historiker', in *Berl.Phil. Woch.* (1908), cols. 189–90.
Bonner, R. J. 'The New Greek Historian', in *CJ* v (1910), 353–9.
—— 'The Boeotian Federal Constitution', in *CP* v (1910), 405–17.
—— 'The Four Senates of the Boeotians', in *CP* x (1915), 381–5.
Bruce, I. A. F. 'Internal Politics and the Outbreak of the Corinthian War', in *Emerita* XXVIII (1960), 75–86.
—— 'The Democratic Revolution at Rhodes', in *CQ* n.s. XI (1961), 166–70.
—— 'The Mutiny of Conon's Cypriot Mercenaries', in *Proceedings of the Cambridge Philol. Soc.* n.s. VIII (1962), 13–16.
—— 'Athenian Foreign Policy in 396–395 B.C.', in *CJ* LVIII (1963), 289–95.
—— 'Chios and P.S.I. 1304', in *Phoenix* XVIII (1964), 272–82.
Bury, J. B. *The Ancient Greek Historians*. London, 1909.
—— *A History of Greece*. 3rd ed., revised R. Meiggs, London, 1951.
Busolt, G. 'Spartas Heer und Leuktra', in *Hermes* XL (1905), 387–449.
—— 'Der neue Historiker und Xenophon', in *Hermes* XLIII (1908), 255–85.
Calder, W. M. and Bean, G. E. *A Classical Map of Asia Minor*. Supp. to *Anatolian Studies* VII (1957).
Castiglioni, L. Review of Lipsius, *Boll.Fil.Class.* XXVII (1921), 146–7.
—— Review of Kalinka, *Gnomon* IV (1928), 18–21.
—— Review of Gigante, *Prolegomena* I (1952), 130–2.
Cloché, P. 'La politique thébaine de 404 à 396 av. J.C.', in *REG* XXXI (1918), 315–43.
—— *La politique étrangère d'Athènes de 404 à 338 av. J.C.* Paris, 1934.
—— *Thèbes de Béotie*. Namur, 1952.
Cook, J. M. 'Greek Archaeology in Western Asia Minor', in *Archaeological Reports for 1959–60*, pp. 27–57.
Cornelius, F. 'Die Schlacht bei Sardes', in *Klio* XXVI (1933), 29–31.
Cousin, G. *Kyros le Jeune en Asie Mineure*. Paris, 1905.
De Sanctis, G. 'La battaglia di Notion', in *Riv.Fil.* IX (1931), 222–9; now also *Studi di storia della storiografia greca* (Florence, 1951), pp. 163–71.
—— 'Nuovi studi sulle "Elleniche" di Oxyrhynchos', in *Atti Accad. Torino* LXVI (1931), 157–94.

Dugas, Ch. 'La campagne d'Agésilas en Asie Mineure', in *BCH* XXXIV (1910), 58–95.
Dunbabin, T. J., *s.v.* 'Orchomenus', *Oxford Classical Dictionary* (Oxford, 1949).
Ehrenberg, V. *The Greek State*. Oxford, 1960.
Ferguson, W. S. 'The Fall of the Athenian Empire', ch. XII of *CAH* V (Cambridge, 1927).
Ferrabino, A. *L'impero ateniese*. Turin, 1927.
Finley, M. I. 'Athenian Demagogues', in *Past and Present* XXI (1962), 3–24.
Fuhr, K. 'Zu dem neuen griechischen Historiker', in *Berl.Phil.Woch.* (1908), cols. 156–8.
—— Review of *OCT*, *Berl.Phil.Woch.* (1910), cols. 165–9.
Fuks, A. 'Note on the nova Hellenicorum Oxyrhynchiorum fragmenta', in *CQ* XLV (1951), 155.
Giannelli, G. *Trattato di storia greca*. Rome, 1948.
Glotz, G. 'Le conseil fédéral des Béotiens', in *BCH* XXXII (1908), 271–8.
Goligher, W. A. 'The Boeotian Constitution', in *CR* XXII (1908), 80–2.
Gomme, A. W. *A Historical Commentary on Thucydides*. Oxford, (I) 1945, (III) 1956.
—— 'Who Was Kratippos?', in *CQ* XLVIII (1954), 53–5.
Griffith, G. T. 'The Union of Corinth and Argos', in *Historia* I (1950), 236–56.
—— 'The Greek Historians', in *Fifty Years of Classical Scholarship*, ed. M. Platnauer (Oxford, 1954), pp. 160–2.
Grote, G. *A History of Greece*. 10 vols., London, 1888.
Hammond, N. G. L. *A History of Greece*. Oxford, 1959.
Hardy, W. G. 'The Hellenica Oxyrhynchia and the Devastation of Attica', in *CP* XXI (1926), 346–55.
Hatzfeld, J. 'Alcibiade et les élections des stratèges athéniens en 406', in *REA* XXXIII (1931), 109–16.
Head, B. V. 'On the Chronological Sequence of the Coins of Boeotia', in *Numismatic Chronicle* (1881), pp. 177–275.
—— *Coins of Central Greece*. London, 1884.
—— *Historia Numorum*. 2nd ed., Oxford, 1911.
Hill, G. F. *Sources for Greek History*. New ed., R. Meiggs and A. Andrewes, Oxford, 1951.
Jacoby, F. *Die Fragmente der griechischen Historiker*. II, Berlin, 1926–30.
—— 'The Authorship of the Hellenica of Oxyrhynchus', in *CQ* XLIV (1950), 1–8.
Judeich, W. 'Theopomps Hellenika', in *Rhein.Mus.* LXVI (1911), 94–139.
Keil, B., *s.v.* 'Notion', *RE* XVII, 1, col. 1,075.

Kirchner, J. *Prosopographia Attica.* Berlin, 1901–3.

Kromayer, J. 'Studien über Wehrkraft und Wehrverfassung der griechischen Staaten', in *Klio* III (1903), 173–212.

Larsen, J. A. O. 'The Boeotian Confederacy and Fifth Century Oligarchic Theory', in *TAPA* LXXXVI (1955), 40–50.

—— *Representative Government in Greek and Roman History.* Berkeley and Los Angeles, 1955.

Lenschau, Th. 'Die Sendung des Timokrates und der Ausbruch des korinthischen Krieges', in *Phil.Woch.* LIII (1933), 1,325–8.

Lipsius, J. H. 'Zu Kratippos', in *Berl.Phil.Woch.* (1917), cols. 1,573–6.

McKay, K. L. 'The Oxyrhynchus Historian and the Outbreak of the Corinthian War', in *CR* n.s. III (1953), 6–7.

Mathieu, G. 'La réorganisation du corps civique athénien à la fin du Ve siècle', in *REG* XL (1927), 65–116.

Meyer, E. *Geschichte von Troas.* Leipzig, 1877.

Momigliano, A. 'Androzione e le Elleniche di Oxyrhynchos', in *Atti Accad. Torino* LXVI (1931), 29–49.

Parke, H. W. 'The Development of the Second Spartan Empire', in *JHS* L (1930), 37–79.

Perlman, S. 'The Causes and the Outbreak of the Corinthian War', in *CQ* n.s. XIV (1964), 64–81.

Picard, Ch. and Avezou, Ch. 'Les fouilles de Thasos (1912)', in *CRAI* (1913), pp. 360–78.

Picard, Ch. 'Fouilles de Thasos (1914 et 1920)', in *BCH* XLV (1921), 86–173.

—— 'Stèle archaïque thasienne de la fin du VIe siècle', in *Monuments Piot* XXXII (1932), 21–32.

Poralla, P. *Prosopographie der Lakedaimonier.* Breslau, 1913.

Pouilloux, J. 'Trois notes thasiennes: I. Le sanctuaire de Déméter', in *BCH* LXXV (1951), 90–6.

Radet, G. *La Lydie.* Paris, 1893.

Ramsay, W. M. *Historical Geography of Asia Minor.* London, 1890.

—— *Cities and Bishoprics of Phrygia.* Oxford, (I) 1895, (II) 1897.

Ruge, W., *s.v.* 'Myndos', *RE* XVI, 1, cols. 1,075 ff.

Rühl, F. 'Randglossen zu den Hellenika von Oxyrhynchos', in *Rhein. Mus.* LXVIII (1913), 161–201.

Salmon, P. 'L'armée fédérale des Béotiens', in *L'Ant.Cl.* XXII (1953), 347–60.

Seymour, P. A. 'Note on the Boeotian League', in *CR* XXXVI (1922), 70.

—— 'Further Note on the Boeotian League', in *CR* XXXVII (1923), 63.

Swoboda, H. 'Studien zur Verfassung Boiotiens', in *Klio* X (1910), 315–34.

—— *s.v.* 'Konon', *RE* XI, 1, cols. 1,319–34.

Tod, M. N. *Greek Historical Inscriptions.* II, Oxford, 1948.

Toepffer, J., *s.v.* 'Alkibiades', *RE* I, 2, col. 1,530.

Treu, M. 'Zu den neuen Bruchstücken der Hellenica von Oxyrhynchos', in *Gymnasium* LIX (1952), 302–19.

Underhill, G. E. 'Theopompus (or Cratippus), Hellenica', in *JHS* XXVIII (1908), 277–90.

Wackernagel, J. 'Orthographica und Verwandtes', in *Philol.* LXXXVI (1930), 133–44.

Walker, E. M. 'Cratippus or Theopompus?', in *Klio* VIII (1908), 356–71.

—— *The Hellenica Oxyrhynchia, its Authorship and Authority.* Oxford, 1913.

—— 'The Oxyrhynchus Historian', in *New Chapters in the History of Greek Literature*, ed. J. U. Powell and E. A. Barber (Oxford, 1921), pp. 124–33.

Westlake, H. D. Review of Bartoletti, *CR* n.s. X (1960), 209–10.

Wilamowitz-Moellendorff, U. von. 'Die griechische Literatur des Altertums', in *Die Kultur der Gegenwart*, I, 8^3, Berlin and Leipzig, 1912.

Wilcken, U. 'Ein Theopompfragment in den neuen Hellenika', in *Hermes* XLIII (1908), 475–7.

Zunkel, G. *Untersuchungen zur griechischen Geschichte der Jahre 395-386.* Jena dissertation, 1911.

INDEX

Milton Keynes UK
Ingram Content Group UK Ltd.
UKHW041927191123
432891UK00008B/44

9 780521 034128